teach yourself

eastern philosophy

eastern philosophy
mel thompson

For UK order enquiries: please contact Bookpoint Ltd., 130 Milton Park, Abingdon, Oxon OX14 4SB. Telephone: +44 (0) 1235 827720. Fax: +44 (0) 1235 400454. Lines are open from 09.00–18.00, Monday to Saturday, with a 24-hour message answering service. You can also order through our website: www.madaboutbooks.com

For USA order enquiries: please contact McGraw-Hill Customer Services, PO Box 545, Blacklick, OH 43004-0545, USA. Telephone: 1-800-722-4726. Fax: 1-614-755-5645.

For Canada order enquiries: please contact McGraw-Hill Ryerson Ltd, 300 Water St, Whitby, Ontario L1N 9B6, Canada. Telephone: 905 430 5000. Fax: 905 430 5020.

Long-renowned as the authoritative source for self-guided learning – with more than 30 million copies sold worldwide – the *Teach Yourself* series includes over 300 titles in the fields of languages, crafts, hobbies, business, computing and education.

British Library Cataloguing in Publication Data: a catalogue record for this title is available from The British Library.

Library of Congress Catalog Card Number: on file

First published in UK 1999 by Hodder Headline Ltd, 338 Euston Road, London NW1 3BH.

First published in US 1999 by Contemporary Books. a Division of The McGraw-Hill Companies, 1 Prudential Plaza, 130 East Randolph Street, Chicago, IL 60601, USA.

Typeset by Transet Limited, Coventry, England.
Printed in Great Britain for Hodder & Stoughton Educational, a division of Hodder Headline Ltd, 338 Euston Road, London NW1 3BH by Cox & Wyman Ltd., Reading, Berkshire.

Impression number   7 6 5 4 3 2 1
Year   2009 2008 2007 2006 2005 2004 2003

contents

introduction

Philosophy is the quest for knowledge and wisdom. It seeks to clarify the general principles that govern our understanding of the world and to examine the language we use to describe it. Sometimes it is speculative, moving out from our limited range of experiences to frame some overall view of reality. Sometimes it is analytical, examining the logic of statements that might otherwise be accepted uncritically, in order to clarify what is being said.

At one level, philosophy is an academic discipline, pursued in universities and presented in weighty tomes that may seem impenetrable to the outsider; at another, it is the natural activity of all thinking people. Everyone who has ever asked why the universe is as it is, or why we call one thing good or beautiful and another bad or ugly, or how society should be organized, is in fact engaging in philosophy.

This book on Eastern Philosophy is therefore concerned with the traditions of thought and wisdom that developed in the Indian subcontinent and the Far East:

- From India, you have the wealth of ideas, mental disciplines, religious and social practices that are collectively known as Hinduism, along with the Jain and Buddhist philosophies that developed within Hindu culture but were critical of Hindu orthodoxy and therefore emerged as separate traditions.
- From the Far East, you have the ancient traditions of Confucianism and Taoism, later blending with Buddhism to form the rich mixture of Chinese thought.
- Then there are two wisdom traditions that are very different in approach – Tantra and Zen – the one based on ritual action and the creative use of the imagination, the other with an intuition of reality that goes beyond concepts.

Together, these traditions have a history that stretches back three thousand years, and they have contributed vastly, not just to the Eastern cultures within which they have developed, but globally. A book such as this can do no more than point to the central themes and issues that Eastern Philosophy has addressed, and to outline its main approaches and conclusions.

But is it philosophy?

Those who are accustomed to modern Western philosophy may be in for a shock as they move eastwards. In the West, both the content and the methods used in philosophy have become carefully defined. Many areas that were once seen as branches of philosophy have been divided off as separate subjects (e.g. natural philosophy has become 'science'). As a result, philosophy has come to be seen as a discipline without a subject matter of its own, its task being limited to the application of rational thought to the presuppositions and arguments used in other subjects, analyzing the language used and the arguments presented.

In other words

In the West during the twentieth century, particularly in Britain and the United States, philosophy became less concerned about the nature of reality itself, but more with the possibility and validity of speaking about reality: not 'What is true?' but 'What does it mean to say that something is true?' Much Western philosophy stopped playing the game and merely analyzed the rule-book.

In the West one does not expect someone versed in the philosophy of mind to work in a psychiatric unit, nor a philosopher of science to be undertaking fundamental research, nor a philosopher of religion to be necessarily practising a particular religion or teaching meditation techniques. Philosophers stand back, look and comment – their quest is generally for truth in the sense of clarity, less often for truth in the form of experience or action.

This has not always been the case. For much of its history, Western philosophy has been broadly based, and it was only really with the rise of modern science that philosophy handed over much of what it had previously considered its subject matter to the emerging scientific disciplines. Only then, reluctant to speak about the world known to science, did it tend to confine itself to the world of meanings.

Moving to the East, the situation is very different. Philosophy has not limited itself to rational argument, nor has it separated itself from those areas in life through which fundamental questions are asked. Hinduism, Buddhism, Jainism, Confucianism, Taoism: these are religious and social systems as well as philosophies. Zen and Tantra are explorations of meditation and sexual power respectively. Such systems have practical and physical consequences: they make a difference to people's lives. But they are also philosophies, in that their religious, social and moral teachings are based on, and give expression to, fundamental views about the nature of reality. So the Wisdom of the East is philosophy and psychology and sociology and religion all rolled into one. Or, to be more precise, it is a wisdom that does not require its insights to be compartmentalized in the Western way.

Sexuality, meditation, ritual, correct behaviour – all of these things have implications for an understanding of the nature of the world and the self, and the quest for insight into them should therefore be considered 'philosophy'. But it is this curious mixture of disciplines, from a Western standpoint, that can sometimes lead to doubts about how much of it should count as philosophy.

But note

Obviously these comments present an oversimplification, and in any case apply mainly to the Anglo-American tradition rather than to European philosophy, which has generally taken a broader approach. They are included here simply to highlight the fact that there is sometimes a reluctance on the part of Western thinkers to accept the broad range of concerns that may be included within Eastern Philosophy.

Eastern Wisdom (*prajna* in Sanskrit) is not simply a matter of logic or speculation, but is also concerned with experience and intuition. Prajna can be applied to all aspects of life.

But that does not mean that the skills of analysis or of the assessment of empirical evidence is absent from Eastern thought – far from it; there are many interesting parallels to Western philosophy. The main difference, generally speaking, is that Eastern Philosophy has not separated itself from other disciplines, and in particular it has retained its links with religion, psychology and mysticism.

What does this book cover?

For the purposes of this book, it has been necessary to set limits to what is being considered as Eastern Philosophy, simply because the subject could embrace the entire civilizations of the Far East, South-East Asia and the Indian subcontinent. The criterion used is this:

• That the ideas being considered touch on ultimate questions about the nature of reality, or society or human nature – questions which (even if framed differently in the West) are universal.

Examples

It is debatable whether Shinto should be included as an Eastern Philosophy. Although it has had a significant influence on Japanese culture, it does not appear to have a developed philosophy as such, but is rather more a religious recognition of local spirits (*kami*) in a way that does not lend itself to universal application.

On the other hand, Zen – which, of all the 'philosophies' in this book, has least interest in rational argument – introduces features of reality and our experience of it which can be examined and compared with those of other approaches.

Therefore, Zen has been included but Shinto has not.

The other important thing to note is that this book will examine the fundamental questions addressed by each religious and philosophical tradition, but descriptions of the ritual or lifestyle of its followers will be introduced only in so far as they illustrate some fundamental insight. Hence, although the chapter titles might look the same, this is not really a book about Eastern 'religions' as such.

Eastern and Western terms

Applying Western terminology to Eastern philosophical positions can lead to distortion. For example, if the Hindu word for absolute reality – Brahman – is translated 'God', there is a danger that Western personal ideas of God will be read into that concept, leading to confusion about how it relates to Hindu devotion to its many gods and goddesses. Questions like 'Is

Brahman really "God", and (if so) why do Hindus also have these other gods?' result from using the Western term for a very different Eastern concept.

As far as is practicable, therefore, Eastern terms will be explained and used in the text.

Western

There are interesting parallels between Eastern and Western ideas and approaches, as well as points of contrast. These are noted in 'Western' boxes, such as this. For example, the ancient Greek philosopher Heraclitus (of 'you can't step into the same river twice' fame) had a view of nature as constantly changing, which is similar to that of the Buddha. This does not imply that Heraclitus was a crypto-Buddhist, nor that there was some literal or esoteric link between the two men, but simply that both sought to explore and explain the same phenomenon.

But please note:

It has not been possible to give an exposition of the Western philosophies referred to in these boxes. Sometimes a particular thinker or argument is mentioned by name only. Those who want to follow up the parallels here might refer to *Teach Yourself Philosophy* or *Teach Yourself Philosophy of Religion*, or the many other introductions to Western philosophy.

The geography of ideas

Ideas not only develop, they also move. Carried along by trade or religion, they find themselves applied to different cultures in separate geographical areas and subsequent developments reflect that geographical separation.

By and large, in studying Eastern Thought, we are looking at the products of two very different geographical and cultural areas: India and China. Indian philosophy and religion (called Hinduism by Westerners) and its offshoots, of which the major traditions to be considered here are Buddhism and Jainism, reflects the culture, and even the climate of that part of the world. You are unlikely to get naked ascetics in polar regions! Its background is very different from Confucian and Taoist thought, which arose in China and reflect respectively the social and individualistic aspects of life there. When Buddhism moved from its Indian matrix northwards to China and then on to Japan, its character changed to reflect the different cultures within which it found itself. Elements latent within its Indian practice flowered in the different circumstances.

In this book, we shall be primarily concerned with the approach taken by each philosophy, and the fundamental ideas that developed within it, but it is important to recognize that – however rationally justified – changes in society, the moving of ideas from one area to another and the passing of time all have an important part to play in the ever-changing pattern of ideas. All we can hope to do here is explore key features of each philosophy, and where possible to hint at their geographical, cultural background and developments.

To sum up

- We shall be looking at key features of Indian philosophy as found in Hinduism, Buddhism and Jainism, and Far Eastern philosophy in terms of Confucianism, Taoism and later developments of Buddhism.

- We shall also examine Tantra and Zen, to explore the total range of what may be considered 'wisdom' and how it relates to fundamental concepts.

- Eastern terms will be explained and used, to avoid confusion.

- 'Western' boxes will point out parallels and contrasts between East and West.

- But, it should be recognized that this book offers no more than an outline and an introduction to a vast and complex range of ideas. It does not claim in any way to be comprehensive. Its aim is to give an overview, and to whet the appetite for further study of a priceless tradition of thought and insight.

01

Hindu philosophies

In this chapter you will learn:

- the background to the philosophies of India
- key concepts in Hindu philosophy
- the principal schools of Hindu philosophy.

Background

The life, religion and philosophies of the Indian subcontinent are expressed through an amazingly rich mixture of ideas, practices and social customs that have developed over more than three thousand years. There is no single Hindu religion or Hindu philosophy, but rather a variety of ways of understanding and relating to the world that are blended from a stock of widely held ideas, some more ancient than others.

Note

Although this chapter is called 'Hindu philosophies' and the religion of the majority in India is generally referred to in the West as 'Hinduism', this is simply a convenient Western term for the ideas and practices to be found in India.

India has been influenced by the many peoples who have invaded it. The earliest of these – about 1500–1200 BCE – was an invasion of Aryan peoples from Central Asia, some of whose beliefs appear to be close to those of the Ancient Greeks, possibly coming from a common source of ideas in the Middle East.

Prior to the Aryan invasions we have evidence of the Indus Valley Civilization (c. 2500–1700 BCE). It is difficult to assess the extent to which the Indus Valley Civilization influenced the development of Hindu thought, since we do not have any written accounts of their religious beliefs, but there are figurines of both gods and goddesses, including one that is like later images of the god Shiva, and the practice of Yoga, which suggest that these ancient people have made a direct contribution to later philosophy and religion.

It is also likely that the blending of the lighter-skinned Aryan and the darker-skinned native inhabitants has produced a range of social and religious phenomena in India, including the caste system, which has been so influential in Indian social life and thought.

But later invasions also left their mark. From about 600–500 BCE there was an influx of Parsi people, with their Zoroastrian religion, native to Persia. Later, 300–100 BCE, the Greeks invaded under Alexander. From 800 to 1800 CE India was influenced by Muslim culture, and finally, from the beginning of the nineteenth century until 1946, it was ruled by the British.

It would therefore be unrealistic to look at Indian philosophy and expect it to form a single, coherent system. It is a wonderful array of social philosophy, along with abstract metaphysics and religion.

Stages of development

One way of getting the wide range of Hindu thought and practice into perspective is to consider it in terms of three different periods, each of which had a particular interest which coloured its philosophy.

- In the earliest period for which we have written evidence – the period of the composition of the early Vedas (see below page 9) – the main concern seems to have been *Dharma* – the right ordering of society in general and of individuals within society in order to achieve harmony and happiness.
- In the second major period – that of the six classical schools of Hindu philosophy, starting in about the second century BCE and on through the first millennium CE – the concern shifted from correct worldly Dharma to the desire for liberation from the world of endless rebirths. Although all that had been said earlier about Dharma remained relevant, the newer concern for individual spiritual liberation (*moksha*) was superimposed over it.
- Then, in a third wave of Hindu thinking, starting about the middle of the first millennium CE, there was an emphasis on devotion (*bhakti*) to one's chosen deity, and here the aim was not so much to escape out of the world as to achieve a unity with the divine in and through one's earthly existence.

Some key concepts

Brahman

In Western thought, under the influence of Judaism, Christianity and Islam, the word 'God' is used to denote a reality that is both creative and also personal – described as the uncaused cause of everything, but also as a personal deity to whom one might pray and by whom one might be heard. Moving to Indian thought, the situation is rather different. At the level of popular religion there are thousands of gods and goddesses – each with a particular sphere of influence, either geographical or in terms of a particular aspect of life. So, for example, the elephant-headed god, Ganesha, is thought to bring good fortune and academic success – and is therefore respected particularly by those concerned with those things.

Beyond this multiplicity there are three gods who represent complementary aspects of life: Brahma, the creator; Vishnu, the sustainer; Shiva, the destroyer. These fundamental aspects of the process of change seen in the world are each acknowledged and portrayed as embodied in the image of their respective god.

But beyond these three there is the idea of Brahman. This denotes ultimate reality, a reality which includes the whole universe with its multiplicity of gods and goddesses. Brahman is seen as the invisible reality within and around everything. All the other gods represent limited aspects of Brahman and make him visible.

Western

In Western terms, one may be monotheist (believing in only one god), polytheist (in many gods) or atheist (believing in no god). Indeed, a major part of the Philosophy of Religion in the West has been given over to the attempt to prove that God does or does not exist. This does not really make sense once we turn to Hindu thought. Individual gods and goddesses exist in terms of their images, and also exist as representations of a particular aspect of life – but they are not really thought of as having an independent, disembodied existence. They are not located; they are aspects of reality, represented by their images. On the other hand, it is difficult to ask if Brahman exists. In a sense, he is above the concept of existence. You cannot sensibly ask if reality exists – it is simply that, reality. All you can do is debate its nature.

Similarly, there are images of goddesses who are taken to represent very different aspects of life. They have one thing in common, however, and that is that they represent feminine power (*shakti*). We shall examine the nature and operation of the power of shakti in the chapter on Tantra.

To sum up

Hindu thought argues that there are a multiplicity of gods, each of which is a way of representing the single ultimate reality, which is called Brahman.

Brahman is sometimes represented by the syllable OM (or AUM). Hindus may chant this slowly, the sound rising through three progressive tones, from the chest, the throat and finally the head.

It is believed to be the vibration of the life-giving energies of the whole universe, emanating from Brahman, but it also represents a gathering together of the whole of the individual in a single expression. This claim, that the chanted syllable is in fact in touch with the universal, reinforces the basic view in the Upanishads (see page 10f) of the identity of Brahman and the self, or Atman. It is a religious symbol for that fundamental unified (monistic) view of reality.

Atman

Whereas ultimate reality is called Brahman, the individual self is referred to as the *Atman*, which is sometimes translated as 'soul'. As we have already touched on, and will refer to later in this chapter, one of the key ideas of the Upanishads and later Vedanta philosophy is the identity of the Atman and Brahman. Whatever your physical limitation within the world, in terms of your own true essence or inner self, you share in a single absolute reality (Brahman). At one level, therefore, the self is identified with the absolute.

At another level, however, what a person is can be defined largely by his or her position in society. This is a person's caste or *varna*. Varna means 'colour', probably referring originally to the contrast between the lighter skinned Aryan invaders and the darker Dravidian peoples they encountered. Below these four varnas come those who are outside the caste system altogether, and take the lowest place in society. (See the section on Hindu life and ethics on page 34.)

This is not a superficial social phenomenon, but is deeply rooted in Hindu philosophy. In the *Rig Veda*, one of the earliest Hindu scriptures, there is an account of the dividing up of a cosmic person (Purusha) each part of whom produces a particular section of human society, or caste. Caste is therefore regarded as the human mirroring of a fundamental structure of the universe, a structure in which there are inherent differences in terms of function and implied value.

Issues to consider

Is equality unnatural? Is the Hindu recognition of fundamental differences within society the logical conclusion from an objective assessment of the natural order? Or is this aspect of Hindu thought simply a later rationalization and justification of what happens when invaders impose their views on a subservient native people?

When we look at the idea of the self, however, we have to consider two very different things. One is the embodied self, which is very much socially determined by its caste. The other is the Atman which is the self in its relationship to the whole, expressed as Brahman.

The Upanishads argue that Brahman and Atman are in fact one; that fundamental self is co-extensive with the reality of the universe. Another way to put this would be to say that there is a single reality; when it manifests globally it is called Brahman, but when it manifests in the self it is called Atman.

> He [Atman] is myself within the heart, smaller than a grain of rice or a barley corn, or a grain of millet: this is myself within my heart, greater than the earth, greater than the atmosphere, greater than the sky, greater than all these worlds.

> (*Chandogya Upanishad* Bk III, 14:3–5)

In one vedic story a young man, Svetaketu, is told to take a pomegranate and cut it open, then he takes a seed and cuts it open, then he cuts again. Eventually he comes to the point of recognition that within the heart of this there is 'nothing'. That invisible, central reality – the nothingness that appears when individual things are divided into their smallest constituent parts – is what a person is. '*Tat twan asi*': 'you are that'.

In other words

The self is only superficially located and defined by the body. In reality the Atman is eternal and infinite in extent. There is no difference between the Atman and Brahman.

Note

The concepts of Brahman and Atman are important because the key feature of Hindu thought seems to have been the quest for an understanding of why the world has come to be as it is, what place the individual self has within it, and how the self might overcome those things that cause it suffering. The range of answers to this run from the impersonal and atheistic through the sense of the unity of the Atman with the ultimate, Brahman, to liberation through devotion to the personal god.

In all this, philosophy is not done in a detached way. It is not purely speculative, but is closely linked to the idea of liberation – once the true nature of things is understood, one is free from the bondage of illusion.

Sanatana Dharma

Sanatana Dharma might best be translated 'the eternal ordering of things'. It is based on the concept that the world has a timeless structure and meaning, and that an understanding of this will allow a person to live in a fundamental harmony with life. Dharma here has the sense of 'reality' or 'truth'. To call Sanatana Dharma 'the eternal truth' might suggest that it can be reduced to a proposition. That would be wrong – it is not truth in the sense of a verbal summary, but the actual experience of reality as it is.

Most Hindu philosophy makes a clear distinction between what is perceived and the absolute reality beneath those perceptions. It is aware of human sensory fallibility. The world of our perceptions is termed *samsara*. It is believed that the self is in some way trapped within the world of samsara, is determined by the working of the law of karma (see below) and is therefore doomed to be born again and again.

Note

Dharma is a much used word, both in Hinduism and Buddhism. Its precise meaning is generally given by the context within which it is used. In Hinduism it can mean 'truth' or 'reality' or 'teaching' or 'order'. In Buddhism it is the word used for the teaching of the Buddha, and thus one of the three jewels to which Buddhists go for refuge. It is also used (with a lower case 'd') to mean 'thing', so that a process of analysis can be said to reveal the dharmas out of which all compound things are formed.

Karma

Karma is a concept found both within Hindu thought and also in Jainism and Buddhism, although for Buddhists it is understood rather differently. Karma literally means 'action'. It is the term used for the process by which actions are believed to have consequences for the person who performs them. These consequences are not merely the practical and obvious results of action but are regarded as spiritual, in that they influence the passage of an Atman through the world of samsara. What is more, Hindus believe that actions performed in one lifetime will influence what will happen to that person beyond death, on the grounds that the consequences that have yet to mature from earlier karma must work themselves out in future lives. As popularly conceived, obedience to the Dharma (reality, or the 'Eternal Law') here and now will bring about a better rebirth.

Moksha

The result of realizing the identity of Atman and Brahman is *moksha* (release) – which is considered to be release from the suffering and limitations implied by a narrow view of the self, and an awareness of one's eternal destiny. All that stands in the way of self-realization is *avidya* (ignorance), which is the state of those who cannot distinguish between the relative unreality of things that are perceived in the limited sphere of this samsaric world, and ultimate reality.

Western

Notice that the aim of the Hindu is to be released from the imposition of endless lives. Moving on to another life after death, although one might strive for an improved situation through avoiding bad karma and performing good karma, is not the ultimate goal. The goal is *not* to be reborn. Contrast this with most Western views of life after death.

On the other hand, there are fundamental parallels (which we shall find many times in this book) between the Eastern contrast of ultimate reality with mundane experience and, in particular, Plato's view of the role of the philosopher. For Plato, most people are as prisoners held deep in a cave who see no more than the reflections of objects projected upon a wall. The philosopher is one who manages to get free and sees reality itself beyond the cave. Most Eastern thought has this same scheme – of seeing an undifferentiated reality in contrast to the mundane, ever-changing and unsatisfactory passing of events.

These are the basic concepts: the way in which they are used in different philosophies will be examined later in this chapter.

Literature

Vedas

The *Vedas* are seen as the touchstone for Indian philosophy – 'orthodox' is what conforms to them, 'unorthodox' is what does not. They are a collection of over a thousand hymns, comprising some 10,000 verses. Many were probably brought into India by the Aryans in the middle of the second millennium BCE, but from the original four collections of these, there has arisen a further body of literature, and all of this together is often referred to as 'The Vedas'. The Vedas are set out in four volumes:

1 *Rig Veda* – the most important, giving most of the core teaching. It is the oldest of the four – about 1200 BCE.
2 *Sama Veda* – which gives music and chanting.
3 *Yajur Veda* – which gives details required for the performance of sacrifices.
4 *Atharva Veda* – contains incantations and spells which may have been preserved from pre-Aryan times.

Each of these Vedas has three other forms of literature attached to it: Brahmanas (epic tales, composed probably between 800 and 600 BCE); Aranyakas (ritual formulas, probably dating from 600 BCE) and Upanishads (philosophical texts, dating from around 600–300 BCE).

The Vedas introduce the pantheon of Indian gods. Indra appears to have been the most popular, in terms of the number of hymns addressed to him. Agni, the fire god, is also important, as is Soma, the god represented by the intoxicating drink taken during religious rituals.

Thus, in the Vedas, cosmic ideas and the world of the gods are presented mythologically, rather than philosophically. The world's origin is seen as an egg, floating on a sea of chaos, or (in the best-known image) as the sacrifice of the cosmic man (Purusha). Towards the end of the vedic period, in the *Atharva Veda*, there appears to have been a dissatisfaction with the mythological form and a move towards speaking of the *asat* ('non-being' or unreal) and the *sat* ('being' or real) – with the aim of the spiritual person to move from the former to the latter.

Comment

In the Vedas, ritual sacrifice is seen as the act that holds the whole universe together and gives it structured form. Acting out a ritual is a way of giving meaning. Surely, what is happening here is the recognition of the need for a personal orientation, a way of seeing the self in relation to the whole. The Brahmin's sacrifice holds the world together – since only with a personal vision can reality move from uncertainty and chaos and become a structured cosmos.

Gradually we see this giving way to more abstract speculation – a more 'philosophical' approach. But perhaps we need to stop and ask a crucial question. Can a sense of meaning and purpose best be grasped through abstract reasoning or through gesture and participation? One of the strengths of ritual is that it enables people to participate emotionally in what is being said or acted out, and it engages the unconscious as well as the conscious mind. Can ultimate truths be grasped by reason alone? We shall need to consider this again in the chapters on Tantra and Zen.

In the Brahmanas, we see a movement away from sacrifice as a means of securing the action of the gods, towards a concentration on the details of the sacrifice itself. The ritual starts to be seen as that which embodies and maintains the universe, it represents reality itself – Brahman. This makes the person performing the ritual (the Brahmin) and the details of that ritual, supremely important. The Aranyakas, which came to be attached to the Brahmanas, recognize that the actual sacrifice can be replaced by a mental one, through meditation. There is therefore a natural progression towards the Upanishads, which move from a mental representation of sacrifice into the area of abstract metaphysical speculation.

In other words

To put it simply, there is a movement away from a 'magic' use of sacrifice in order to influence divine forces, through sacrifice as expressing the nature of reality, and the idea that the sacrifice can be performed mentally, towards the idea that the universe can be understood rationally and philosophically.

Upanishads

Upanishad probably comes from 'upa – ni – sad' which means 'to sit near', and refers to the teachings given by a guru to those disciples who sit nearest to him – in other words, it is aimed at the initiated, rather than the people at large. They were composed towards the end of the Vedic period and introduce key features of later Hinduism, such as the unity of Atman and Brahman, the cycle of samsara and moksha, or release from this cycle. Whereas the earliest Upanishads are similar in style to the Brahmanas, as time went on the Upanishads reflected the early Vedic literature less and less and the sacred power of the sacrifice became seen as the power that lies within and behind the whole cosmos.

In the *Chandogya Upanishad* (5:3–10) we have the idea of rebirth depending upon actions (karma), and the description of the Atman as the separate individual self. The *Chandogya Upanishad* also contains the story (see page 6) of Svetaketu splitting the seeds.

Comment

The Upanishads present the earlier teaching in the form of monist philosophy – in other words, they argue that there is a single reality to which everything belongs. The appearance of separateness, for example, between the individual self (Atman) and the ultimate reality (Brahman) is simply an illusion; the ultimate truth is that they are one and the same. However, our understanding of the Upanishads today is probably influenced by later philosophical expositions of them – especially that by Sankara (see page 25).

The Epics

Hindu thought makes a distinction between what is known as *shruti* ('hearing'), which applies to the Vedas and implies eternal truth, and *smriti* ('remembering') which may be used of other literature which does not have that status. Among the smriti literature are the great epics, the *Mahabharata* and the *Ramayana*.

The *Mahabharata* contains the *Bhagavad Gita* (6.23–40), dated probably second century BCE or a little later. This is the most popular of all Hindu texts, and it marks an important step in the development of Hindu philosophy. It tells of Prince Arjuna, troubled about going into battle against the slaughter that will ensue, being advised by his charioteer, who is the god Krishna. Krishna explains that the self (Atman) is indestructible and eternal. Therefore Arjuna will not be killing the real self, but only the body, which is like an outer garment.

The *Gita* (the commonly used shortened form of *Bhagavad Gita*) offers a synthesis of many existing Hindu teachings within an overall framework of belief in God. Krishna declares that all action done from selfless motives becomes a sacrifice, that disinterested action is true renunciation and that there is no point in withdrawing from the world in order to follow a spiritual vocation, but rather that one should stay but act in a selfless way. In other words, one's karma depends on right motivation. This becomes the first of three ways of achieving release – the 'way of action', *karmamarga*. This is followed by the way of understanding (*jnanamarga*), and finally the way of devotion (*bhaktimarga*). Here Hinduism has moved beyond the necessity of sacrifice, as in the earliest Vedic literature, through the way of understanding and mystical identity offered in the Upanishads, and has arrived at a point at which release is achieved through devotion to the deity.

After the time of the *Gita* you come on to the period of classical Hinduism – represented by the great philosophical systems. But we need to be aware that these schools were not entirely innovative, but drew on the implications of earlier teachings.

Philosophical schools

Hindu philosophy may be divided up into various schools, which are either *astika* (orthodox) if they accept the authority of the Vedas, or *nastika* (unorthodox) if they do not. The unorthodox schools include Buddhism and Jainism. There are six orthodox schools, which are generally considered in pairs: Nyaya/Vaisesika, Sankhya/Yoga and Mimamsa/Vedanta.

Nyaya/Vaisesika

These two schools started independently in about the fourth century BCE, but gradually came together (their unity generally being attributed to Gangesa, a twelfth-century thinker) to form a single system of philosophy.

The Nyaya school was concerned with epistemology – in other words, it asked about how we know that something is the case. So, for example, it argued that there were four valid sources of knowledge: perception, inference, testimony and comparison. And, based on these, it systematically set out to decide what one could know. The Vaisesika school was more concerned with metaphysics – in other words, it wanted to know about the underlying structure and reality of our experience. It undertook a process of analysis, starting with the basic substances of earth, water, fire and air, and their particular qualities of taste, colour, touch and smell. It argued that everything is divisible into smaller and smaller parts, and ultimately you come to that something which is theoretically indivisible, called *paramanu*. Everything is therefore composed of paramanu.

This philosophy takes experience as the starting point for knowledge: all that we can know comes through the senses. Whatever is experienced can be analyzed into *padartha* (category) which is that which has existence, can be known and can be articulated. There were seven of these: substance; quality; action; class character; individual character; inseparability; and non-existence. All of them were seen as 'real'. Thus, what is experienced has an underlying substance, particular characteristics and relations with other things. But those characteristics and relations are as real as the substance of that which displays them. They are all part of the phenomena of the world as we experience it.

Western

The Nyaya–Vaisesika philosophy has interesting parallels with Western Empiricism. And notice that it makes the basic assumption that what is real is the same thing as what can be known and described – with the implication that, if it can't be known, it can't be real. There are parallels here with the Logical Positivist approach to language and meaning. It would also be interesting to explore parallels with Wittgenstein's *Tractatus* in this respect.

There are parallels between Vaisesika and Western 'atomism' – from the Greek 'atomists' Leucippus and Democritus in the fifth century BCE, through Hume's view that the world is comprised of atoms of experience, to Russell's 'logical atomism' of 1918 – where he sees the whole world as made up of logical atoms, each representing a predicate of some sort.

The Nyaya–Vaisesika system sees a quality that inheres in a number of individual things as a reality in itself. Thus there is a quality of 'treeness' that inheres in and makes individual things trees. That quality may be divided and may inhere with other

Western

There are parallels here with Plato's idea of 'Forms'. For Plato, the 'form' (of 'the good', for example) has a reality greater than that of individual good acts, a reality in which those individual acts participate in so far as they may be called 'good'. We intuitively know the form, and can therefore identify it in the individual things we encounter. (The opposite approach would be to take a 'nominalist' view that goodness does not have any independent reality, but is merely the name we give to show that a number of acts have a common quality ascribed to them.)

A great issue for both Eastern and Western thought is the existence or otherwise of universals. Are they simply part of our language and the way in which our brains organize their experience of the world, or do they exist 'out there'?

qualities in an individual thing (after all, the tree will also – at an appropriate time of year – have the quality 'green'), but each quality still retains its own distinct reality.

If all knowledge comes through experience, what does the Nyaya–Vaisesika approach make of the Atman (self)? The body, mind and senses all depend on the Atman, which is their animating principle. But how can we know about the self, either in terms of our own Atman or that of others? It cannot be identified with the body (since it remains the same while the body changes – you were very different as a baby), nor can it be identified with a person's experiences, since they constantly change. We therefore come up against the usual problem with any empiricist philosophy:

• What do you do with things that are known, but cannot be identified with any of the things that are experienced through the senses?

According to Nyaya–Vaisesika philosophy, you know your own self by direct awareness. It is the 'I' of your experience. When it comes to other people, however, they are only known by inference from your experience of them. You can see bodies and their actions, and from these you infer that they are 'selves' of the same sort as that which you experience directly as your own self.

The self cannot be identified with bodies, minds or sensations, but is known (directly in the case of myself and by inference in the case of others) as the 'I' or the 'You' that remains constant while all else changes.

Comment

This could be presented as a Western argument about the self from an empiricist point of view, but it is given a distinctively Hindu slant here, in that the self remains eternal, while the body is discarded at death and another one taken on in the process of rebirth. Personal characteristics and habits which cannot be accounted for solely with reference to experiences in this life, can be attributed to experiences in previous lives.

Note

Buddhist philosophy comes to a very different conclusion from the same observed phenomena, arguing that there is no fixed Atman. Since no empirical evidence can be found to decide between these two positions, it comes down to personal awareness. The Nyaya–Vaisesika system points to the experience of an ongoing, permanent 'I' through all the changes of life; the Buddhist sees this is an illusion. For Buddhism, the 'I' is no more than a conventional way to describe yourself. There is no 'you' over and above the things you think, feel, say and do, no hidden, unchanging Atman behind the scenes.

When it comes to the Supreme Self (which we are here referring to with the Western term 'God', because there is more of a parallel here than in other Hindu philosophies) this philosophy has an argument based on effects and agents. In its simplest form it can be presented like this:

- every effect has an agent
- the world is an effect
- therefore the world must have been produced by an agent and
- the name given to such an agent is God.

It then goes on to present such a God as both omnipotent and omniscient.

There are several problems with such an argument, even from the Nyaya–Vaisesika point of view. One is that the premiss that every effect has an agent is not empirically provable. The second is that some things (e.g. the Atman) are said to be eternal. Now, that which is eternal cannot be an effect, since there was no time when it did not exist and therefore could not have been brought into existence. This would imply that individual selves are not subject to the creative action of the Supreme Self, which would seem to make God rather less than omnipotent and omniscient!

Western

See Aquinas and the traditional cosmological arguments for the existence of God, for the Western equivalent of this.

There is another argument put forward for the existence of God, to be found in *Nyana Kusamanjali* by Udayana, a tenth-century philosopher. It says simply:

- people use the word 'God', so that word has meaning
- that word must refer to something (since meaning is given in terms of that to which a word refers)
- therefore God exists.

There are two ways of understanding this argument. The most obvious one, from a Nyaya–Vaisesika point of view, depends on the basic assumption of that philosophy that whatever is real both exists, is knowable and is describable:

- if people use a word, it refers to something
- that something must be knowable, or there would be no reason for the word to have come into use
- Therefore there exists something to which that word refers.

Its theory of knowledge shows this philosophy to be thoroughly empirical. Everything that is known is based on experience (perception), and the other ways of gaining knowledge (inference, testimony and comparison) depend upon it.

In other words

This philosophy accepts that knowledge is not simply raw experience, but that it depends on an understanding or assessment of an account of experience.

When it comes to language, the Nyaya-Vaisesika approach makes the individual word, rather than the sentence as a whole, the basis of meaning. The meaning of a word is given by that to which it refers. If there is no external reality as a referent, then the word has no meaning. All meanings are, of course, conventional – people simply agree together that a certain word is going to refer to a certain external reality.

Like most Indian philosophy, it is concerned with moksha, liberation from the sufferings of this world. Effort may be required in order to achieve moksha, but that effort needs to be based on understanding. So in this system, there is no distinction between knowledge for its own sake, and knowledge for the

> **Western**
> There are parallels here with the Logical Positivists, whose view
> of language sprang from a similarly radical empiricism. They held
> that the meaning of a word was its method of verification and
> that anything for which no empirical referent could be given was
> meaningless.

sake of liberation; the two are part of one and the same process. Understanding is a necessary step towards freeing yourself.

As with all the philosophies in the Indian tradition, there is a delight in detailed analysis and subtle distinctions. This section has done no more than hint at some of the broad areas of approach. Of all the Eastern philosophies, the Nyaya–Vaisesika is possibly the one with the most parallels with Western philosophy – particularly in its empiricism, its approach to language and also the place it gives God within its overall metaphysics.

The other important thing to realize about this philosophy is that it is not the product of a single person or era, rather it describes one broad tradition in philosophy that has developed over more than two thousand years.

Sankhya

Sankhya is generally claimed to be the oldest of the Hindu philosophical systems, for there may be references to it in the *Svetasvatara Upanishad* and the *Bhagavad Gita*. On the other hand the word sankhya means 'knowledge' or 'wisdom', so the references may simply have that general meaning. Two key features of Sankhya thought – *prakrti* and *purusha* (representing matter and consciousness) are certainly found in the *Mahabharata*, so elements of Sankhya are certainly as old as that epic. Traditionally, the founder of this school is thought to be Kapila, who lived sometime between 100 BCE and 200 CE, but we do not have any of his writings. The oldest extant Sankhya text is from the fifth century CE.

Basically, like other philosophical systems, Sankhya seeks to give an account of reality and a means of avoiding suffering and achieving liberation. Yoga, the tradition with which Sankhya is paired, sets out the principles of discipline required for achieving such liberation.

According to Sankhya, there are two ultimate realities: prakrti (matter) and purusha (consciousness). Prakrti is the reality out of which the world as we experience it is formed. It is made up of three *gunas* (meaning 'strands' or 'ropes'): *sattva* (reality, illumination – at the psychological level this guna produces happiness); *rajas* (foulness, constant restless activity – leading to pain); *tamas* (darkness – referring to dull inertia, leading to ignorance and apathy).

Prakrti and its three gunas are encountered in all the particular things we experience, and each of those things is limited and has a cause. But prakrti itself, lying behind all of its particular manifestations, is eternal and uncaused. It cannot be experienced directly and it is an unconscious, non-intelligent reality.

In other words

Underlying everything we experience, there is a neutral, material reality, out of which the world as we know it develops. It has different qualities (the gunas) but is impersonal.

In contrast to this, purusha is pure spirit. It is not the same thing as mind, ego or intelligence, since in Sankhya these are thought of as refined forms of matter. Purusha is the knower – eternal, free, beyond time and space. There are various arguments put forward for the existence of purusha – including the fact that there must be a subject to experience the pleasure, pain or apathy that is encountered in prakrti. There is also the sense that the longing for liberation from this material world only makes sense if there is a separate spirit that is capable of such liberation.

Notice that purusha is not located outside the self, it is not some external deity (indeed, Sankhya philosophy is in itself atheistic). Rather, purusha, since it is universal and eternal, is also found within the self – but as a pure spiritual self, not the self of the ego or the intelligence.

Sankhya then claims that prakrti, having come into contact with purusha, goes through a cycle of evolution and dissolution, producing the intellect, then the sense of individual egos, then mind, sense organs, the bodily organs and the elements. It is not clear why this happens under the influence of the eternal purusha, or why it should produce things in this order, but the basis of the whole evolution and the emergence of the world of particulars, is the neutral prakrti.

According to Sankhya, an individual person (*jiva*), comprises purusha joined to an ego (*ahankara*), senses and a body. In other words, it represents the two fundamental features of the whole world. But unenlightened individuals do not realize that their true identity is purusha, for they are engrossed in their ego, entirely motivated by their senses and their bodily needs. Liberation occurs once the difference between purusha and prakrti is seen.

In other words

Once you recognize that you have a pure spiritual nature that is not the same thing as your ego, your intellect, your senses or your body, then you will be free.

The method of achieving such liberation, however, is left to Sankhya's sister philosophy – Yoga.

Before leaving Sankhya, however, it is worth noting its epistemology (theory of knowledge), and particularly its views on cause and effect. First of all, knowledge of the world through the senses, in Sankhya, comes in the form of images in the mind, produced by the operation of the senses in contact with things in the world. Although Sankhya never doubts that the external world exists, it claims that we cannot know that external world as it is in itself, only the sense impressions that are produced in the mind as a result of it.

Western

Kant also makes this distinction between things-in-themselves, which are unknowable, and things as we perceive them to be.

This is the first of three sources of knowledge, the other two are inference (much as we saw above in the Nyaya school) and shruti, knowledge from scriptures. In practice, however, Sankhya seldom appealed to the scriptures, generally using just perception, inference and analogy.

Notice

We have a contrast here with Nyaya philosophy. In Nyaya, the world is what is experienced – simply that. In Sankhya, the world is out there, unknowable in itself and distinct from the sense impressions that it gives rise to in the mind.

Much argument in philosophy uses the concept of cause and effect. Sankhya has a distinctive way of approaching this. It argues that you cannot just get any effect from a given cause, but that the effect is related to qualities in the cause. For example, that you can produce cheese from milk, but not from water. That implies, so it is argued, that when something causes something else to happen, it is simply making actual what was previously potential. Cheese is a potential within milk. Milk is the material cause of the cheese, but it also requires the efficient cause of churning and so on to make the potential cheese actual.

> **Western**
> It might be worth considering Sankhya in the light of Aristotle's four causes – material, efficient, formal and final. Both East and West have struggled with this basic problem of causation. How are cause and effect related? Is the effect already there as a potential in the cause? For both Aristotle and Sankhya this appears to be the case.

The conclusion that Sankhya reaches on this is that cause and effect are not two separate things at all, but are different states of the same substance.

Comment
Perhaps, in the light of this, one might look back at the Sankhya idea of the constant evolution and dissolution of everything in the world. There is a constant process of change, with causes leading to effects which themselves appear as causes for yet further effects. In reality, Sankhya is inviting us to consider that this is not simply a matter of separate things reacting to one another, but rather that it is the outworking of the potential of a single undifferentiated prakrti.

Yoga

Yoga offers a set of disciplines that lead to liberation. Its origins are ancient, but Patanjali (who may have lived around 200 BCE or perhaps as late as 400 CE), wrote the *Yoga Sutra*, the oldest of the Yoga texts.

Although in general Yoga follows the philosophy of Sankhya, there is one very significant difference. Unlike Sankhya, it includes the idea of a personal God – *Isvara*. The argument used within Yoga for the existence of Isvara is based on the different grades we give to qualities. We say that one thing is greater than another, which implies that we have some measure by which we can assess them. This in turn implies that there must be some Being who possesses them to the highest possible degree. In other words, making value judgements implies knowledge of that which is of supreme value – Isvara.

Western

Notice parallels with Anselm's ontological argument for the existence of 'that than which no greater can be conceived'. Also, Aquinas put forward an argument from degrees of quality as the fourth of his 'Five Ways' of proving the existence of God.

Notice, however, that in Yoga, Isvara is eternal, omniscient and omnipotent, but is *not* regarded as the creator of the world of matter. This concept of God is therefore very different from the Western one and from that of the Nyaya-Vaisesika system.

The task of Yoga is to release purusha, and this requires spiritual discipline. Yoga sets out an eightfold path:

1 Abstention – from harming life, from lying, from theft, from sexual activity and from greed.
2 Observance – of internal and external purification, of contentment, of asceticism, of the study of philosophical works and of devotion to God. (These first two steps provide the moral basis of Yoga.)
3 Posture.
4 Regulation of the process of breathing.
5 Withdrawal of the senses. (These get the physical body ready for spiritual experience.)
6 Fixing the mind on an object.
7 Contemplation of that object.
8 Samadhi – a state of deep meditation.

At this last stage, the mind may still be aware of the object of its meditation and have an intuitive awareness of what is happening, or it may have gone beyond the process of thought into a state where the mind is totally absorbed in the process of meditating. It is in this last state that the purusha is liberated from matter.

Clearly, this process reflects a practical response to the nature of reality (purusha and prakrti) as set out within Sankhya. The function of God (Isvara) within Yoga is to provide a source of inspiration – since the proof of his existence is through the intuitive knowledge of that which is highest, and since devotion to him is seen as preparing the practitioner of Yoga for the physical and mental disciplines that follow.

Mimamsa

Mimamsa is concerned with an understanding of the Vedas, which includes the vedic hymns, the Upanishads and the Brahmanas. There are two traditions within Mimamsa:

- Purva (earlier) Mimamsa: This is concerned with the Dharma; with the principles of right action as they are set out in the Vedas. It is sometimes referred to as the Dharma Mimamsa.
- Uttara (later) Mimamsa: This is concerned with Brahman, with the ultimate cause of everything. It examines the nature of reality, rather than the principles of conduct. It is sometimes called Brahma Mimamsa.

The Uttara Mimamsa is also called Vedanta, the last of the six philosophical schools we shall be considering. It is important to realize that Purva Mimamsa is not 'earlier' in a chronological sense, but only in the sense that the Vedanta pressed beyond it to look at the ultimate principles that lay behind the vedic literature.

Note

The origins of both schools are obscure. Traditionally the Mimamsa goes back to the *Mimamsa Sutra* by Jaimini, written down somewhere between the second century BCE and the second century CE, after a long period of oral tradition. It is known mainly through the interpretation of Bhasya of Sabara, in the third or fourth century CE.

Mimamsa has as its starting point a basic proposition that only statements that prescribe a course of action are meaningful. The reason it makes this surprising claim is that it regards the Vedas as eternally true. Individual events – facts, in other words – could only be known to be true or false depending on evidence. But no evidence can be given for something that is eternal, since you cannot localize it or define it. Therefore, if the Vedas are eternal, they cannot offer mere contingent facts.

What then do we make of the apparent descriptions of facts in the Vedas? Mimamsa's answer to this is that their eternal meaning is given in so far as they introduce or explain some principle for living, some rule or prescription.

Western

In the West, prescriptivism is the term used for a philosophical view that statements about value are really just recommendations about a course of action. If I say something is good, there are no external facts that correspond to the word 'good', it is simply a way of saying that the action I am describing is one that I prescribe.

Mimamsa comes to a similar position. To say that the Vedas are eternal is to give them ultimate value. But such value cannot be expressed in terms of contingent facts. Therefore, the Vedas must be concerned with the prescription of a course of action.

If everything meaningful in the Vedas is in some way associated with the rules for living (the Dharma, in other words), then there is no point in asking if the Vedas are true, or in trying to check them against independent facts – that would be quite irrelevant. All that one needs to do is explore how one can most appropriately apply the particular Dharma to one's own life. In other words, Mimamsa does not challenge or assess the Vedas in any way. It merely interprets the rules it finds within them.

The view Mimamsa takes about the nature of knowledge follows from its claim that the Veda is eternal: all knowledge is said to be self-evident, and is known by self-awareness. In other words, mere facts do not yield true knowledge.

We see a radical dualism here. The mind is quite separate from the everyday objects of which it is aware. Knowledge is not something that the mind generates on the basis of experience, but something eternal that is there to be discovered. But it cannot discover eternal truths through facts, so it has to accept them as given in the Vedas. This position emphasizes the universal nature of karmic cause and effect. Everything that we do will have its results, and everything we do is determined by our previous actions.

The overall effect of Mimamsa within the Hindu tradition was to emphasize the role of correct performance of Dharma. The

Vedas provided a wealth of detailed rules, eternally valid, which needed to be constantly interpreted and applied. And alongside this went the implied threat that failure to perform correct Dharma would result in bad karma, and therefore in future suffering.

Vedanta

Vedanta remains influential to the present day. The term itself means 'end or purpose of the Vedas' and it is primarily concerned with Brahman – the absolute reality described in the Upanishads. Vedanta is also concerned to produce a philosophically consistent interpretation of the wide variety of vedic material. The earliest existing work of this school is the *Vedantasutra*, although this summarizes debates that took place earlier.

A key feature of this approach is that ultimate truth (Brahman) cannot be known by reason or logic but it can be perceived through devotion and meditation. The reason for this is straightforward:

- Brahman has no attributes (it is not 'this' or 'that'; not part of the world of phenomena)
- reason can only deal in concepts and attributes
- therefore reason cannot comprehend Brahman.

How then can Brahman be related to the world? The answer given in Vedanta is that Brahman transforms himself into the things that form the world, but does so without himself changing. In one sense, Brahman is therefore seen as the cause of the world. But it cannot be that simple, because cause and effect are separate things and if Brahman is eternal then nothing can be separate from him. Therefore Brahman and the world are actually identical. There is nothing that is not Brahman, but at the same time, there is no 'thing' that is Brahman.

Western

In many ways the Vedanta understanding of Brahman is rather like the Western idea of 'panentheism' – namely, that God is within everything and yet distinct from everything.

Although Vedanta attempted to create a single consistent philosophy out of the material in the Upanishads, there are inevitably some differences of view. One problem concerns the extent to which Brahman can be said to be an agent. After all, if he transforms himself into the things of the world, then he takes a direct role in their coming into being. On the other hand, Vedanta (like other Indian philosophies) includes the idea of karma – that everything is the result of good or bad actions already performed. Does that mean that some things are caused by karma and others by the direct transforming action of Brahman? Vedanta does not seem to be consistent on this point.

Sankara (c. 788–820 CE)

Sankara's *Brahmasutrabhasya* is one of the most important works on Indian philosophy. In it he comments on the Upanishads, the *Gita* and the *Brahmasutra*. He claimed that the ordinary world as we perceive it is in fact illusion – *maya*. The only fundamental reality is Brahman. This approach is termed *advaita* which means 'non-dualism' – there are not two realities, only one.

Sankara takes the general Vedanta line that reason cannot comprehend Brahma, since perceptions are only applicable to the empirical world. You cannot get 'beyond' the senses. On the other hand, the self or soul is an aspect of Brahman, it is therefore possible to know Brahman directly through the self. In fact, Brahman is the 'I' that acts – separate from the body and other aspects of the self that can be seen and described.

Sankara also distinguished between *Nirguna Brahman* (unqualified reality) and *Saguna Brahman* (qualified reality). Nirguna Brahman could be known only as pure consciousness, whereas Saguna Brahman was seen acting as a vital force in everything and also as Isvara – the general term used for 'God'.

Western

Sankara is often likened to Kant – for both pointed out the limitations of what could be known through the senses. Equally, Kant held that God could be known through the experience of human freedom (God, freedom and immortality were, for Kant, postulates of the practical reason – in other words, we presuppose them every time we make a free choice and act upon it).

In some ways one could also see Sankara's distinction between Nirguna and Saguna Brahman as being like Kant's noumenal and phenomenal realms.

There are therefore two levels of truth: conventionally and pragmatically Sankara saw the world as an evolving and changing system, produced by a divine person, rolling through its cycles, but ultimately he believed the world was unreal. As all experience is open to misinterpretation, we may be deceived and the world as we know it may be like a dream through which we are living. The only absolute reality is Brahman, identical with the self, the Atman.

The soul is trapped within layers, the outermost of which is the physical body. The layers are determined by our karma – and they may gradually be shed, until, at the very centre of ourselves, there is the Atman. Release, for Sankara, is by knowledge (jnanamarga) and it is release into *satcitananda* (or *saccidananda*), a term made up of three components: *sat* = existence, *cit* = consciousness and *ananda* = bliss).

Comment

There would seem to be a basic problem with *satcitananda*. Does that state – as suggested by the term *cit* – imply consciousness? If so, of what could someone in such a state be conscious? If it is a state of being an eternal and infinite Atman, at one with Brahman, what else is there to be aware of? Also, if the Atman is in some way self-conscious (and what else can it mean to be in a state of bliss), that implies that Atman/Brahman has personality. But Sankara claimed that Brahman was above personality.

To a certain extent this can be resolved by making the distinction between Nirguna and Saguna Brahman: the second is known but the first is not. But it seems to me that Sankara always wants to have it both ways:

- to be able to speak about Brahman, but at the same time identifying him absolutely with that about which one cannot speak, and
- to suggest a state of awareness and bliss without being able to give any content to either the awareness or the bliss.

Sankara tried to express the relationship between the absolute and the particular, within which it participated, by using the following image. A number of pots are filled with water. The sun is shining and is reflected on the surface of the water in each pot. It is the same sun, but it is seen in many different reflections. In the same way, Brahman can appear to each individual as his or her Atman – whilst still remaining the one Brahman.

In the same way, just as light is refracted through a pure colourless crystal giving a whole spectrum of colours, so we tend to assume that the reality we see with our senses is a true reality, but in practice it is limited, part of the world of illusion (maya).

Sankara criticized the Sankhya argument that an effect pre-exists in its cause, on the grounds that this would lead to an infinite regress: if everything depends on an earlier potential, which in turn depends on an earlier potential, and so on, how can anything become actual in the first place? Instead, he argues that, in reality, cause and effect are identical. We merely see them as different because that is the conventional way in which we are able to experience them.

> **Western**
>
> This is another point at which Sankara comes close to Kant. Kant argued that space, time and causality were part of the way in which we perceive things, rather than being features of things as they are in themselves. In the same way, Sankara argues that cause and effect, as separate things, are merely conventional – ultimately, they are identical.

Sankara also argued that:

- no insentient thing (lacking consciousness), unless it is an instrument used by a sentient being, can do anything in order to achieve a purpose or goal
- but the world appears to have purpose
- the world should therefore be seen as the product of an intelligence.

> **Western**
>
> This is Sankara's version of what was (much later) developed in the West as the 'argument from design'. Used by Aquinas and later (using the well-known analogy of coming across a watch, examining its parts and concluding that there must be an intelligent watchmaker) by William Paley, this argued for the existence of God on the basis of the perceived purpose and design in the world.

To use his own analogy – the clay needs a potter before it can become a pot.

Sankara made a point of criticizing rival philosophies. Among those, we have already mentioned his criticism of Sankhya, but he also criticized Buddhist philosophy on a key issue: Buddhism holds (see page 43f) that everything is radically impermanent, and the Dharmas, of which everthing is made, are momentary events. Thus, in Buddhist philosophy, the self is not permanent, but comprises five *skandhas* which are constantly changing and which come together to make a unique individual at every point in time. Sankara would not accept this. In particular he argued that, if there were nothing that persisted from one moment to the next, it would be very difficult to account for the phenomenon of memory or of recognition. If I remember something, according to Sankara, it implies that there is an 'I' that was there both in the past and in the present. And, of course, for him this 'I' is the Atman, ultimately at one with Brahman, the fundamental reality. This remains constant, even if everything else within the world of experience is merely maya and subject to change.

His system left little scope for religious devotion, which he saw as no more than a starting point. A person needed to move on to develop profound knowledge, gained through meditation, in order to achieve moksha.

Between the eighth and the fifteen centuries CE different schools of Vedanta developed. The three main traditions are:

1 Advaita (non-dualism)
2 Visistadvaita (qualified non-dualism) and
3 Dvaita (dualism)

The Advaita tradition developed the approach taken by Sankara. At its simplest it may be summed up as:

- What is real is permanent and cannot change.
- The objects we experience in the world are not real because:
  – they change
  – it is impossible to say at what level they might be real.

In other words, which is real, the cloth or the threads, the clay or the pot?

- The self is not part of the world we experience, rather it is self-evident. It cannot be the same as 'my' body, for it is the 'I' that is implied by 'my'.

- Therefore what is ultimately real is Brahman/Atman – the 'self' that is within everything. It is Pure Being and Pure Consciousness.
- Even if, conventionally, things are said to exist; ultimately, everything other than Brahman/Atman is like a dream.

Ramanuja (1017–1137 CE)

The *Visistadvaita* tradition affirmed the objective reality of the material world (*acit*), of individual souls (*cit*) and of God (*Isvara*). It is particularly associated with the work of Ramanuja. He taught the way of devotion, and held a theistic view of reality. Devotion leads a person to see himself or herself as a dependent fragment of God. Whereas for Sankara, the absolute is impersonal, for Ramanuja it is personal – Isvara.

This has implications for the nature of the self. For Sankara, the self (Atman) is in fact the same as Brahman – and the awareness of this brings moksha. But for Ramanuja, although the self becomes at one with God, it is not identical to God – there remains a distinction, without which the self would have no identity of its own. (This is why this approach is called 'qualified non-dualism'.)

Western

As in Westerm theism, Ramanuja holds that creation is an expression of the personality of God.

This Visistadvaita approach set out a straightforward test for what could be considered real. If something was perceived in two contradictory ways, then one of those perceptions must be false. Thus, in the much-used example, if I think that a length of rope is in fact a snake, but someone else sees it as rope, then one or other of those perceptions must be false. On the other hand, if there is no dispute about what is perceived, then there is no reason why that thing should not be accepted as real. In many ways Ramanuja's approach here seems rather more in line with common sense than that of the Advaita.

Madhva

Dvaita Vedanta was an approach associated first with the thirteenth-century philosopher Madhva. Like the Visistadvaita approach, it accepts:

- a personal God (in this case Vishnu)
- the real existence of finite selves
- the real existence of the objective world and
- devotion as necessary for liberation.

But he went further, by setting out a basic dualism between God (the only independent reality) and everything else (which is totally dependent upon God). Individual things are therefore distinct (i.e. this is the opposite of the advaita approach) but they are not totally independent (as was the case with the Nyaya–Vaisesika tradition) because they all equally depend on God.

In effect, Madhva was claiming that God was the efficient cause of everything, but that he was not the material cause – matter was eternal, and so were individual souls, but they only continued to exist because willed to do so by God. For Madhva, God cannot be the material cause of the world, because the sentient and the insentient are totally different from one another, and the one cannot convert into the other.

Western

This dualism is rather like the Western Deist tradition, in which God is seen as the originator and external controller of the universe, but in fact it is more what would be called panentheism – in that God, in Madhva's philosophy, is concerned with the ongoing existence of everything in the world.

Madhva introduced a very different view of the liberation of souls from the earlier schools. He suggested that there were three, intrinsically different categories of souls:

- those that would eventually achieve moksha (liberation)
- those who would stay for ever within samsara and
- those who would remain in a state of eternal suffering.

The justification for this is that, although progress towards liberation depends upon karma, each individual has an innate disposition which leads him or her to perform particular actions and therefore to suffer (or benefit from) their consequences.

One crucial difference between the souls that are bound for liberation and those that are doomed is that the latter think they are independent, whereas the former know they are totally dependent upon God. But Madhva goes one step further and argues that liberation or otherwise is totally dependent upon the will of God – so presumably God established the inherent dispositions, which led to the karma, which led to liberation.

Western

There are many parallels with Christian thought here, and particularly with later Calvinist ideas of predestination. It is widely believed that Madhva was influenced in his thinking by contact with Christian communities in southern India.

It will be clear by now that Vedanta is a vast area of Hindu philosophy and includes many differences within it, both obvious and subtle. In general, however, we need to remember that it represents the philosophical development of the Upanishads and that, alongside the authority of scriptures, it accepted both preception and inference as valid sources of knowledge.

Non-orthodox philosophies

The philosophical schools set out above developed within the main Vedic tradition. Others – including Jainism and Buddhism, which we shall consider in later chapters – developed separately, and are particularly associated with the area of north-eastern India, in what was then known as Magadha and is now West Bengal and Bihar.

But there were other non-orthodox schools as well, and a fascinating outline of these is given by Karel Werner in the Routledge *Encyclopedia* (1997, see 'Further Reading'). He describes the area as ruled by the Vratyas – a confederation of Aryan tribes.

Vratya philosophy is found referred to in the *Atharva Veda* and in scattered references elsewhere. It was a mystical philosophy in which the term Vratya is used for a cosmic creative power, individualized in Ekavratya (also called Mahadeva, the great god). From him comes the cosmic wanderer – Brahmacari – who establishes the Earth, impregnates it and thus gives rise to the multiplicity of our experienced world.

This trinity (Vratya, Ekavratya and Earth) was re-enacted in a fertility rite – with master, student and female assistant – in a ritual involving sexual intercourse, *maithuna*.

In religious terms, the aim was to reverse this process and regain a simple transcendence beyond the multiplicity of our experienced world. This led to a renunciation of the world as a celibate 'brahmacari' and, once accomplished, one was known as an *ekavratya* or *arhat*.

Note

What you have here is a ritual re-enactment of the process of creativity, with human sexuality mirroring a fundamental creativity in the universe. Then, in response to this, there is a reversal of the process, rejecting the world and seeking a higher mystical unity.

This sexual imagery, and the use of sexuality as expressing creativity, also appears in Tantric practice (see Chapter 07) although any linkage with Vratya remains speculative.

Lokayata philosophy was materialist – it claimed that only those things that are perceived are known to exist. There is no other world, and no survival of death. Belief in such things is thought to be fantasy. No logical proof for the existence of the unseen is possible, for inference cannot be used as a valid source of new knowledge, since it cannot be proved unconditionally. Inference should only be accepted if its results are at least, in principle, perceivable. But, as Werner points out, the basic materialist assumption (what cannot be seen, does not exist) cannot itself be proved true or false. It is therefore simply a metaphysical postulate, a choice about how experience is to be interpreted.

Consciousness – for the lokayata – is simply the result of the coming together of the elements that form the person, just as the property of intoxication is the result of the process of fermentation within a drink.

There were various lokayata schools, some identifying the self simply with the material components nourished by food (very much a 'You are what you eat' approach), some with the power of sensory perception, a third school is said to identify the self with vital forces, yet another accepts the distinct existence of the mind, although it too was regarded as perishable.

Western

This is rather like the weak form of the Verification Theory as developed by the Logical Positivists. They held that, to say that something exists, one should be able to say what sort of evidence could count for or against its existence.

The lokayata idea of the self would, in Western terms, be called 'epiphenomenalism'; namely, that the mind is a phenomenon that arises on the basis of the physical body.

The lokayata ethics follow from the conviction that there is no survival beyond death: that one should enjoy pleasures to the highest measure possible, and the highest bliss was said to be the embrace of a beautiful woman. Sacrifices and studying the Vedas were said to achieve nothing, and were therefore best left to those who lacked intelligence and manliness.

On the other hand, lokayata teaching held that the pursuit of pleasure should not be such as to cause suffering to others. Animal sacrifices and warfare were therefore opposed.

Western

The most obvious parallel here is with Epicurean philosophy. In its approval of pleasure as a valid goal in life, but in the limitations it imposed on its pursuit – for example, not causing suffering to others – there are parallels with Western utilitarian ethics.

Note

No lokayata texts have been preserved, and we know of it only through the attempts of the orthodox schools to refute it. I have no doubt that it was popular!

When we come on to look at Buddhism, we shall see that it refers to itself as 'The Middle Way'. This can be understood in a number of ways (as a balance between luxury and asceticism, or between eternalism and nihilism) but one of them, in the context of its origins, probably refers to its position between orthodox Hindu asceticism and this materialistic hedonism of lokayata.

Life: goals and ethics

The Vedas describe a natural order of things (*rta*, a concept which was later rather displaced by the ideas of Brahman and Dharma) which will lead to the welfare and happiness of all. All the various gods described in the Vedas are there to help maintain this *rta*. Humans can maintain it through the rituals of sacrifice and through performing their duty. If these things are done, they receive the benefits of following their *rta*.

From the Vedas, therefore, we have the basic moral concept: dharma. Dharma (which can be translated as right or appropriate action, or duty) is that which sustains society, ensuring that it conforms to the natural order of things. Later, in the *Gita*, this is expressed in the term *svadharma*, which is 'dharma for oneself' – in other words, each person will have particular duty to perform, and one's svadharma is the dharma as it applies to you as an individual.

Varnasramadharma

Clearly, the svadharma will vary between individuals according to their particular circumstances. One's dharma depends on one's colour (*varna*) and stage in life (*asrama*).

Within Indian society, from an early stage, there were caste differences within four main groups, or varnas, a term possibly used as a distinction between the fair-skinned Aryans and the darker skinned indigenous peoples whom they had conquered and with whom they co-existed. One's dharma within society therefore depended upon one's position within this social system.

There are four varnas:

1 the *Brahmin* (priestly) caste
2 the *Kshatriya* (ruler or warrior) caste
3 the *Vaishya* (merchant) caste
4 the *Shudra* (worker) caste.

These were set out in the Purusa Sukta of the *Rig Veda*, and their origin was expressed graphically in terms of the division of primal man (Purusa) – with the Brahmin as his head, the Kshatriya as his arms, the Vaishya as his thighs and the Suhdra as his feet. Such an image suggests mutual dependence and harmony, in spite of radical differences in status and function.

Alongside varna, another determining factor for one's dharma is the stage of life, or *asrama*. There are four of these:

1 *Brahmacarya* (student)
2 *Grhasta* (householder)
3 *Vanaprasta* (retired)
4 *Sannyasa* (renunciate).

Taking these two factors together, therefore, one's duty was seen as *varnasramadharma* – duty set according to one's stage in life and by one's 'colour'.

Comment

A key feature of Hindu ethics is this flexibility in recognizing that different people, at different stages of life, will have different norms of behaviour. Such an approach will always have the advantage of not having to constantly adapt generalized laws to the needs of particular groups of people. On the other hand it is difficult within such a system to distinguish between what is right or wrong in any absolute sense, and what is merely a reflection of the social structure. It is also difficult not to allow society to institutionalize what (in absolutist terms) may be seen as injustice. Hence the criticism of the Hindu caste system that can be made from a Western humanist perspective, where it is assumed that all should be treated equally.

The four aims of life

Within the Vedic literature there is a group of sutras particularly concerned with the exposition of Dharma, the most important of which is the *Manudharma Sastra* (or *Manusmrti*). This sets out four aims of life:

1 *Dharma* (virtue/right conduct)
2 *Artha* (wealth)
3 *Kama* (pleasure)
4 *Moksha* (liberation)

The fourth of these has been considered already, since it is an important feature of the classical philosophical systems. The second and third recognize the role of sexual and other pleasures and the gaining of wealth as a valid part of life, provided that they do not go against Dharma or harm others. Clearly Artha and Kama are particularly appropriate for the householder stage of life, where a person is expected to be economically and sexually active.

Ways to liberation

Just as Dharma is the principle that underlies all four of the aims of life, so *moksha* (liberation) is the ultimate goal, and we have seen this in the classical Hindu philosophies. There are three different *marga* (paths) leading to *moksha*:

Karma marga

Traditionally there were two different ways of behaving that would lead to liberation. The first was to follow the path of the renunciate (the *sanyassin*) and withdraw from life as far as possible, living as an ascetic. The other was to remain within society, but to behave with moderation and in a way that reflected one's svadharma. These two come together in the concept of *karma marga*. This is a path advocated in the *Bhagavad Gita*, and it is to act without attachment to the results of that action. In other words, there is both the sense of renunciation (not looking for personal gain) and yet one can practise this whilst still involved with worldly activity.

Of course, this reflects the earliest teaching of Dharma, which was to act for the good of society but also in accord with one's inner self. The path of action includes the *yamas* (rules concerning things to avoid) and *niyamas* (qualities to cultivate).

The yamas are:

1 *ahimsa* (not killing)
2 *satya* (speaking the truth)
3 *asteya* (not stealing)
4 *brahmacarya* (continence in matters sensual)
5 *aparigraha* (avoiding avarice).

The niyamas are:

1 cleanliness
2 contentment
3 pure concentration
4 study along with others
5 devotion to God.

Jnana marga

We have already seen that philosophy has played a large part in the Hindu tradition. The path of knowledge (*jnana*), as we saw above, may involve a recognition of the identity of the Atman with Brahman, a perception thought to lead directly to liberation. Notice also that study is one of the qualities to be cultivated on the path of action.

Bhakti marga

We saw, in examining the development of Vedanta, how, by the end of the first millenium CE, the Bhakti (devotional) tradition exerted a powerful influence over the whole philosophical tradition. This may be traced back to the time of the *Gita*, where devotion is seen as a means of achieving liberation. Of course, the whole Bhakti tradition implies the existence of a personal deity, and it is therefore not an option for those who take a non-theistic philosophy.

Ahimsa

We have already seen that killing is the first thing to be avoided. *Ahimsa* within Hindu thought is not merely abstaining from killing, but involves developing a positive attitude towards all living things. Mahatma Gandhi took the principle of ahimsa as the basis of his whole campaign to free India from British rule. In terms of the overall Hindu view of life, ahimsa is crucial. It relates both to the idea of karma and to the key notion that all beings have a svadharma: to do violence to another is to deny that other's right to live in an appropriate way. Ahimsa is also a recognition of the interconnectedness of all life.

Comment

Notice that ahimsa is also the key feature of the two non-orthodox philosophies that we shall be considering separately – Jainism and Buddhism. It is deeply ingrained in the whole of Indian philosophical and social thinking.

Western

Within this chapter, we have been concerned with the basic themes that have shaped Indian thought, and there has been no opportunity to examine particular modern thinkers. Those wishing to follow up on Hindu philosophies might wish to look particularly at the work of: Swami Vivekenanda (1863–1902), Mahatma Gandhi (1869–1948), Sri Aurobindo (1870–1950) and Radhakrishnan (1888–1975).

02

early Buddhism

In this chapter you will learn:
- the basic teachings of the Buddha
- the place of philosophy and meditation in the Buddhist tradition
- key features of Buddhist ethics.

Background: The Buddha

In the previous chapter it was pointed out that, alongside orthodox Hinduism, there developed a number of non-orthodox schools of thought which flourished particularly in the kingdom of Magadha in northern India. These non-orthodox schools included both extreme forms of spiritual discipline (asceticism) and also lokayata philosophy, which was materialistic and hedonistic. Two of these non-orthodox schools flourished and established themselves as separate traditions: Jainism and Buddhism.

Anyone living in northern India in the sixth century BCE would therefore have been familiar with three basic philosophies of life:

1 There was orthodox Hinduism, dominated increasingly at that time by the authority of the Brahmins, based on the Vedas and the correct performance of rituals.
2 There were what amounted to freelance spiritual teachers (*shramanas*) who offered ascetic training and meditation. Those shramanas who did not accept the absolute authority of the Vedas were regarded as unorthodox.
3 Finally there was the materialistic and hedonistic philosophy of the lokayata school, which fully justified the pursuit of pleasure as a valid aim in life.

It was also a time of increasing commerce and urbanization, weakening the links that individuals had with their family homes and village traditions, and fostering a spirit of questioning and spiritual exploration.

Siddhartha Gautama (563–483 BCE), later to be called the 'Buddha' (meaning 'the fully awakened or enlightened one'), is described as having lived a life of princely luxury and then given it up to follow forms of extreme asceticism. His quest was to find the cause of suffering and the means of overcoming it, and in pursuing this quest, he acknowledged having trained under various Hindu teachers prior to the experience that Buddhists accept as his enlightenment.

In the earliest sutras (the written records of his teaching), we find ourselves in a world where there is wealth and commerce, alongside the phenomenon of large numbers of people who deliberately retire from worldly concerns as part of a personal religious quest. Spiritual people, often referred to as 'ascetics and Brahmins' in the sutras, were generally supported in their efforts by wealthy patrons. It is against this background that the Buddha taught his 'middle way' between the extremes of hedonism and asceticism, of materialism and a nihilistic rejection of all material values.

Religion or philosophy?

It has often been difficult to know how to categorize Buddhism. Today it is generally referred to – with justification – as one of the world religions. At one time it was more common to see it referred to as a philosophy, or an ethical philosophy. Viewed from the perspective of Western religion, Buddhism appeared to be a philosophy rather than a religion, since it required no belief in God, nor in the immortality (or even the existence) of the soul. It also expected its followers to accept its teachings only to the extent that each individual could understand and be personally convinced by them.

On the other hand, from the standpoint of Western philosophy, Buddhism appears quite religious, especially since the Buddha himself did not encourage abstract speculation on metaphysical matters. What he claimed to offer was a practical path leading to full insight into things as they really are (insight which was thought to render speculative questioning unnecessary), along with a set of precepts and practices.

As we shall see later, the key feature of Buddhist philosophy is the idea that everything arises in dependence upon conditions. This is applied not just to the physical world, but morally and personally. Thus, the precepts and practices of Buddhism may be described in terms of creating the conditions under which insight and happiness might arise and suffering might be overcome.

So it should be remembered, as we look at Buddhist philosophy, that it needs to be thought of as a description of insight, rather than simply the conclusion to a logical argument or straight inference from experience. On the other hand, at the core of Buddhism there are a number of concepts, centred on the idea of the 'interconnectedness' of all things, which provide a conceptual clue to the whole of its spiritual and moral approach. It is these concepts that make it radically different from both orthodox Hinduism and the other non-orthodox schools.

Comment

In effect, Buddhism is saying 'Take a look at life this way. Now, does it make better sense to you?' In Western terms, that is certainly closer to philosophy than religion, since it asks no initial commitment other than the honest examination of its claims. That does not mean that Buddhism does not require subsequent commitment from those who choose to follow its path – that was always the case both for monastic and lay disciples – but commitment is expected to be based on personal conviction rather than 'faith' in a Western sense.

It is also important to recognize at the outset that Buddhist philosophy is based on the analysis of experience. The goal of the Buddhist path, exemplified by Siddhartha Gautama, is enlightenment, which is a matter of seeing things as they really are.

Relationship to Hindu thought

Some Hindus regard Buddhism simply as an unorthodox form of Hinduism. On the other hand, Buddhists see the teachings they follow as quite separate from the Hindu tradition. In any case there are two fundamental differences between orthodox Hinduism and Buddhism:

- Hinduism accepts the idea of a single divine reality (Brahman) which may be expressed through many different images of gods and goddesses. It also accepts the idea of an immortal soul which is lodged in the body and will, after death, pass on to other lives. Buddhism rejects both the reality of an eternal God (Brahman) and of the self. Nothing is permanent; everything is interconnected and in a state of flux.

- Hinduism is based on tradition and on acceptance of the Vedas. Buddhism rejects all external authority, and insists that teachings are accepted on the basis of reason and experience.

It is these two fundamental differences, rather than any details of moral teachings or styles of worship, that distinguish Buddhism from Hinduism.

Key concepts

Note

Buddhist terms are found in both Pali and Sanskrit. Pali was used for the earliest collection of the Buddhist scriptures, and has continued within the Theravada tradition. The Sanskrit versions are generally given here, simply for convenience, since we are also considering other religions that use Sanskrit, and to save any confusion.

Pratitya samutpada

Pratitya samutpada is the fundamental concept to all Buddhist philosophy and is a distinctive feature of Buddhism. It may be translated as:

- dependent origination
- conditioned co-production and
- interconnectedness.

In its simplest form it may be expressed as 'This being so, that arises. This no longer being so, that ceases.' In other words, things only come into existence because of certain conditions, and if those conditions change, they will cease to be. Their origins are dependent. Looked at in another way – whatever is about to happen will do so because of a variety of factors that exist now. Those factors themselves will depend on other things being the case, and those will depend upon yet others. In other words, everything is interconnected.

As we look at the world, the temptation (especially for those schooled in Western philosophy) is to divide the world up into 'things', each of which has its own separate existence. That is not the Buddhist perspective. For Buddhism, the world comprises an infinite network of conditions – and everything that exists is the temporary manifestation, in this particular time and place, of that whole network.

Example

Think of the conditions that enable you to read this book. First of all, you require air to breathe and light to be able to see. Your life depends on food and drink, on a whole network of practical things that maintain you, as well as generations of people who have met and coupled to produce children who in turn have produced children, who have become your parents. Imagine the vast number of chances that have determined your heredity. And it is not simply the sexual attraction between couples stretching back through generations, but all the other factors that led each of them to meet one another.

So much for your own existence, but consider also the book, its materials, its publication, its distribution, the circumstances that led me to write it, and which led to you to read it.

In short, it has taken a theoretically infinite number of chances (conditions) to enable you to be born, and for you to be here reading this book.

In other words
If anything in the universe were different, everything would be different, for everything is interconnected. Equally, you are not separate from the rest of the world, you are part of the world, and are totally dependent on the rest of it. When the conditions which enable you to live are no longer there, you will cease to be.

This view might sound fatalistic or determinist, but it does not deny human freedom, since your present actions contribute to what the future holds. If everything else makes a difference to you, then it is equally the case that you make a difference to everything else! This feature of the Buddhist view can be appreciated by a reflection on all the possible consequences of a present action or choice.

Three Marks of Existence

Pratitya samutpada gives rise to three universal features of the conditioned world in which we live:

Anicca
Nothing is fixed, but everything is in a constant process of change. We may have a concept of that which is eternal, we may long for the eternal, but in reality, everything we experience in this life is subject to change, because everything is dependent upon the conditions that maintain it in existence.

Anatta

Not only is everything changing, but nothing exists in and of itself. At every moment, each existing thing depends on everything else. But interconnectedness implies even more – that there is no such thing as an inherent 'self' (like the Hindu Atman). What appears as 'self' in conventional language is – in absolute terms – an illusion, devoid of reality. As Western philosophy has found, the self is elusive; we cannot find something that is the self that is not also something else. Buddhism has no such problem, it sees individuals as a collection, a bundle of five *skandhas* (see page 51) – body, feelings, perceptions, volitions and consciousness. They come together at birth, and are conventionally given an overall term 'oneself'. At death they cease to operate together, and so this conventional 'self' ceases to exist. Like pratitya samutpada, anatta is absolutely crucial to Buddhist philosophy: nothing has inherent and therefore independent or permanent existence; there is no fixed self. The radical implications of this single idea dominate the Buddhist view of reality.

Dukkha

If we do not have a permanent self, and if everything is changing and dependent upon conditions, then life will inevitably involve frustration, suffering and death. These things are not imposed on us from outside, but are the natural consequence of being limited, dependent beings. Dukkha is a broad term used to cover all that is unsatisfactory in life. Not getting what one wants is dukkha; getting what one does not want is dukkha. Even pleasant things can be dukkha, for we know that nothing lasts and will have to be given up. To pretend that life does not involve dukkha is seen by Buddhists as deliberate refusal to face the facts.

All that follows on the Buddhist path is the result of a radical recognition of the nature of conditioned existence and the dukkha (often rather narrowly translated 'suffering') that follows from it. The whole of Buddhist philosophy is aimed at overcoming dukkha. This does not imply that Buddhism seeks to change the reality of the world – that would be quite impossible – but it argues that an understanding of the mechanism by which dukkha comes about, and the response that people have to it, will in itself help them to overcome it. And since everything happens as a result of conditions, the Buddhist path seeks to create the conditions within which suffering may be overcome.

Note

Buddhist philosophy is sometimes introduced with a bald statement that all life is suffering. In one sense this is correct, for Buddhism teaches that all conditioned things are eventually liable to decay, and that pretending otherwise is wilful delusion, leading to frustration. Yet it can give entirely the wrong impression of Buddhist philosophy. For reasons we shall see later in this chapter, Buddhism is not negative but realistic, and the statement that all life involves suffering is not to endorse suffering, but to recognize those things that cause it in order that they may be overcome. Buddhism itself does not focus on suffering, but on the means of overcoming it.

The Four Noble Truths

Using a common form of reasoning (parallel with that of a doctor giving a diagnosis and cure) the Buddha is said to have set out his *Dharma* (teaching) in the form of four propositions, each following from the previous one:

1 All life involves *dukkha* (suffering or unsatisfactoriness).
2 The cause of suffering is *tanha* (craving; longing for things to be other than they are).
3 If this craving ceases (*nirodha*), suffering too will cease.
4 The way to eliminate craving is to follow the Noble Eightfold Path – called *magga* ('the middle way').

Let us examine the implications of each of these:

Dukkha

As has been outlined above, this claims to be a realistic assessment of the human condition. It does not imply that life is devoid of happiness. Indeed, the Buddha recognized that the quest for happiness and the avoidance of suffering was fundamental not just to human life but to that of all sentient beings. It is simply a recognition of the implications of living in a world where everything is interconnected and constantly changing. Reality can never match our dreams, or if it does so, that ideal state cannot be sustained permanently.

Tanha

Tanha is *not* the same thing as the natural desire for those things that sustain us or bring happiness. It denotes craving for something to be fixed and permanently available in a world where that is not possible. In other words, it is a form of wanting that is fundamentally at odds with the way the world is.

Tanha may take three forms:

1 sensual craving (*kamatanha*): seeking permanent satisfaction through sensory pleasure and avoiding situations of sensory deprivation
2 craving for existence (*bhavanatanha*): the longing to survive as an individual
3 the third form of craving (*vibhavatanha*) can mean two very different things. Vibhava can mean 'prosperity', in which case it is craving for success and wealth, but it can also mean 'annihilation', and so would refer to the desire to leave the world altogether, presumably by suicide. Vibhavatanha is therefore an 'all or nothing' approach, attempting to avoid the changing and dependent nature of life by opting for one extreme or the other.

Comment

In this context, it sounds likely that the third form of craving should be for wealth, but it is possible that this was set out to counter the extreme asceticism of some of the non-orthodox groups. Remember that, in coming to the 'middle way', the Buddha rejected extremes. Perhaps this third form of craving can therefore be taken to refer to both the extremes of luxury and asceticism.

Nirodha

Nirodha means 'cessation': if tanha (craving) ceases, then dukkha (suffering/unsatisfactoriness) will also cease. It is tempting, from a Western perspective, to interpret this negatively – 'If you don't expect anything from life, you won't be disappointed.' Within Buddhism it is not seen that way, for two reasons. The first is that craving for annihilation is just like any other craving and leads to suffering – so nirodha cannot mean annihilation. Secondly, this third Noble Truth is often referred to as *Nirvana* (*Nibbana* in Pali) which (as we shall see on page 58) is the state of happiness and peace to which Buddhists aspire, marking the point at which the 'triple fires' of hatred, greed and ignorance are burnt out, to be replaced by love, generosity and wisdom. So the point at which tanha ceases is thought of as bliss, not surrender.

Magga

This is the 'Middle Way', and it sets out eight features of the Buddhist path. These are set out below.

Note

The 'Middle Way' can sometimes be taken to refer to the middle way between the extremes of luxury and asceticism, following the example of Gautama Buddha. It also has a more philosophical background, as the middle way between nihilism and eternalism. A nihilist will deny the reality of things, including the self. An eternalist, by contrast, will claim God and the soul as eternal self-existing realities, and may see people as being souls embodied in this world but fundamentally independent of it. The idea of interconnectedness and of a lack of inherent existence leads to this middle path – things have reality, but it is a changing reality, always dependent upon conditions.

The same applies to concepts of value. To the nihilist, nothing in the world has value; to the eternalist things are accorded their own permanent value. The middle way here shows that things have value exactly in their arising in dependence upon conditions and in their relationships with everything else.

The balance of the middle way, in philosophical terms, is not simply one of compromise, but one which reflects the Buddha's fundamental vision of the nature of conditioned reality. In a world in which everything is interconnected, things have their existence and their life insofar as they connect. *Reality does not inhere in the whole only, nor in the individual only, but in the ever-changing set of relationships that lie between them.*

Western

The shift from a Hindu to a Buddhist perspective is interestingly parallel to shifts in the understanding of language in twentieth-century Western philosophy. Early in the century it was argued (e.g. by Wittgenstein in *Tractatus*) that words had meaning to the extent that they corresponded to some sense datum. If you could not point (literally or metaphorically) to something and say 'that's what the word stands for', then it had no meaning. Later, it came to be recognized that words took their meaning from their use within various forms of speech (language games). Thus, to understand a word, you need to see the context within which it is used; it takes on a life and meaning of its own within that context, without the need to try to pin it to some external fixed datum.

Buddhism goes through a similar process with respect to the existence of individual things. They are not independently self-existent – like a word whose meaning is guaranteed by some external fact; their meaning and their reality comes from their interconnectedness.

The Eightfold Path

Although generally referred to as steps on a path, these eight features of the Buddhist life are not intended to be taken in sequence, but simultaneously. They represent features of attitude, lifestyle and spiritual practice which are helpful in setting up the conditions under which a person may move towards the goal of the Buddhist path, namely, seeing things as they really are.

1 Right (or perfect) view
This refers back to interconnectedness and the fundamental features of the Buddhist view of life. Without such a view the path does not make sense.

2 Right intention
This step introduces the element of personal, existential commitment. The Buddhist path cannot be a matter of detached academic interest, but requires commitment. This is not to take some moral high ground against intellectual frivolity, but implies that the path can only be followed in engagement, not in detached reflection.

3 Right speech
Various forms of speech are to be avoided: false speech, harsh speech; speech liable to cause dissension; idle chatter. The opposite – truthful, gentle, constructive and purposeful speech – is to be cultivated.

4 Right action
The moral precepts that form this part of the path are discussed on page 68. In brief, they are: not to take life (but cultivate compassion and goodwill towards all living things); not to steal

(but to cultivate generosity); not to indulge the senses harmfully (but to cultivate stillness, simplicity and contentment); not to practise wrong speech (see above); not to cloud the mind with intoxicants (but to practise mindfulness).

5 Right livelihood

Clearly, Buddhists are encouraged to follow a livelihood that is in line with the fundamental Buddhist vision and particularly the five precepts given in step four.

6 Right effort

There are four right efforts:

1 eliminating harmful thoughts/desires that already exist
2 preventing these from arising in the future
3 encouraging the arising of positive thoughts/desires
4 maintaining those positive thoughts that have already arisen.

In other words, it is the process of consciously refining thoughts and wishes in line with Buddhist principles.

7 Right mindfulness

We shall consider this again under 'meditation' (see page 65). Basically, the Buddhist path requires a person to cultivate awareness of the body, feelings, mental processes and the objects of thought. This follows from the basic Buddhist view that lack of awareness leads to suffering, and that the goal of the spiritual path is to be fully awake or aware (in other words 'buddha').

8 Right contemplation

As we shall see later (page 65) meditation of various kinds plays a crucial role on the Buddhist path. In general one might say that the taming and gentle controlling of the mind, calming it and harmonizing the various conscious and unconscious urges that determine its activity, is the means by which the path can be followed. Without it, the insight and determination will be lacking (or will be forced, rather than natural), and the practical steps of speech, action and livelihood will not spring from a naturally integrated vision and desire.

Triple Way

The Noble Eightfold Path is only one way of setting out the working out of the Buddhist dharma. Another common division is between:

- *Sila* (morality) – particularly the Precepts
- *Samadhi* (meditation) – including the step of mindfulness
- *Prajna* (wisdom) – reflecting the first two steps, but in practical terms the most subtle of the three, since it cannot be forced, but arises either in a moment of spontaneous insight, or as a result of practising both Sila and Samadhi.

Wisdom is regarded as accessible on three levels:

- *Shrutamayi prajna*: This is the wisdom that arises as a result of listening to or reading the sutras. It is accepted wisdom from the tradition in which one stands.
- *Cintamayi prajna*: This is the wisdom that develops as a result of personal reflection and thought.
- *Bhavanamayi prajna*: The highest form of wisdom comes as a result of an understanding that arises in the course of *bhavana*, spiritual practice.

Clearly, these levels are seen as leading on from one to another. First comes an understanding of the tradition, then a conscious, personal reflection on it, and finally the influence of that personally accepted wisdom into meditation and other practices, at which point the wisdom engages both the unconscious mind and the emotions, leading to spiritual insight.

Comment

It is important to appreciate this threefold process of deepening wisdom in Buddhism, because it highlights the difference between Eastern and Western philosophy. In the West, philosophy has generally been regarded as a matter of intellectual and logical debate. Arguments are examined for logical coherence. Even with existentialist philosophy, where we explore the implications of personal choice and meaning, the aim is to relate these in a rational way to an overall view of life.

Buddhism regards all such philosophy as a starting point, not an end product. Its teachings are presented as a basis for meditation, allowing personal and unconscious influences to shed light upon them. As a result, much Buddhist philosophy does not appear to have the honed logic of a good western argument, and it may often appear less rigorous because it may employ flowery imagery or be conveyed through the medium of story. But this merely reflects this three-layer approach to philosophical truth – the deepest level is not necessarily that which can be most easily set down on paper.

The self

Implications of anatta

The Buddha's teaching reflects the Hindu spiritual practice and language of his day, either by way of development, or by way of contrast. His views on the self may therefore be seen in contrast to those of the majority of Hindu philosophers, as set out in the previous chapter.

Hinduism generally accepts that there is an eternal self (Atman) which is linked with, but essentially independent of the physical body. Thus, for example, in the *Gita* there is the famous passage in which the god Krishna, disguised as a charioteer, explained to Prince Arguna that people neither kill nor are killed in battle. The body is destroyed but the self (Atman) continues and lives again. Equally, in the earlier Upanishadic literature, the goal of the spiritual life is the unification of the Atman with Brahman, absolute reality. The 'true' self for a Hindu is not subject to change with the changing fortunes of the material world, and its true nature is revealed only in its identitfication with the absolute.

One implication of this was that people were largely fixed by their unchanging identities, which in turn reinforced caste distinctions and – so it may be argued – led to a fatalism in terms of one's inability to shape one's own destiny.

In teaching anatta, the Buddha rejected the Hindu concept of the eternal Atman. By teaching interconnectedness the implication is that each 'self' has no inherent or permanent reality, but arises in dependence on conditions, is constantly changing as those conditions change, and will cease to exist in its present form at death.

In Buddhist teaching the self is described as made up of five skandhas (or 'heaps'). They are:

- *rupa* (form)
- *vedana* (feelings)
- *samjna* (perceptions)
- *samskara* (volitions)
- *vijnana* (consciousness)

Each of these is a temporary and changing 'bundle' of phenomena that, when put together, I conventionally call 'myself'.

It is very important, in examining the Buddhist view of the self, to set aside all Western, dualistic notions of mind and body. So let us ask: What am I?

I am, first of all, a changing physical entity on its way from birth to death, a physical body that requires food, drink and oxygen, a body that is processing food into energy to maintain itself, a body that is totally dependent upon the rest of the physical world for its existence.

I am also aware of a constantly changing sequence of feelings, some good, some bad and some neutral. They arise in response to perceptions – knowledge that comes to us through the senses. As a result of our feelings and perceptions we have desires, we decide to act, we make decisions; these are our volitions (and they form our *karma*, see below) and express our response to life.

But arising as a result of these four skandhas is consciousness. There are different forms of consciousness, depending on the organ of the body in which it arises – sight, sound, smell, taste and touch (the usual five senses recognized in the West) along with mind, which Buddhism sees as the faculty of thought (just as the eye gives the faculty of sight).

Consciousness is the process of seeing, touching, smelling, tasting, hearing and thinking.

Comment

Notice that there is no separate 'thing' that is consciousness. There is no mind other than the process of thinking, just as there is no sight other than the process of the physical eye picking up and recording light. Consciousness, the last of the skandhas, simply arises in dependence upon the other four.

Mind is therefore not a 'thing' at all, it is a process (the Pali term for this is *santanna*). As individuals, we are the sum total of our actions of body, speech and mind. To have a mind that is more harmonious, more integrated, more sensitive (which is what Buddhism seeks to promote) does *not* imply that there is some separate entity that has these qualities. It is simply a way of describing the processes of speech and thought to which these qualities can apply.

In other words

Remove the thought and there is no thinker that remains. There is no separate soul or self – what we conventionally call 'ourself' is but the sum of all those processes by which the faculties engage with the rest of the world, including the mental processes by which we conceptualize and reflect upon our experience.

Western

In Western terms, this approach to the self is called 'epiphenomenalism': mind arises as a result of other phenomena, and is not independent of them.

It is important also to note a 'nominalist' aspect of Buddhist thought here. We conventionally give names to things – 'self', 'mind' – but giving a name does not mean that there is a separate physical entity to which the name is given.

For example, you would not dream of examining an eye and its optic nerve, along with the source of light that it is detecting, and then ask 'Where, over and above these things, is "sight"?' Sight is the name we choose to give to this process of seeing. Mind is the faculty of thinking, and consciousness is the name we give to that process of thinking and being aware.

Here we could explore parallels with Gilbert Ryle's, *The Concept of Mind*, where the traditional Western idea of a separate self or soul is termed 'the ghost in the machine'. The main difference, however, is that Ryle comes at the problem from a linguistic point of view, whereas within Buddhism it is simply part of the overall view of all life as comprising an interconnecting web of ever- changing phenomena.

What is the 'real' me?

To this question Buddhist philosophy has a simple answer. The real you is what you are – what you feel, see, think and choose to do with your life. There is no elusive 'real' you somewhere else. Buddhism therefore denies the validity of the quest for some definitive self other than the present ever-changing psycho-physical organism.

Western

Descartes, prepared to doubt everything known through the senses, could not doubt the fact of his own thought, and therefore concluded *cogito ergo sum* – 'I think, therefore I am'. The task he set himself was one that a Buddhist would see as futile. He sought to separate the self off from the world, to eliminate everything that could be something else, to arrive at a basic, independent, permanent 'self'.

In Buddhist terms, the task of separating self from world is futile, because the self is part of the world and is totally integrated with it. Descartes tried to see all sensations and so on as part of a material world, but could find no location for mind (it was not the same thing as the brain), and therefore set up a great gulf between the material and the mental – the two independent worlds being joined by the pineal gland, since he had to find some link to allow the one world to interact with the other.

Comment

The Buddhist despairs of that Cartesian process and says in effect: 'There is one world, you are part of it, you live within it. Your part of the world has faculties that enable it to encounter and respond to the rest of the world, and when those faculties are working, you have consciousness. That is what you are, there is no mystery, no ghostly soul to be sought elsewhere. *The secret of the elusive self is that there is no secret elusive self.* You are exactly who you are – a physical, feeling, sensing, willing, thinking, conscious entity.'

This is absolutely central to the Buddhist view of reality. There is no 'self' (anatta). Now that does not mean that you do not have a personality. As you act (in other words, as you build up new karma, and respond to you old karma – see page 56) you are weaving a pattern of characteristics. The memory (conscious or otherwise) of all that you have experienced in the past, informs your feelings and choices for the future, and so on. No 'self' does not mean no personality. Everything is just as we perceive it, you are you, with your feelings thoughts and habitual tendencies. All that has gone is the idea that there is some other 'self' over and above this process.

The middle way on the self

In presenting the radical difference between the Hindu and the Buddhist view of the self, notice that Buddhism attempts to avoid what it sees as two fundamental errors: eternalism and nihilism.

- An eternalist view (Hindu) disengages the self from any interconnectedness, and claims that it has an eternal essence. This may be seen as an attempt to gain some permanence and security in a world where the body so obviously changes and decays.
- At the other extreme, the nihilist denies that there is any such thing as the self. It does this by denying that there is any value, meaning or (by implication) connections within the world.

Both views attempt to make the self a separate 'thing' and then consider whether or not it exists, and if so what its nature can be. Buddhist teaching denies this as a valid way to approach the 'self'. For Buddhism, it is quite impossible to isolate a self from the conditions and connections within which it is embedded and operates. Without them it is nothing but, arising in dependence upon them, it has an interconnecting and changing reality.

Comment

It is important to keep this last point in mind. The idea of anatta (or the later term *shunyata* – which is generally translated as 'emptiness') seems to imply, from a Western point of view, non-existence. But within Buddhism both have a positive role. To put it crudely: you exist in so far as you share (your body is part of the physical world, your thoughts and language part of culture, your emotions part of relationships and so on). Without your connectedness, your self appears to vanish, it becomes (to use the Western term) 'elusive'.

Buddhist philosophy and ethics only make sense in the light of this philosophical position. It is a philosophy of connections, or consequences, of ever-changing patterns. It is about recognizing a flow of life within which one participates. In a conventional sense, you exist, and it is convenient to label the bits that make you up as 'you'.

Even at a physical level, however, that is not actually how things are. The atoms that make up your body have existed elsewhere and will do so again; you are but the name given to their present, temporary arrangement. Billions of years ago, before the Earth or our Sun and its solar system came into existence, the atoms which at this present moment form your body, were forged in the thermonuclear reactions in the heart of a star. With that star's 'death', the material was flung outwards and has re-gathered. You are the product of that re-cycling process. Such a vista, offered by modern cosmology, appears to endorse the Buddhist perspective.

When defensively separated from their context in an ever-changing, interconnected world and forced to be the bearer of all values, Buddhism considers individuals a sorry sight, for their future inevitably involves decline and death. From that perspective, nothing seems worthwhile, since all ends in dust.

Once interconnectedness becomes a habitual way of seeing things, however, the existential power of suffering is broken. Sickness, old age and death continue, but as a natural part of a world in which an individual has links throughout time and space. This view is expressed through the ideas of karma and (particularly in later, *Mahayana* developments) of a 'Buddha nature' within all things. That is why, as a personal philosophy, Buddhism can be absolutely positive in its appreciation of life, and at the same time hold that only frustration and suffering can come from what it sees as the illusion of an independently existing self.

Karma

The opening verse of the *Dhammapada*, an early collection of Buddhist teaching, says:

> What we are today comes from our thoughts of yesterday, and our present thoughts build our life of tomorrow: our life is the creation of our mind.

Buddhist philosophy does not take interconnectedness in a fatalistic way. Although everything arises in dependence upon conditions, once it has arisen it forms part of the conditions which allows the next thing to arise. In this sense, everything has a constructive part to play in the process of change.

Within its physical limitations, life is shaped by thoughts and decisions – both one's own and those of others. One's intentional actions have consequences. Karma simply means 'action', but within Buddhist philosophy it refers to actions done as a result of conscious act of volition. It is those things that you *choose* to do that shape who you are. There is, therefore, a constant process of creating new karma and also experiencing the results of past karma.

Note

There is a tendency to think that what one *is* determines what one *does*. Thus, if you are a good person, you will be expected to display that inherent goodness by doing good deeds – the existence of the deeds displaying the essence of 'goodness'. For Buddhism it is the other way round: if you do good deeds, you are called 'good' and the doing of them might be referred to as 'goodness'. For example, you do not play music because you are a musician, you are a musician because you play music. 'Musician' is not some invisible essence, it is simply the name given to someone who plays music.

In Buddhism, there is no fixed essence, so what you will be in the future is determined by what you do now – by generating good or bad karma. In that sense, existence comes before essence – or, more correctly, essence is simply a conventional name given to certain features of existence.

Re-becoming

Although in popular usage, Buddhists are said to believe in 'reincarnation', that is not strictly accurate. Reincarnation implies that there is a soul that lives in a body and then, at death, moves on to be 'incarnated' in another body. Clearly, such a view is quite incompatible with the Buddhist view of the self as an ever-changing collection of skandhas.

For a Buddhist, what you are today is the result of what you were yesterday, and in turn shapes your tomorrow. You are constantly changing, shaped by your karma. Re-becoming is therefore something that happens throughout life. The correct Buddhist term for this process is not reincarnation, but *punabhava* (re-becoming). At death, however, the whole network of interconnections, and their karma, do not simply come to an end. They are still there, and what you have chosen to do today will have some impact on tomorrow, even if you die in the night. So Buddhists see karma as continuing to mature and bear fruit in some future life. *Not*, that you disappear out of this world into some other world where you get a replacement, disembodied existence, but that in this world there will be lives that take on and work though the karma that you have created. This is expressed as a series of twelve links in a chain, called the *nidanas*.

The image given for this is of the flame of one lamp lighting another. The second flame is distinct from the first, but it is burning as a result of the burning of the first flame. Nothing physical passes from one to another, but the burning of the second depends upon the prior burning of the first.

Nirvana

There is some debate about exactly what the word *Nirvana* (or *Nibbana* in Pali) means. The literal interpretation is probably 'blowing out', in the sense of extinguishing a flame. It does *not* mean extinction however, so Nirvana is not the point at which the self ceases to exist. Rather, Nirvana is described as the point at which the triple fire (of hatred, greed and ignorance) is extinguished because it has no more fuel to keep it burning. Put in a positive way, it is a point of absolute love, generosity and insight.

Nirvana is generally contrasted with *samsara*. Samsara describes the ordinary world, whose changes are the results of karma generated by hatred, greed and ignorance. The whole process of karma – leading from one action to another, from one state of mind to another, from one life to another – is regarded as inherently unsatisfactory. Fulfilment, in terms of Buddhist philosophy and spirituality, comes in getting beyond samsara. This does not imply removal from the world, but achieving a state in which a person is untouched by those things that bring suffering, and also ceases to cause suffering in others.

Within the earliest Buddhist traditions, Nirvana is seen as the ultimate point in the spiritual path and a natural consequence of enlightenment. One who has achieved this is known as an *Arhat*. The other term used for one who has achieved this state is *tathagata*, which means 'one who has gone beyond', and it is generally used of the Buddha.

Note

Buddhism, of course, does not include belief in God – so there is no union with some external, transcendent God at the end point of one's spiritual journey. Rather, the transcendence of Buddhism consists in progress towards ever higher levels of human consciousness – leading ultimately to enlightenment.

In other words

According to Buddhist philosophy, ego identity ultimately fails, and comes from a very limited awareness of the nature of the self and of reality itself. It also leads to suffering, since it makes central an ego that does not have inherent existence and is constantly vulnerable to conditions. From an ego-centric point of view, life is always, ultimately a failure.

The opposite quest is to become more and more aware of the interconnected nature of reality and therefore less ego-centric. This process, turning away from the ego's cravings (which lead to hatred and greed and are based on ignorance of the true nature of things) leads to a blissful state of Nirvana. The basis of this is an ego-less awareness of things – which frees a person from craving and suffering, and also (as a natural consequence) leads them to avoid inflicting suffering on others.

The scope of the idea of Nirvana in Buddhism is illustrated by the names used for it. These include *amata* (immortal) and *asamkhata* (uncompounded). What is certain, is that Nirvana does not mean the annihilation of the self, only the annihilation of the illusion of a self. Nirvana is also described as *mutti* (freedom).

Nor should it be thought that the state of Nirvana is such that, following it, there could be no more ordinary or painful experience. Rather, Buddhist philosophy suggests that the person who has experienced Nirvana still experiences sensations as being pleasant, painful or neutral, but unlike other people, he or she does not become bound by them, recognizing that they are impermanent. The Buddha, following his enlightenment, was believed to be in exactly that state. Thus, although he ended up dying in considerable discomfort from what was probably food poisoning, the Buddha saw that as quite natural, and never suggested that he should be exempted from such things.

The Abhidharma

Abhidharma means 'higher dharma'; in other words, higher or more developed teaching. It is found in the Buddhist scriptures alongside the *Sutras* (discourses of the Buddha – often presented in the form of dialogues) and the Vinaya, or monastic rules of conduct. The Abhidharma represents philosophical analysis of the Dharma and its implications.

The Abhidharma sought to provide an overall theoretical framework for the Dharma, so that it could be presented in a way that was both clear and also comprehensive. This contrasted with the teachings of the Buddha as they are found in the Sutras, for we have there collections of particular teachings, each set in the context of a particular encounter or situation.

Alongside individual accounts, the Buddhist Sangha gathered together lists to help the understanding and transmission of the teachings. The Abhidharma grew out of these lists, as an extension of the earlier process of systematizing the enormous number of individual teachings that formed the early oral tradition. Between about the third century BCE and the first century CE, each of the early Buddhist schools (see page 62) would have developed its own Abhidharma, but much of this material is now lost.

The analysis of Dharmas

Note

Whereas dharma means 'teaching' and indeed 'following the Dharma' is the preferred way of speaking about following the Buddhist path, the word dharma has a second meaning – 'thing' or 'entity'. Since the individual things we see and know do not have their own inherent selfhood (anatta), they are seen as composed of 'dharmas'.

We saw earlier that the basic teaching of 'anatta' was that all compound things lacked inherent existence, and were constantly subject to change. At a conventional level, we see individual people, tables, chairs and all the other objects of experience. Each appears to be a separate 'thing'. At the ultimate level of truth, however, they do not exist separately, they are simply a conventional way of gathering together, in something like a bundle, the various bits and pieces of which they are made.

As the process of analysis of complex things into their constitutive parts continues, there is reached a bottom level at which things cannot be further divided. These are the simple building blocks of life – the 'dharmas'. The Abhidharma considered that these 'dharmas' were ultimately real in a way that complex entities were not.

Comment

From a modern perspective, there is an interesting dilemma at the heart of the whole process of analysis of dharmas.

First, as the process of analysis continues, you can never reach a point at which you can be certain that you have the very basic building blocks. So, for example, physicists at one time considered the atom to be basic, then came the subatomic particles, now the various quarks. What next? Is it possible to say that the quark is indivisible? Clearly, the process of analysis is theoretically limitless.

Second, the Abhidharma generally gives the impression that reality lies with the dharmas, rather than with the compound entities that they make up. Thus through analysis, one comes to see things as they really are, rather than as they are conventionally perceived. But the problem with this is that we can never know whether we have achieved reality, since the dharmas are always theoretically divisible again into even more subtle forms. Reality, therefore, remains theoretical, never actual. *But* enlightenment is seeing things as they really are. Therefore, following the logic of this argument, enlightenment must always be theoretical, never actual. One way out of this dilemma is to say that enlightenment is a matter of the experience of reality, and that is not necessarily the same as the analysis of reality, for you can experience something without being able to give an exhaustive analysis of it.

Third, following pratitya samutpada (interconnectedness) things arise in dependence upon conditions. Their reality is not inherent but is contingent upon those conditions. If each thing only becomes itself in connection with the whole (since everything theoretically influences everything else), then reality lies with the whole and in the process by which the whole causes particular things to arise, rather than with the particulars. If that is the case, then analyzing dharmas in order to understand reality is a bit like counting individual bytes of memory on a computer chip in order to understand the software program!

Perhaps the whole process of the Abhidharma analysis can be seen as a Buddhist extension of the Hindu Upanishadic story of Svetaketu dividing the seeds, and arriving at a self that is identified with the invisible essence (see page 6). The analysis into dharmas is a quest for reality. What is distinctively Buddhist, however, is the conclusion that everything that is 'put together' is devoid of self-existence, simply a compound and therefore liable to change.

The early Buddhist schools

Because Buddhism did not have a fixed creed, but rather encouraged individual investigation, it was quite inevitable that there would, given time, develop a wide range of philosophical traditions. What is more, as Buddhism developed with the passing of time, it took into itself new cultural and religious phenomena and interpreted them in the light of its distinctive teachings.

It is usual to divide Buddhism into three *yanas* (or 'vehicles'):

- the *Hinayana* (a rather derogatory term, meaning 'small vehicle'), used of those who kept to the early and, arguably, narrow interpretation of the Dharma. There were many early schools which were later to be regarded as Hinayana, and it is with these that we are concerned in this section. Of those early schools, the main tradition extending to the present day is the Theravada (meaning 'Tradition of the Elders').

- the *Mahayana* (meaning 'large vehicle') which developed alongside the early schools, incorporated many of the devotional approaches that are also found to have been developing within Hinduism in the first millenium CE. It became established in the more northern countries, especially China and Japan. We will examine Mahayana philosophy and Zen in later chapters.

- the *Vajrayana* (meaning the 'diamond vehicle' or 'thunderbolt vehicle'), which incorporated Tantric elements. This is found particularly in Tibetan Buddhism. Tantra is also found within Hinduism and is covered in Chapter 07.

Although later traditions claim to go back to the teaching of Gautama, the historical Buddha, it would be widely accepted that the Early Schools, as they have come down to us through the Pali Canon (the oldest surviving collection of Buddhist scriptures), and preserved today within the Theravada tradition, represents the closest we can get to the original Buddhist Dharma.

The Sthaviravadin School

At the Second Council, a gathering of the leaders of the Buddhist monastic community in about 345 BCE, there was a basic split between the Mahasanghikas (who wanted a broader interpretation of monastic practice) and the Sthaviravadins, who were traditionalists. Of the Sthaviravadins, the only remaining representative today is the Theravada tradition. The Sthaviravadins held that Buddha was an ordinary mortal, and that his enlightened followers (called Arhats) had equalled his attainment. They promoted traditional analytic meditations involving the systematic analysis of dharmas, and tended to reject whatever seemed to be elaboration or speculation in connection with the Buddha.

They held that what we perceive with the senses *is* the external world, and it is independent of our perceiving it. Our experiences are not representations from which we have to deduce external facts, they *are* those extenal facts, as mediated through our senses. Hence the practice of analysis in meditation – one simply becomes more aware of the subtleties of what exists.

Their opponents, the Mahasanghikas, considered that the apparent ordinariness of the Buddha was actually an illusion, and that in reality he was supramundane, born out of his mother's side and having no mundane impurities. This approach was a forerunner of the Mahayana schools of Buddhism. In particular, they started to speak of the Buddha as having a career spanning many different births, in each of which the *Bodhisattva* (meaning 'Buddha-to-be') developed his spiritual qualities. This opened the way for the consideration of many different Buddha images.

The Sarvastavadin School

This school divided off from the Sthaviravadins in the third century BCE. Their distinctive philosophy is summed up in the expression *sarvam asti* (everything exists). They argued that all dharmas exist, but in three different modes – past, present or future. When you remember something that happened in the past, you are actually having knowledge of a present dharma, but one which exists in 'past' mode. They argued that the simultaneous existence of all things in this way provided the basis for the operation of the law of karma, for the cause and the effect existed at the same time, albeit in different modes.

Two other features of the Sarvastavadin School were developed within the Mahayana tradition and will be considered here – one is the popular image of the 'Wheel of Life'. The other is the idea that a Buddha-to-be should practice Six Perfections (*paramitas*).

The Sautrantika School

This branched off from the Sarvastavadin School. It rejected the Abhidharma of the other schools, and argued that dharmas were only momentary, and that they could not exist in three modes. It reasoned that, when you perceive something, all you are actually aware of are mental images. There might indeed have been a dharma that gave rise to the mental image, but you cannot get independent evidence for it – by the time you have the image, the dharma has already vanished.

Western

Bishop Berkeley had a similar view – that all we can know are our perceptions, and that it is impossible to speak of something existing if there is nobody perceiving it. In other words, the claim that something exists is the claim that it can be perceived (see also Logical Positivism).

The Sautrantika approach also has parallels with Kant's distinction between the noumanal and phenomenal realms, since things-in-themselves remain essentially unknowable.

One of the problems that this raises is how it is possible, if dharmas have no continuity, for the law of karma to work. How can something that no longer exists affect your present state? The answer given by this school was that actions 'perfume' one's ongoing mental state, and thus influence what will happen later.

Comment

This view may have given rise to the later Mahayana view of the 'seeds' that are planted by present action, waiting to ripen at an appropriate time in the future.

There were many subgroups of these schools, concerned with the description of the nature of perception and the nature of reality. Their variety was inevitable, given the freedom from doctrinal orthodoxy within Buddhism, and the requirement that everyone should examine and come to his or her own personal conviction. One of the main thinkers representing this early core of Buddhist thought is Buddhaghosa, who lived in the fifth century CE. His main work *Visuddhimagga* (The Path of Purification) gives a synthesis of the teachings found in the Pali Canon.

Meditation

Buddhism is not based on belief in God, but on becoming progressively more aware of reality and living in accordance with the insights gained in that process. The mental practices associated with Buddhism do not therefore take the form of prayer to some external deity for help, but exercises designed to cultivate greater sensitivity and awareness.

There are many forms of Buddhist meditation, but they can be divided into two basic forms: *samatha* (which seeks to develop calm, one-pointedness of mind) and *vipassana* (which seeks to develop insight into the nature of reality). Within the Buddhist tradition, these were later developed and augmented by visualization and other practices, some of which we shall consider in the chapters on Mahayana Buddhism, Tantra and Zen.

Samatha

The most basic samatha practice is 'mindfulness' – *sati* (in Pali) or *smrti* (in Sanskrit). The literal meaning of this term is 'remembering' or 'recollecting', and it refers to any process in which a person consciously seeks to become immediately aware of his or her body, feelings, mental processes or the objects of thought. Mindfulness is a matter of being aware of what is happening in the present moment, while still being fully engaged in that moment.

This last point is most important in any understanding of the place of meditation within Buddhism and of the philosophy that lies behind it. It is possible to stand back from immediate experience and gain a detached, almost alienated awareness of one's body, feelings or thoughts. This would attempt to separate off the observing self from the process that is being observed. But this would not fit Buddhist philosophy at all, for it implies that the self (which is doing the observing) is a separate, fixed 'entity' – something which exists independent of the body and its various sensations, feelings and thoughts. But Buddhism teaches that there is no such fixed self: we are the sum total of the processes through which we are living. It is not that we observe sensations or feelings as though they had a separate existence from ourselves, but that we become aware of ourselves experiencing those things.

The other essential feature of meditation, as it relates to Buddhist philosophy, is that it takes place in the present. The past no longer exists and the future has not yet come into existence. Reality is only to be encountered in the present moment, and even then it is a present moment that is constantly changing. A basic skill to be learned in Buddhist meditation is catching the fleeting experience as it is happening.

A possible analogy for the experience of this kind of meditation is that of a surfer riding a wave. At the start of meditation the wave is mounted and the experience becomes one of forward movement, but that which moves forward is constantly changing, and a subtle balance is required to stay with the wave of experience.

Once a person loses the immediate experience and starts to think about it, he or she moves back from the present moment and mentally starts to describe or categorize what is happening, or to dwell in the past (memory) or future (fantasy based on desires or fears). When that happens, the wave of immediacy is lost. The meditator has re-entered the more habitual state, in which past, future and self-consciousness dominate. Once the meditator recognizes what has happened – in other words, he or she becomes aware of being 'distracted' – the process has to start over again. The surfer has to paddle back and mount the next wave!

In other words

Meditation is the art of being creatively aware of what is happening in the present moment.

This is where Buddhist philosophy and Buddhist meditation practice reinforce one another. The experience of the fleeting moment is an experience of anicca and anatta, and that experience reinforces change and interconnectedness as an habitual way of looking at reality.

The other crucial thing to be aware of in samatha practice is that it is an end in itself, as well as being a preparation for insight meditation. For those who meditate within this tradition, it brings its own benefits and leads to an intuitive grasp of reality, as well as an experience of integration and calmness.

One of the most basic practices is the mindfulness of breathing. In this, attention is focused on the process of breath entering and leaving the body. The apparent simplicity of this is deceptive, as the beginner soon discovers, but the process of awareness of breath leads to calmness and a sense of integrity. Notice that awareness is not focused on a theory, or any external concept, but on an actual process – which is indeed the most basic and essential process for life. This is exactly in line with basic Buddhist philosophy, which rejects speculation in favour of immediate experience.

Vipassana

Vipassana meditation aims to go beyond the quest for calmness and receptiveness to include a direct development of insight. As a result, within vipassana, one may meditate on one or more of the Buddhist teachings in order to engage with that teaching with the whole of oneself – unconscious as well as conscious. The reason why such meditation is needed is that teachings are merely verbal formulae, aiming to express insights. The words themselves are mere vehicles of that insight. Understanding the words is a matter of looking at a finger, rather than looking at the moon to which it is pointing. In meditation, the attempt is made to get a 'feeling' for the teaching, rather than accepting it intellectually.

Comment

Is it appropriate to have a section on meditation in a book on philosophy? I think it is and have included it because it highlights that crucial difference between Eastern and Western philosophy – that Eastern Philosophy is concerned with experienced reality as well as conceptualized reality. The concepts within Buddhist philosophy are not determined on the basis of logic (even if logic can subsequently justify them) but on an intuitive grasp of reality, and that process is underpinned by meditation.

Ethics

Buddhist ethics does not generally use terms for good or bad, right or wrong, but speak of thoughts and actions being either:

- *kushala* (skilful) – if based on compassion, generosity and wisdom,
- *akushala* (unskilful) – if based on hatred, craving and delusion.

The reason for this is that an action, if analyzed objectively, may have quite different interpretations depending on the circumstances within which it is performed. Skilful actions are those that are able to bring about an increase in happiness and are conducive to following the Buddhist path. Unskilful actions are those that do not lead to happiness and make it more difficult to follow the Buddhist path.

Examples

Taking a knife to someone's chest has very different implications depending on whether one is a surgeon or a robber.

An act of sexual intercourse has quite different implications depending on whether those involved are friends or strangers, married to one another or to other people, willing or unwilling participants.

Buddhist ethics therefore takes into account the context of each action and the motivation of those involved. Notice that this is another implication of the fundamental principle of interconnectedness. Things are not good or bad in themselves, but are only deemed so because of the way in which they relate to those involved. Actions have consequences (we considered this principle under karma). Equally, actions take place because of existing conditions. An action cannot exist in isolation from its conditions or consequences.

Once again then, we see that Buddhist philosophy has no fixed building blocks, but only a fluid pattern of connections in assessing anything from a moral point of view. Having said that, it is also true that there is a substantial body of precepts and rules that are available to guide Buddhists.

The Five Precepts

Precepts are not fixed rules, but principles of training. They illustrate the qualities that would be expected of a person who was enlightened, and are therefore a guide for those seeking enlightenment. They are most commonly set out in their negative form – as things to be avoided:

1 I undertake not to take life.
2 I undertake not to take the not-given.
3 I undertake to abstain from misuse of the senses.
4 I undertake not to speak falsely.

5 I undertake to avoid those things that cloud the mind.

Each of these principles of training gives rise to a positive counterpart:

1 To develop loving-kindness and compassion towards all living things.
2 To develop generosity.
3 To cultivate stillness, simplicity and contentment.
4 To seek to speak truthfully, gently, positively and with purpose.
5 To develop mindfulness.

Buddhism aims to balance morality, meditation and wisdom (sila, samadhi and prajna) in its spiritual path. Buddhists do not present morality as a means to an end, making it a necessary requirement if one is to achieve enlightenment. Rather, since everything arises in dependence upon conditions, Buddhists claim that basic morality is a condition which enables other features of the Buddhist path to arise.

It is important to note that these are not commandments, given by some external deity, with the threat of punishment if they are broken. They are simply the Buddha's summary of the kind of life that allows wisdom and compassion to arise. Buddhists have these guidelines, but are free to decide how best to apply them to individual situations, recognizing that every moment and event is unique.

Of course, Buddhist ethics need to be seen in the light of the theory of karma. Volitional intentions determine future states, and it is the intention that counts, not just the carrying out of the deed – although the karmic consequences are likely to be more serious if the deed is subsequently carried out.

Western

There is a parallel here with Jesus' moral teachings, for he argues that the attitudes of lust or hatred, as well as the subsequent deeds of adultery and murder, are to be punished. The reason for this would seem to be that both Jesus and the Buddha were approaching the matter of morality primarily from a soteriological point of view. In other words, they were primarily concerned with the effect that the action would have on the spiritual life of those concerned. Neither was considering it solely from the point of view of the right ordering of society, from which perspective it is the action that is crucial and the intention is of secondary importance.

Monasticism

The majority of Buddhists have followed the Dharma while continuing to live a family life. On the other hand, monasticism has always played an important role in Buddhism, and many accounts of Buddhism as a world religion emphasize it to the point at which lay Buddhism may seem but a preliminary or inferior form of the religion.

Following the Hindu tradition of his day, the Buddha had left the family home to enter into the life of a wandering seeker after truth (a *shramanera*), and his first followers were drawn from these ascetic circles. Like many religious movements, it was these 'full-time' members who spread the teaching, and handed on its oral and later written traditions. Much of the Buddhist literature is concerned with rules for those who have chosen to be under monastic discipline, and this reflects the centrality of the monastic community for the transmission of the teachings.

On the other hand, in his teaching (as recorded in the Sutras) the Buddha regularly taught lay people. Although the monastic life makes it easier to follow the Buddhist path, by providing an ordered structure to life and by avoiding obvious distractions, monasticism is not immediately relevant to the fundamental philosophical concepts of Buddhist Dharma with which we are concerned. The basic Dharma remains the same, whether practised by monk, nun or lay person. Similarly, when it comes to ethics, the rules of the monastic vinaya are presented in addition to the basic Buddhist precepts, and it is these that illustrate the ethical application of the fundamentals of Dharma.

Buddhism and philosophical speculation

It will be clear by now that Buddhism is certainly not against philosophy. At its peak, before being destroyed in the Muslim invasions of northern India, the Buddhist University of Nalanda had some three thousand scholars drawn from all over India and also from China, Korea, Tibet, Mongolia, Sri Lanka and Sumatra. Systematic study was at the heart of Buddhist training and Nalanda offered courses in grammar and philology, medicine, logic, the fine arts and metaphysics.

On the other hand, the Buddha was concerned to distinguish between things that could be examined profitably and those metaphysical questions that would never be resolved and which might prove to be no more than a distraction. Questions the Buddha refused to answer include:

- whether the world is finite or eternal
- whether the enlightened person does or does not exist after death.

Now this may seem a major oversight, especially since we are looking at the Buddhist contribution to Eastern Philosophy. On closer inspection, the matter becomes clearer. What the Buddha was refusing to do was to take sides in contemporary philosophical debate. One reason for this may well have been that all such debate depends on the acceptance of key terms and concepts, and by refusing to enter into metaphysical debate he was emphasizing the inadequacy of existing concepts. As in many areas, the Buddha sought to take a middle path. To have said that the world is eternal would have been inadequate to the point of being wrong. On the other hand to say that it is not eternal would have been equally misleading. He therefore affirms a 'neither this, neither that' approach and refuses to give an answer that can be subsequently misunderstood.

More importantly, however, by denying the validity of such questions, and by insisting that his sole aim was to resolve the problem of human suffering, he effectively makes speculation for its own sake a sideline, emphasizing the place of the problem of suffering and the means of overcoming it at the heart of the philosophical quest.

In one of the collections of early sutras (the *Majjhima Nikaya*), the Buddha says that any idea of 'I am this' is a conceiving, or 'I shall be formless' is a conceiving. He wants none of this speculation and declared:

> ... conceiving is a disease, conceiving is a tumour, conceiving is a dart.

> (*MN*, 140)

By overcoming all such conceiving one may become 'a sage at peace'.

Those who concentrate on the cultural or religious artefacts of Buddhism – the temples, monks and images – may miss the very radical nature of the Buddhist view of reality. It is a view which cannot be encapsulated in conceptual terms alone. But above all else, it is a view of the world as dynamic, as a process of interconnecting relationships and conditions.

Western:

For a Western thinker – schooled since Descartes in the idea that 'I think, therefore I am', and thus the self as an indubitable fixed point, or since Aquinas in the idea of God as an unmoved mover, uncaused cause, source of all values, the intelligent and purposeful designer – the twin certainties of much traditional Western metaphysics are removed by Buddhism. In their place is an ever-changing reality which is only known in its immediacy and through participation, never captured conceptually.

For Western philosophy that takes this element of change and process seriously, one might look at Heraclitus among the ancients. Among modern philosophers, process has been a major theme of H. Bergson and A.N. Whitehead.

A pragmatic philosophy

If Buddhism were simply a philosophy, the term used for it would be *darsana*. In fact, another term is used – *yana*. The meaning of this is 'vehicle'. Buddhism is therefore seen as a spiritual vehicle, a means of making progress. Those things that do not contribute to the liberation of human beings from suffering and ignorance may be ignored as irrelevant.

The *Mahaparinibbana Sutta* contains a list of essential teachings, believed to have been given by the Buddha, shortly before his death, to his cousin and companion Ananda. The list contains seven key features, broken down into what are known as the '37 Aids to Enlightenment'. What is interesting, is that the summary contains no speculative propositions of any kind. It includes the cultivation of awareness of body, feeling, mental states and objects of thought, moving on to describe the right efforts required, spiritual faculties and powers to be explored, even enlightenment factors including mindfulness, awareness of Dharma, enthusiastic effort, rapture, serenity, concentration and equanimity. It also includes the Eightfold Path, described above.

Such a summary should come as no surprise, since pratitya samutpada (interconnectedness) – which is the key concept at the very heart of the whole of Buddhist philosophy – points out that things arise in dependence upon conditions. What the Buddha set out in his summary of teachings was the set of spiritual parameters which aimed to help individuals to create the conditions which would allow them to become enlightened.

Western

In scientific research, the observer and method of observation may influence the conclusions reached. So, for example, in psychoanalysis the analyst is trained to recognize and eliminate the influence of his or her own prejudices. In other words, there is a recognition of the connection between conditions, method and conclusions. The former must be specified if the latter is to be assessed correctly.

Similarly with Postmodernism, the material, the medium and the method of artistic creation are the object of attention. One cannot pretend that there is some abstract 'reality' to be communicated which is external to and independent of the vehicle of its communication. By emphasizing the conditions required for insight, rather than its conceptual content, Buddhism has the philosophical and spiritual equivalent of this.

In a traditional Buddhist formulation, the *Ti Ratana Vandana* (Salutation to the Three Jewels), the Buddha's teaching is described as:

Sanditthiko akaliko ehipassiko opanayiko paccatam veditabbo vinnuiti.

A broad translation of which would be:

Immediately obvious; always available; something to be examined by trying it out; progressive; to be understood individually by those who are wise.

In other words

Buddhist teaching claims to be an undogmatic, rational and pragmatic approach to understanding reality.

03

Jainism

In this chapter you will learn:
- the background to and teachings of Mahavira
- the basic ideas of Jain philosophy
- how Jain philosophy compares with Buddhist and Hindu thought.

Background

Jainism is a philosophy and a religion in which the principle of *ahimsa* (non-violence) is absolutely central to both theory and practice. Like other Eastern philosophies, its aim is not disinterested speculation, but rather the development of a means of helping people overcome the suffering inherent in ordinary human existence. It seeks to achieve this salvation by conquering worldly limitations, and the word *jina* (from which the name Jainism comes) means 'conqueror'.

Jain tradition claims that there have been a succession of 24 teachers, over a very long period of time. They are known as the 'ford-makers' (*tirthankaras*) since they help their followers to cross over the stream of this world to a place of security and salvation. Of the ford-makers, only the last is recognized as an historical person. He was known as Mahavira (meaning 'great hero') and lived in the fifth or sixth century BCE.

Thus Jainism, as it is known today, stems from the teaching of Mahavira, although Jains claim that it is far older and that Mahavira was simply repeating the teachings given by the earlier ford-makers. This claim implies that Jainism is not limited historically, but is of permanent and universal validity. It also serves to divide time into periods when life on earth is so dominated by either good or evil that it is impossible for Jain teaching to be received. The ford-makers appear when there is a balance between the two – a balance that allows for spiritual development, but recognizes the reality of suffering and change.

Mahavira

Vardhamana Mahavira was an heterodox ascetic who lived and taught in the area of India now known as Bihar and Uttar Pradesh, and was probably an older contemporary of the Buddha. His dates are sometimes given as 599–527 BCE, although he may have lived rather later – 540 to 468 BCE.

Shramana background

Whatever eternal validity is claimed for his teachings, it is worth considering the background against which Mahavira taught. Although there is great variety within it, Orthodox Hinduism depends on two things:

1 the authority of the Vedas (scriptures)
2 the validity of ceremonies performed by Brahmins (priests).

Also, two central features of Orthodox Hinduism are belief in the eternal reality of God (Brahman) in his various forms, and in the human soul (the Atman).

During the sixth century BCE, there were a number of religious and philosophical approaches taken, particularly in northern India, which challenged these beliefs. There was, for example, the lokayata philosophy of Charvaka (see page 32) who held that all knowledge is ultimately based on the senses, and therefore only what can be perceived in this way can be real. Thus he held that there could be no soul and no life after death. The logical conclusion to draw from his position was that happiness in this life was the only valid pursuit, and he therefore took a position of pure hedonism and amoral materialism.

But there were some who went to the other extreme, emphasizing the eternal nature of the soul, but challenging the authority of the Brahmin sacrifices and engaging in ascetic practices as the method of gaining moksha (liberation). Groups of these freelance spiritual teachers and ascetics wandered about, gaining converts and operating quite outside the orthodox pattern of Hindu rituals and caste system. These teachers were generally known as Shramanas. Two present-day philosophies originated within these groups in the sixth century BCE: Jainism and Buddhism.

Mahavira's life

Mahavira is said to have left his home at the age of 30 in order to become an ascetic, and then spent 12 years as a naked ascetic, during which time he became associated with Gosala, the founder of the Ajivikas (another heterodox Hindu sect). At 42 he is believed to have achieved enlightenment, and is therefore known as a *jina* (a conqueror). His followers are known as *Jainas* (usually shortened to Jains) or 'followers of the conqueror'.

After teaching for a period of about 30 years, he died of voluntary starvation at Pava, near modern Patna, which has become a place of Jain pilgrimage. By the time of his death he had a very large following, both in terms of monks and nuns (women outnumbering men), who were supported by lay followers. He is mentioned in Buddhist scriptures, where he is known as Nigantha

Nataputta, and the situation described there is one in which there is a generally friendly rivalry between the followers of Mahavira and those of the Buddha. Some Buddhist sutras (e.g. Sutra 56 of the *Majjhima Nikaya*) set out philosophical debates between representatives of the two traditions.

The teachings of Mahavira

Sometimes, where there are different sects within a religion, it is difficult to assess which of competing doctrinal claims is the authentic voice of the founder. This is not a problem for Jainism, for although there are two main sects (the *Svetambaras* and the *Digambaras*), the disagreement was on a matter of practice (whether or not their monks should wear clothes) rather than on their interpretation of basic Jain philosophy. We may therefore be fairly confident that the concepts that have been handed down within the Jain tradition do actually reflect the original teachings of Mahavira.

He rejected Brahmin rituals as a method of achieving moksha (release), reinterpreting the Hindu concept of karma, which in orthodox Hinduism had been applied primarily to the results flowing from the correct performance of rituals. He also denied the existence of an eternal, divine realm, believed that the human soul was entrapped within the material world and needed to be released in order to achieve fulfilment, and he made ahimsa (not taking life) absolutely central to his philosophy and practical ethics.

His teachings were not set down in writing, however, until the second century CE, and not until the fifth century CE was there an overall edition of the major Jain scriptures. For understanding Jain philosophy, the key work (accepted as authoritative by all Jain sects) is the *Tattvartha Sutra* ('A Manual for Understanding All That Is') written by a philosopher-monk, Umasvati in the second century.

Basic concepts

A superbly succinct summary of Jain philosophy is given by Nathmal Tatia in the introduction to his translation of the *Tattvartha Sutra*:

The central themes of the *Tattvartha Sutra* are non-violence, non-absolutism and non-possession. Non-violence strengthens the autonomy of life of every being. Non-absolutism strengthens the autonomy of thought of every individual. Non-possession strengthens the interdependence of all existence. If you feel that every soul is autonomous you will never trample on its right to live. If you feel every person is a thinking person you will not trample on his or her thoughts. If you feel that you own nothing and no one, you will not trample on the planet.

Tattvartha Sutra, p. xvii

As with other Eastern philosophies, its purpose is not speculation but liberation, which it sees as the goal of human life. It therefore combines a rigorous analysis of experience with corresponding ethical injunctions.

There are three basic features of Jain philosophy that need to be appreciated before we can move on to consider the Jain idea of the self and Jain ethics: non-absolutism in terms of philosophy; the atomism and animism that form the basis of Jain cosmology; the atheistic interpretation of the cosmic process.

Anekantavada (no absolutes)

Jainism is radical in challenging the basis of its own teachings. In particular, it makes no claim to absolute truth, but highlights the fact that all truths depend on the perspective from which they are viewed, and therefore that all knowledge is partial. Thus (in terms of the nature of the self) it argues that:

- the self may be permanent
- the self may not be permanent
- the self may, from different perspectives, be both permanent and non-permanent
- the matter may be ineffable.

But these four options may be combined, so, for example, the soul may be permanent, but the matter may also be ineffable (so that it *may be so*, but we cannot *know* that it is so). In which case there are seven different combinations possible.

Thus we can know things both directly and indirectly, but nothing (given the limitations imposed by the samsaric world) can be known completely or with absolute certainty. What is more, it is argued that the truth or distortion of our knowledge is not determined by our ability to grasp facts, but rather because of the ethical and spiritual values that form our particular standpoint.

An example

Suppose I look at a tree. I may say –

- there's some useful shade or shelter
- that would be good to climb
- there's some useful timber
- it is an oak
- it has grown since I saw it last
- it will have to be felled.

Each of these perspectives is valid, whether it is concerned with past, present or future and whether the tree is seen in itself (and categorized in terms of species) or simply viewed as a commodity or source of entertainment or comfort. Each has an element of truth, but limited by its particular perspective.

Because absolute knowledge (even if we possessed it) could not properly be communicated in limited concepts, all philosophy is relative. All teaching is therefore provisional and differences are assumed to be the result of differences in perspectives. This does not prevent Jainism from making definite statements. Rather, it adds a qualification to every part of Jain teaching – a qualification that recognizes the standpoint from which it is made, and therefore its limited validity. Jainism always accepts that others may see things differently.

Comment

There is a traditional story of a number of blind men touching an elephant and attempting to describe what it is. Depending on the part touched – trunk, side, tusk – each gives a different description. The descriptions are all valid, but none is able to define the whole elephant.

Atomism and animism

In traditional Jain teaching, the atom is the smallest element of matter, and there are four kinds of atoms: air, fire, water and earth. These atoms gather together to form *skandhas* (compounds), which form objects within the world as we experience it.

But there are other, non-physical elements that also form part of the world: joy, sorrow and life itself – the last of which, in the form of the soul, or *jiva*, is most important in Jain philosophy.

Mahavira taught that everything has a soul within it. Not just humans, animals and plants, but even rocks, earth and wind; and not just permanent entities, but even brief events have a soul that is born within them and lives for as long as that event takes place. Jain philosophy therefore recognizes a constant process of interaction between material and spiritual reality. Whatever capacity a soul has – for example to sense things – it has because of the world of matter (sense organs are physical). On the other hand, those organs are nothing if they are not informing a living soul. Although they are equally real and distinct, soul and matter are inseparable in terms of ordinary life.

But beneath this atomism, so to speak, there is another level of reality, for Jainism also holds that there are eternal substances, each of which has fixed qualities. The highest of these substances is jiva. In itself jiva is perfect and eternal, but under the influence of the phenomenal world it can take on a body and be born over and over again within the world, taking the form of celestial beings, humans or any other creatures, including the most simple forms.

Thus you have a universe in which everything is a compound, made up of both physical and non-physical elements. The phenomenal world, structured by the elements of space, time, motion, rest and matter, is permeated throughout by spirit, which – although linked now to compounded bodies and events – is eternal.

Western

Within Western philosophy, atomism was one strand of Pre-Socratic Greek thought. See particularly the work of Heraclitus (best known for the comment that you can't step into the same river twice). In terms of the relationship between matter and spirit, the dualism here is not really the same as that of Descartes, for Descartes was making a radical distinction between the thinking self and materially extended bodies, and in Jain thought the jiva is really a substance, part of every compound thing. The nearest Western tradition to explore might be Gnosticism, since the Gnostics held a view of eternal souls, trapped within material bodies, and their goal – like that of Jainism – was release from material limitations and achieve awareness of one's eternal nature.

Atheism and the ever-changing universe

Jainism is atheistic. There are no absolutes and (unlike Hinduism) there is no final unification of the Atman with an eternal Brahman. Instead, final release is the recognition that one's spirit is actually the ultimate reality (the point of recognizing this is a state called *kavala*). The world is without beginning, but it is seen as moving through periods of evolution and devolution. It requires no external explanation, and the process of change comes about because of the working of the laws of karma, and because everything is inherently unstable and compounded. It is karma, not God, that drives the universe.

Comment

Any system of philosophy which holds that the world is without beginning or end tends towards atheism, since any belief in God requires the world to find in him a reason, support or origin. Without the need of those things, God becomes redundant.

Jainism appears to hold together two contradictory views of things: that they are permanent, but also that they are in a constant state of flux. It does this by saying that something 'real' continues in existence, although it passes through an innumerable number of 'modes'. At any one time, these modes are changing, and the thing appears therefore to be coming into existence and passing out of existence. On the other hand, it remains real – and therefore continues to exist – throughout this process. This is another example of Jainism recognizing that truth depends on perspective. Things both have and do not have permanent existence, it all depends on the way in which you look at them.

Comment

It is interesting to compare this view with the Buddhist one. Buddhism holds that everything is subject to change and therefore that there are, for example, no permanent souls, just a series of changing features that make up the self. Jainism is just as radical in terms of analyzing the process of change, but is then able to say that, from another perspective, there is an enduring 'self' that continues in spite of the changes.

The self

Like other Indian religious and philosophical systems, Jainism is not primarily a speculative attempt to understand the world, but a method of spiritual development and release. Its aim is to help people to escape from the limitations of the material world within which it sees their souls as trapped. What is says about the self is therefore of key importance, for it is in the light of its idea of the self and its destiny that all else is interpreted. We need to keep in mind, however, what has been said above about the *anekanta* world view – namely that there is more than one way of looking at things, and therefore that souls both have and do not have permanent existence, depending on how you consider them.

Souls (jiva) and physical bodies (ajiva)

An individual consists of a soul born in the form of a physical body, and salvation lies in releasing the soul from its material constraints. The body needs to be controlled in order for the soul to make progress. This approach is similar to that of the Hindu Sankhya school of philosophy.

One's path through *samsara* (the ever-changing world that we experience) is determined, and one can only reach moksha (release) after a long period during which the soul moves through a very large number of different lives. The existence of the soul is not something that Jains feel the need to prove, because they believe that the soul is acknowledged in every act of cognition. Thinking, feeling and being aware of being alive is therefore what being a soul is all about.

It is quite difficult to conceptualize the Jain view of the soul. On the one hand it is present everywhere, but on the other it is in a sense, material. It is almost an animating physical substance, available everywhere and capable of bringing an appropriate body to life. What is clear however, is that there is a difference between an individual soul and the 'soul material' of which it is formed. Thus there are innumerable soul units in the soul, just as there are innumerable space units in space (*Tattvartha Sutra*, 5.8; 5.9).

In other words
Just as material atoms clump together to form a physical object, so the soul comprises innumerable soul units gathered together to form the individual self.

Karma-vada (action and consequences)

Jainism holds a radical and literal view of the general Hindu idea of karma. In the round of incarnations within the samsara world, one's lot in life depends on one's previous karma.

Unlike Buddhism, which regards karma as being generated by one's volitional actions (and thus one's ethically significant actions), Jainism sees karma in a broader sense of all that conditions a person. You are affected by karma even without any conscious choice on your own part. The only way to escape from the rounds of rebirth is to achieve a state of perfect tranquillity and knowledge (kavala), and this requires a person to progressively set aside all desire for things that limit and trap you – thus you enter an ideal state of no desire. What is more, Jains believe that the soul should be omniscient (i.e. it should know everything that it is possible to know), but in this world it has lost this omniscience and is limited in what it can know by its karma.

Comment

What Jainism has done is to accept the mechanism of karma, which had developed within Hinduism, and take it to its logical conclusion. If karma is a mechanism for improving the self within a world of change, then nothing beyond that mechanism is needed. Any intervention by a god or gods only confuses the issue – by claiming to override one's karma in order to improve one's spiritual destiny. If karma is the central spiritual fact of life, then its outworking cannot be subject to divine interference.

Liberation (moksha)

Although Jainism teaches that your soul (jiva) is eternal and omniscient, it doesn't appear to be so in this world, because it is limited now by its material form and by its karma. Of course, the task of the many lives through which the jiva passes is to achieve that state of absolute purity and knowledge which is the jiva's true nature.

Liberation (*moksha*) comes about when the self is freed from all the implications of past actions. Therefore one must rise above all action. Good actions are not enough, since they only benefit the soul while within samsara, they do not allow it to rise above it.

Comment

In the end, Jainism is fundamentally dualistic. Even though, in the ordinary course of events, souls inevitably interact with matter, the point of liberation is the point at which matter is left behind.

The goal of Jains is to become a *siddha* (perfect one) – siddhas are said to have infinite knowledge, vision, strength and bliss. In this state, one realizes that the self (Atman) is the ultimate reality. At this point the soul separates from the body:

> When all karmic bondage is eliminated, the soul soars upwards to the border of cosmic space.

> (*Tattvartha Sutra*, 10.5)

Reinterpretations of Hindu concepts

Atman and jiva

For orthodox Hindus, the Atman (soul) is ultimately identified with Brahman (the ultimate reality and spirit within everything), although the direct awareness of that identity is the final goal of the spiritual journey, rather than something apparent to everyone. The soul is spiritual, in contrast to the material body.

Jains also make a distinction between the physical and the spiritual, but for them the jiva is a subtle physical substance which animates the body – in that a jiva is described as having the size and shape of the body within which it has taken form. It is in itself the ultimate reality (or would be seen to be such by those who attain moksha), but that does not mean that jiva is then identified with any other, external reality (i.e. there is no place for Brahman).

The other key difference here is that, for Jains, the soul is composed of innumerable 'soul units', and its uniqueness is therefore explained in terms of that composition. For Hinduism, since the Atman is in reality at one with Brahman, there does not appear to be any desire to analyze the soul into its atomic constituents.

Karma

Within orthodox Hinduism, karma is related to a large extent to the correct performance of ritual. It is ritual that aligns one's life with that of the universe as a whole and thereby wipes away the results of past actions, where these generate unwelcome results. The Buddhist reinterpretation of this was in terms of karma being ethically significant action (moral, therefore, rather than ritual). For Jainism, however, karma includes all those things which bind a person to his or her world, whether moral or immoral, good or bad.

Comment

It would seem that within Jain philosophy, karma is almost like a physical structure within which everything has to operate – it is not selective as in Hindu and Buddhist philosophy.

Parallels with the Sankhya school of philosophy

For both Sankhya and Jain philosophy, the world is eternal. Equally, they both make an absolute distinction between matter and consciousness, with matter being morally neutral. The same term (jiva) is used in Sankhya and in Jainism for the individual self. Both systems, since they accept an eternal material universe, are atheistic.

These parallels do not point to a simple conclusion that the one borrowed from the other. We only know Sankhya as a system from the period after about 100 BCE, but its origins might be (and probably are) very much older. Kapila, traditionally regarded as its founder, may have lived as early as the seventh century BCE. Perhaps it is safest to say that there is a common stream of thought found in both Sankhya Hinduism and Jainism.

One important difference, however, was that Sankhya remained an orthodox Hindu tradition, whereas Jainism was unorthodox. Sankhya achieved this by saying that the scriptures were one of the three sources of knowledge (see page 19). In practice, it used this source rather seldom, but its inclusion allowed it to remain within the Hindu orthodox fold.

Parallels with Buddhist philosophy

We have already noted some of these. They should not be surprising, since Siddhartha Gautama and Vardhamma

Mahavira were contemporaries and had spiritual lives that resembled one another so closely.

- Both are atheistic, and both see the world as in a constant state of flux.
- Both place great stress on ahimsa as a key feature of the moral and spiritual life.
- Both allow a spiritual progression from the domestic to the monastic life.
- Both reject the authority of the Brahmin rituals and the Vedas.
- Both reject the Hindu requirement that a person's action should be determined by his or her hereditary caste.
- Both promoted the ascetic life (but whereas Jainism held that it was necessary to follow the ascetic tradition and become a monk or nun in order to gain salvation, the Buddha regarded the monastic life as desirable but not necessary, and there are accounts in the Buddhist sutras of lay followers gaining enlightenment).

There is, however, a fundamental difference – and it is absolutely crucial with regard to Buddhism. That is, for Buddhism there is no fixed self, no jiva that is lodged in an alien material environment waiting to be released. Rather, the self is a conventional concept only. In ultimate terms it is an illusion. There is no dualism in Buddhism, rather everything – both material and spiritual – form conditions which allow other things to arise.

It is also worth noting that some things (e.g. whether or not the universe is eternal, and whether the enlightened person lives on after death) are matters that Jainism (and Sankhya Hinduism) are happy to address, but which Buddhism is not. From a Buddhist perspective they are speculation and therefore a distraction.

Comment

Both Buddhism and Jainism have often been portrayed in a negative way as offering salvation through an escape from the material universe. To some extent this is inevitable, given the importance of monasticism within both traditions. On the other hand, through the interconnectedness of things and the operation of the law of karma, both explore the interaction between the self and its material environment – an interaction which both teach should be characterized by an attitude of non-violence and compassion – and thus offer a very positive view of the contribution people can make to their world.

Both encourage the practice of self-restraint, mindfulness and the development of analytic meditation in order to make progress towards enlightenment/omniscience. The fundamental difference is that Jainism sees both the view that the self is impermanent and the view that it is permanent as different but equally valid perceptions, and claims that both can therefore be true at one and the same time. Buddhism, on the other hand, regards the permanent self as an illusion, and – at best – a conventional (rather than an ultimate) way of describing reality.

Ethics

Jainism sees danger in identifying human life exclusively with either the physical or the spiritual. If the spiritual is not recognized, then people may be tempted to ignore a basic feature of life, which is that souls are there to help one another and that life is essentially about interdependence. A key verse of the *Tattvartha Sutra* states:

> Souls render service to one another
>
> (*Tattvartha Sutra*, 5.21)

On the other hand, if the physical is ignored, humans are unlikely to take responsibility for their actions *vis-à-vis* the material world, with adverse implications for the environment within which they live and on which they depend. Jainism therefore insists that the interdependence of the physical and the spiritual needs to be recognized, and this is the foundation for Jain ethics.

The five vows are: non-violence (ahimsa); truthfulness; not stealing; chastity (or faithfulness within marriage); and non-possessiveness (limitation of goods). Of these vows the most important by far is ahimsa. Not harming living things is taken in a more literal and extreme way in Jain philosophy than in either Hinduism or Buddhism. It is important to avoid bad karma and particularly the effects of destroying life – therefore Jain monks and nuns take ahimsa as far as is possible, wearing a mask over the mouth to prevent accidentally swallowing some insect, straining the water they drink and even (where possible and appropriate) brushing the road ahead of them as they walk, to avoid destroying small creatures. Naturally, Jains are vegans since they would not want to harm or exploit animals for food. But even fruit and vegetables are living things, and therefore any nourishment is going to involve some harming of life. The logical response to this is for Jains to limit what they take to the minimum necessary to sustain life.

Not all Jains are able to follow the vows in the same way or to the same extent. So, for example, some will practise chastity, while others take that vow to require faithfulness within marriage. Since it is assumed that people go through many incarnations before they can attain release (moksha), those who are still involved in business and family life are likely to have rather more incarnations to go than those who live the ascetic life.

Asceticism takes precedence over ritual. Thus, although lay members of the Jain community may make daily offerings before stone images of the ford-makers, ascetics do not. They are beyond making offerings, and in any case should have nothing to offer! Interestingly, however, for a religion which rejected Brahmin ritual, there is considerable emphasis on paying for rituals to be performed, and this is a matter of pride and self-respect within the Jain lay community.

Key features

Chastity and non-attachment are the twin features of a key ethical quality of Jainism: *self-control*. This is even reflected in the term 'Jain' which refers to a follower of one who has 'conquered', in the sense of having conquered the self and one's personal needs. Naturally, being atheistic, Jainism does not have the sense of an external deity who is there to accept devotion and facilitate the spiritual path of followers. In the absence of God, progress requires a measure of spiritual self-help, although there is the teaching of the ford-makers to inspire and guide.

The other major quality is generosity and non-attachment to material goods. These things find expression in key features of the Jain life:

- generosity in supporting monks, nuns and temples
- the desire to avoid hurting any living thing
- living in the most simple way possible.

Thus, the Jain ethic can be summed up in the fundamental precepts of compassion and self-control, as is seen in asceticism (for those who choose monastic orders) or restraint and generosity for those who remain lay followers.

Although, as with all vows that lead to an ascetic life (or the simplified version of an ascetic's vows taken by a householder), the impression can be negative – that life is dominated by things to be avoided. This is not the intention of Jain ethics, however. The *Tattvartha Sutra* sums up the positive qualities that the vows are intended to cultivate:

> The observer of vows should cultivate friendliness towards all living beings, delight in the distinction and honour of others, compassion for miserable, lowly creatures and equanimity towards the vainglorious.
>
> (*Tattvartha Sutra*, 7:6)

Apart from particular issues that only really apply to monks and nuns, the discipline accepted within Jainism forms a single, graded system that includes both monastic and lay members. Naturally, because of their more extreme asceticism, it is the monks and nuns who are regarded as nearer liberation; lay people have many more lifetimes to go – but that does not mean that their efforts are wasted. Indeed, everything they do in this life contributes to future incarnations and goes towards their final release.

Two issues

There have been two features of Jain ethics which, although they may seem remote from modern philosophical debate, illustrate the fundamental insights of Jain philosophy: monastic nudity and death by voluntary starvation.

Monastic nudity

There is a division within Jainism between the Digambaras ('sky clad', whose monks are naked) and the Svetambaras ('white clad', who allow each monk to wear three pieces of white cloth), a division that originated in about 300 BCE. Although the division appears to be over monastic nudity, in actual fact there were other important issues involved, particularly the preparation of an edition of sacred texts in Patiliputra (modern Patna) while a considerable body of monks were away in Nepal. Those who stayed in Patna, and committed their version of the scriptures to writing, formed the basis of the Svetambara sect, and those who returned from Nepal and disputed the newly written edition of the scriptures, formed the Digambara.

As an ascetic ideal, all opportunities for attachment to worldly things are to be rejected. Therefore, since even simple clothes are potentially objects of attachment, a Jain monk should go naked.

Both sects held that complete nakedness was ideal, but the Svetambaras compromised and wore robes, whilst the Digambaras maintained nakedness – although in modern times Jain monks are clothed in public.

Nudity has always been a feature of Indian asceticism, and Mahavira himself practised as a naked ascetic during the 12 years before he became a jina. Although nudity *per se* is not a philosophical issue that divides Jains (since both groups accept it as the ideal), and it is not a fundamental teaching, it highlights the overall philosophical approach which sees a spiritual person as 'naked' in the broadest sense, living without attachment or material status.

Comment

Within the Judaeo-Christian tradition, a sense of shame at public nakedness is associated (through the story of Adam and Eve) with disobedience and loss of innocence. In the popular mind it is also associated with sexuality, since, naturally enough in the absence of its broader social appreciation and acceptance, the intimacy of shared nakedness is seen as inviting sexual activity. In Indian religious culture, nakedness is a means of overcoming shame and sexuality, not encouraging it. Indian culture therefore does not have a problem with nudity, and images of naked men and women abound in religious art. Nor does it have a problem with depicting sexuality, but that is another matter.

Nakedness is a spiritual state as well as a physical one. As practising naturists will confirm, the joy of nakedness is not primarily sexual, but is a more general sense of natural well-being and self-acceptance. It is standing on the surface of the Earth, free and entire, feeling the touch of wind or sun, and shedding all that is superficial. It is an expression of reality, in contrast to the artificiality that comes with clothing.

Even though clothed, a Jain should therefore remain naked.

There were two other issues that divided the Digambaras and Svetambaras. The former held that an omniscient being would no longer perform any worldly activities or functions. Thus it would be impossible to be omniscient and also continue to eat. The latter held that a person could become omniscient and still carry on normal functions for the rest of his or her life. The other issue concerned women. The Digambaras held that women could not directly attain liberation. Thus, a woman would have to be reborn as a man at some point further along the spiritual path. The Svetambaras accept spiritual equality between men and women.

Today there are very few who are able to take on the full discipline of a Digambara monk. Far more belong to the Svetambara tradition, and in this there are about three times as many nuns as monks – although it should be noted that nuns of neither tradition have ever been allowed to go 'sky clad'.

Comment

Clearly, allowing nuns the benefits of nudity might have caused problems for the male monastic community, since one of the practices aimed at supporting the vow of celibacy is:

> To avoid: listening to lewd stories about women, looking at sexually arousing parts of a woman's body, recalling past sexual experience, stimulating or delicious food and drink, decorating one's own body.

(Tattvartha Sutra, 7.7)

Clearly, the unfettered inclinations of the male have not changed much over the millennia! It appears to have been assumed, however, that women would not be similarly afflicted.

Death by voluntary starvation

In general, the Jain guideline about the consumption of food is that it is to be taken in order to maintain life, not simply for the pleasure of eating. This is because all food requires the destruction of life and should therefore be kept to a minimum. Jainism also promotes fasting as a spiritual exercise.

This is the context in which to understand the Jain idea of *sallekhana*, the practice of preparing for death through meditation and voluntary starvation. It is most important to understand that this does *not* mean that an individual should choose, while in good health, to starve to death. That would be utterly against Jain ethical principles. Rather, as with all Indian religious traditions, it is believed that one's spiritual state as death approaches is most important for preparing oneself for rebirth or for liberation.

The reason for the practice of sallekhana is to help a person to die in full awareness of what is happening, and able to maintain his or her vows right through to the end of life. It is a total fast, and should only be undertaken once death is imminent due to some other cause. It is the point at which a person consciously accepts that the time has come to die and enters into that experience by ceasing to take food.

Comment

Understood in this way, voluntary starvation is the ultimate sign of self-control. A person accepts that life has come to its end, makes that acceptance known by the decision to take no more food, and thereby chooses to enter into death in a state of religious discipline – the mark of a true 'conqueror', a 'Jain'.

Jain lifestyle today

Although Jainism maintains an ethic of non-attachment, there has been a tradition within the Jain community that lay followers should take up businesses, and should seek to prosper. Within the lay community the element of non-attachment is shown through generosity, for they are encouraged to use their wealth to contribute to the building of temples and the support of the monastic community. Within the lay community, wealth and generosity are signs of piety.

A key feature of Jain ethics today is care for the environment. This springs naturally from the desire to show compassion and to avoid the taking of life. It is also prompted by the Jain insistence that jiva (self or soul) is a feature of all things and all situations, and is not simply a human phenomenon. Jains today see themselves as promoting a philosophy based on non-violence, compassion and love. As such they believe that they have an important contribution to make to modern society.

Although in the present day, followers of the Jain religion interpret the emphasis on ahimsa (non-violence) as encouraging an engagement with social concerns that benefit the environment, the traditional Jain teaching, as we have seen, emphasized that in order to achieve salvation it was necessary to reject society and all the material clutter that comes with it. Jainism has therefore often been portrayed as taking a negative view of the world because of its emphasis on renunciation. All kinds of action, both good and bad, lead to consequences and bind the individual to the material world. Therefore, the logical way to avoid this is by practising ascetic detachment.

This has led to a certain frustration within the Jain community in that, although Jains claim to have made a great contribution to art, literature and culture, their philosophy is widely perceived as being concerned only with a liberation beyond death. To a certain extent such tension appears inevitable in any philosophy which includes an ethical and practical way of life for lay followers and also an ascetic monastic community.

04

Mahayana Buddhism

In this chapter you will learn:

- the difference between the principal schools of Buddhism
- some key Mahayana Buddhist teachings
- the teachings of two principal Mahayana philosophies.

Background: development of Buddhism

Over a period of two or three hundred years, starting probably around 100 BCE, but tracing its origins back to the Mahasanghikas of the Second Council in the fourth century BCE (see page 62), there developed within the Buddhist community a strand of thinking that criticized some traditional ways in which Buddhist Dharma (teaching) was presented. This criticism focused on two things:

1 It argued that the goal of individual liberation, as it had been presented in the early schools, was too narrow and selfish. In its place, it sought a new ideal (which became known as the Bodhisattva Path) of working towards Buddhahood not simply for one's own benefit, but for the sake of all sentient beings.

2 It also saw the Abhidharma as promoting a form of wisdom that was too simply analytic, an exercise in breaking down all complex experience into its constituent dharmas (which, in this context means the basic components out of which every compound thing is made). But it argued that becoming aware of dharmas was not in itself the end of Buddhist wisdom – there had to be something more (what came to be called the 'Perfection of Wisdom').

In other words

These two criticisms may be summed up in two key terms that describe the thrust of Mahayana philosophy – compassion and wisdom.

In this chapter we shall start by looking at the compassion implied in the Bodhisattva ideal, and the ethical implications of this. We shall then look at the philosophy that developed as a result of the new approach to prajna (wisdom).

The Bodhisattva ideal

A *bodhisattva* is literally an 'enlightened being'. It was used as the term for a being that was on its way to becoming a Buddha, but who had deferred that final step in order to assist others to make spiritual progress, and thus to show compassion for all suffering creatures.

In early Buddhism, Siddhartha is described as a bodhisattva prior to his enlightenment. Stories of his previous births also provided images of himself as a bodhisattva, and it was believed that at some time in the future, when the present teaching of the Dharma had died out, another teacher would appear, the Bodhisattva Maitreya.

Mahayana Buddhism enlarged the scope of the bodhisattva considerably. It included all beings who aspired to enlightenment – thus all practising Buddhists were regarded as apprentice bodhisattvas. It also included a whole range of archetypal beings who could be visualized in meditation and who represented aspects of the enlightened consciousness (see page 114).

The Bodhisattva ideal thus introduced into Buddhism not merely a spiritual goal for the individual, but also a whole range of spiritual beings to whom devotion could be paid. This is what makes Mahayana Buddhism very much richer in terms of its religious practice, when compared with the simplicity of the earlier Theravadin approach.

The paramitas

There are traditionally six qualities of the enlightened being, termed *paramitas* (perfections):

- *Dana* (generosity)
- *Shila* (morality)
- *Kshanti* (patience)
- *Virya* (energy, expended in pursuit of what is good)
- *Dhyana* (meditation)
- *Prajna* (wisdom).

These are seen as principles of self-transcendence. They do not prescribe any particular course of action, but indicate the qualities that would inform the actions of an enlightened being – and therefore those that an aspiring Bodhisattva should seek to adopt.

Ethical implications

By emphasizing the paramitas as the qualities of an enlightened being that all Buddhists may seek to follow, some ethical issues take on a different emphasis, and one that reflects the household rather than the monastic setting.

In early Buddhism, the ethics of the Buddhist community focused on the five precepts (see page 68), which applied to all Buddhists, monastic and lay, along with the additional precepts that were accepted full-time by the monastic community and might be accepted for limited periods by the laity. There built up, in addition to these precepts, a whole body of rules and traditions, which became the monastic Vinaya. It was always recognized that these were not absolute rules, but principles by which conduct could be assessed. In the absence of any concept of God, and recognizing the fact of constant change, there was no basis for an absolutist approach to ethics. The development of the bodhisattva ideal did not go against this earlier ethic, but it provided a new way by which one's actions could be assessed – a way based on imaginatively entering into the situation of one who is enlightened.

In other words

Instead of saying 'What, according to the teaching, should I do in order to make spiritual progress?' it asked 'What would I do in this situation if I were already an enlightened being? How, if I were enlightened, would I display the qualities of generosity, morality, patience, energy in pursuit of the good, meditation and wisdom?'

These place emphasis on the qualities displayed in, and the intention that lies behind an action, rather than on the action itself. This reflects the general Buddhist ethical view that actions are not so much good or bad as skilful or unskilful. Every action is an expression of a person's awareness (reflecting his or her wisdom) and intention (reflecting his or her compassion). It is the wisdom and compassion behind an action that decides its ethical quality.

There are some distinctive ethical issues that developed particularly within the Mahayana. For example, within the Tantric practice which was developed by some of those within the Mahayana (see Chapter 07) there is a view of sexuality which encourages the use of sexuality as a vehicle for insight. This is in contrast to the earlier view, where sexuality is voluntarily given up for the sake of the spiritual quest within monasticism, and for the laity is seen as at best neutral and at worst a hindrance to the spiritual life.

There is also a distinctive Mahayana contribution to the issue of vegetarianism. Clearly, the first precept (against the taking of life) would suggest that meat should be avoided, but in the

Lotus Sutra (one of the most important Mahayana scriptures) there is the suggestion that rebirth can take the form of plant as well as animal life. This has radical implications, since the taking of vegetable life is therefore in principle no different from the taking of animal life.

In practice, the guidelines used for overcoming this dilemma are that although all intentional killing is unskilful, it is less so in the case of animals than of humans, and therefore by implication, less so in the case of vegetable than animal life.

Comment

If everything is linked to everything else in this world, then there is a price to be paid for maintaining one's life – none can be absolutely harmless. The dilemma is that, if you were desperate to harm no living thing, you would end up harming yourself – which would also be against the first precept. This dilemma cannot be solved in terms of a moral rule – it has to be a matter of developing sensitivity (which is what the Mahayana emphasis on wisdom and compassion is all about).

Of course, unintentional killing is not considered an offence, since it is the intention that gives rise to an act that determines its karmic implications, and thus whether – for that person at that time – it can be seen as skilful or unskilful.

Comment

This last point is important for Buddhist ethics in general. If I am held responsible for all that I could change, but do not, irrespective of where it is happening or my individual involvement, then, for example, I am responsible for starvation in another part of the world even if I did not directly bring it about, simply on the grounds of whatever action I knew I could take to alleviate it but chose not to take. I cannot be held responsible for that which I cannot do, but can be held responsible for anything that I could have done but consciously declined to do.

Notice however, that ethics in this context is quite different from the assessment of guilt or otherwise. What we have here are the ethical implications of following an ideal – that of the Bodhisattva. An enlightened being, displaying all the qualities of wisdom and compassion, would understand what is needed in every situation and would respond accordingly. The paramitas give an outline of just such qualities.

As we have seen, in assessing a situation, this approach asks in effect: 'What would an enlightened being do in these circumstances?' Again, remembering the basic Buddhist view that there is no inherent selfhood, it is no excuse to say 'but I am not enlightened', as though enlightenment were an inherent quality to be possessed. Rather, it is the actions of an enlightened being that demonstrate enlightenment – so one's own actions (or lack of them) demonstrate one's own spiritual state. To be able to see and respond accordingly *is* to make progress towards enlightenment.

Comment

This approach may sound selfish – that doing the right thing is precisely for the purposes of helping one's own progress towards enlightenment. But that would be to misunderstand enlightenment, for, from the standpoint of the bodhisattva ideal, to be enlightened is to behave with selfless generosity and wisdom. To perform an action simply in order to gain merit would be counter-productive, since the *intention* would be selfish, and for Buddhists it is the intention that counts morally.

Once again, the key feature of Buddhist ethics, springing from its fundamental philosophy, is overcoming the illusion of ego-identity. The enlightened being can act with compassion towards all, simply because he or she is free from the selfishness produced by the illusion of a permanent and independent self.

Reason tinged with emotion?

All Buddhist philosophy is based on reason and analysis. One is encouraged to examine propositions and test them out in experience; one is also encouraged to become increasingly aware of one's present experience and one's response to it. It is this fundamental orientation that has enabled us to study Buddhism as a philosophy. On the other hand, reason divorced from emotion turns its back on a significant part of human experience. To have a philosophy of life that does not engage the emotions is a contradiction in terms.

The criticisms made of the earlier schools by the Mahayanists, particularly as reflected in their development of the Bodhisattva ideal, were in part an attempt to engage the emotions in the Buddhist path, and thus prevent the whole philosophical and religious enterprise from becoming excessively analytic and dry.

Part of the process of engaging the emotion took the form of a more imaginative approach to meditation. Whereas all Buddhist practice had involved developing awareness and analysis of states, the Mahayana tradition included the visualization of a range of images of enlightened beings – images with which the meditator could identify and also use as an object of devotion. We shall see later in this chapter how this developed into the *Trikaya* (three bodies) idea. For now we need to recognize that the bodhisattva ideal gave rise to an imaginative development in which there could be a great variety of bodhisattvas – from the ordinary Buddhist practitioner, who was considered an aspiring bodhisattva, through a range of imagined forms used in visualization.

From the image of early Buddhism as an analytic discipline leading eventually to arhatship and personal enlightenment, there developed a rich variety of forms within which the Buddhist path could be explored, with images to inspire whatever qualities of wisdom or compassion a particular person needed to develop. The Bodhisattva ideal provided the vehicle for much of this development.

In other words

The Bodhisattva ideal, by offering images of enlightened beings with which individuals could identify, provided a means of engaging the emotions in a process that had previously been seen as primarily rational. This did not deny the validity of the earlier approach, but sought to supplement and enrich it.

Madhyamaka philosophy

The two principal schools of philosophy within Mahayana Buddhism developed out of a tradition of interpreting those sutras that had not been accepted as part of the Pali Canon.

The Madhyamaka school interpreted the Perfection of Wisdom sutras and the Yogacara school interpreted a range of other sutras which, in Western terms, we would call 'idealist'. The two schools of philosophy were later divided into various subgroups, and attempts were also made to synthesize them. For the purposes of this book, however, we shall be concerned only with the basic approaches of the Madhyamaka and Yogacara. It is important to recognize also that those using the Mahayana scriptures did not think that they were innovating. They believed that the traditions embodied in these sutras had been taught by Siddhartha Gautama himself, and had remained part of the oral tradition – albeit (as we shall see later) a part that was reserved for the initiated rather than preached to those who were not yet ready for their more advanced ideas. In this way, the Mahayana schools saw themselves as part of the original stream of Buddhist teaching, not as importing anything new or as setting aside earlier traditions.

The *Prajnaparamita Sutras*

The *Prajnaparamita Sutras* are a collection of philosophical works, compiled and reshaped over a considerable period of time, on the theme of 'The Perfection of Wisdom'. The most succinct of these (and one of the latest) is known as *The Heart Sutra*. It is particularly important because, being short, it is easily memorized and recited and has thus been a key way of gathering and propagating this particular philosophy.

The Heart Sutra deals with issues that are key to an understanding of Mahayana Buddhism, and we will be examining these in the course of this chapter. They may be summarized thus:

- All phenomena lack inherent existence; they cannot exist independent of one another.
- Although complex entities (like the body) exist conventionally (i.e. for practical purposes we need to be able to speak about them as single entities), careful analysis shows that they do not exist over and above their constituent parts (i.e. there is no 'body' other than the sum of all the bits and pieces that make up the body).
- All phenomena are therefore mere appearance. (I may see a tree in front of me, and conventionally I may call it a tree. In fact, it could be analyzed into individual molecules and atoms, into subatomic forces even. The tree is simply an accumulation of all these atoms, it does not exist independently of them – and of course, they do not exist independently of all the rest of the world and the way in which the universe is made up.)
- Everything is both form and emptiness. (Where 'form' is the tree, and 'emptiness' the fact that it does not exist in itself but only as an arrangement of constantly changing atoms etc.). Neither exists without the other.

- Unless we are enlightened, we cannot see both form and emptiness simultaneously.
- The goal is to become enlightened, to see everything as being 'empty' of inherent existence, and therefore accepting it as it is, in its ever-changing reality, without grasping at it or attempting to project our own fixed ideas upon it.

Inevitably, this is an over-simplification of a very complex set of ideas, but it is necessary to grasp this basic idea of form and emptiness in order to understand the philosophies of the Mahayana.

Note

The Abhidhamma of the earlier traditions concentrated on breaking down all compound things into their constituent dharmas. The intention of this process was to make a person aware of the compound and therefore impermanent nature of things. The problem with this, from the standpoint of the Perfection of Wisdom tradition, was that it suggested that the dharmas were themselves permanent. But for those sutras, and for Nagarjuna interpreting them, it was a key feature of the whole Buddhist view of reality that absolutely *nothing* has *svabhava* (own-being, inherent existence).

Comment

The reason why it is always important for Buddhism to deny svabhava, is that it implies permanence. Once you locate something that is permanent you can attempt to cling to it and rely on it – and that leads to suffering. Buddhism insists that *nothing* is permanent, and thus that seeking permanence is always an illusion.

Modern science tends to agree. Whereas atoms might have been thought to be permanent (as opposed to the molecules and more complex entities that they combine to form), it is clear that all matter only comes into existence below a certain temperature and that it can be re-converted into radiation. Some things in the universe are of very long duration, but none has svabhava, for none can exist in complete independence of conditions.

What is the 'perfection' of Wisdom? That is a reasonable question to ask, since the perfection of wisdom (prajna) is the name of this body of literature. Clearly, the key is in the idea of 'emptiness' (shunyata), but it involves more than an intellectual grasp of that concept. An important feature of Mahayana philosophy is that it is not to be taken exclusively at an intellectual level; it is a view of life into which a person can enter. Seeing things as 'empty' changes a person's attitude to them, which in turn influences moral choices and actions. Emptiness is therefore an attitude of mind in dealing with life, not just a way of highlighting the impermanent nature of life. The Mahayana claim is that such an attitude of mind is, and has always been, fundamental to Buddhism.

Nagarjuna

The Madhyamaka school of Buddhist philosophy was founded by Nagarjuna, a monk who lived in the second century CE. The name of this school means 'middle position', which reflects its central teachings:

- things do not exist absolutely
- nor do they not exist at all
- therefore they exist relatively.

Nagarjuna claimed that this was simply an explanation of the Buddha's original teaching, in rejecting both eternalism and annihilationism.

The Madhyamaka philosophy of Nagarjuna systematizes the Perfection of Wisdom sutras, a key feature of which is the emptiness (shunyata) of all dharmas. Another important feature of Mahayana philosophy that we will consider here is the distinction made between ultimate and conventional truth.

In interpreting the sutras, Nagarjuna did not offer any new philosophy, other than to emphasize the absolute centrality of the idea of shunyata in the Buddhist view of reality. Instead, his main thrust was to use reason to show the logical incompatibility of the claims of others, using *reductio ad absurdum* arguments.

Western

His approach was like that of Socrates: look at a commonly held belief; examine its implications; show the logical absurdity of these; then re-evaluate the original assumptions.

Nagarjuna's arguments are set out in the *Mulamadhyamakarika* (Verses on the Fundamentals of the Middle Way).

Conventional and ultimate truth

Clearly, there is going to be a problem with language that claims that everything is 'empty', since in ordinary day-to-day speech we need to say of people, animals, physical objects, even events that last only a very short time, that they 'exist'. And in saying that, we are not trying to say that they will exist for all time, nor that they are independent of everything else – merely that they are, rather than that they are not.

The Madhyamaka way out of this dilemma is to speak of two kinds of truth – the conventional and the ultimate:

- *Samvrti satya* – conventional truth (the concepts we need to use on a day-to-day basis).
- *Paramartha satya* – ultimate truth (the way things really are, shorn of conventional concepts).

Thus, for example, conventional truth requires us to speak of individuals as though they were discrete and permanent entities (otherwise we could not deal with them on a day-by-day basis), but ultimate truth says that there is no such thing as a permanent self.

In other words

On a conventional level, I exist. Other people know me, interact with me, and can (if asked) describe me. But on an absolute level, I do not exist – I am a temporary 'put together' part of the world. My anticipated life span, once deprived of oxygen, is very limited. I am composed of cells that have grown because of the food I eat. I am in a constant state of flux physically – as is every living thing. But equally the 'I' that relates to people is also constantly changing and responding to relationships and environment.

Conventionally, therefore, 'I' am all this. In absolute terms, however, I do not exist. By making this distinction between absolute and conventional, Mahayana philosophy was able to continue to make very rigorous analysis of everything, whilst not thereby making normal life and conversation impossible.

Comment

Remember that for Mahayana Buddhism, as for all Eastern Philosophy, the key thing to appreciate is the personal and religious implications of its view of reality. The conventional world, in which we all appear to exist as individual, permanent selves, is one that can lead to jealousy, pride, competitiveness, love, hatred and all the other passions. Once this is tempered by the awareness that ultimately we are 'empty', there is hope that a less selfish, more balanced view may prevail. Equanimity is not a matter of not caring what happens, or of finding no distinction between one option or another, but of seeing everything in a balanced way, and recognizing that everything is temporary and subject to change.

There are two ways of overcoming the conventional notion of self-existence:

- For those things that have been learned – for example, the existence of gods, or that one has a soul – they can be refuted by showing logically that everything is dependent upon other things and therefore not self-existent.
- At a deeper level, there is the ordinary way of looking at the world as though the things we see are permanent entities. This does not yield to rational argument – the only way to overcome it is by meditation.

Of these, the Madhyamaka generally emphasizes the way of rational argument. Therefore, everything is just as it is. The Buddhist term *tathata* (suchness) expresses this – that things are just what they are in a temporary and relative way. That is not a negative statement, it does not deny anything. It is simply a term which corresponds to things as they really are, letting go of any eternalist fantasy.

In other words

Don't try to say 'this is for ever' – because you know it is not, and that attitude will only lead to craving, grasping and suffering. Just say 'this is as it is' – then it may be enjoyed for itself, without forcing it to comply with our eternalist fantasy about what it should be for us.

This philosophy may not sound very different from the earlier Buddhist thinking (and we have seen that Nagarjuna simply regarded it as a logical exposition of what the Buddha had taught) but there was an important distinction between some of the earlier schools (particularly the Sarvastivadin) and the Madhyamaka – a distinction in the status of 'emptiness' and dharmas.

Shunyata (emptiness)

Shunyata means 'emptiness'; everything is described as being empty of svabhava (own-being). Although this sounds a rather negative view of reality, that is not its intention. In early Buddhism there was the recognition of two universal features of reality: anicca (everything is constantly changing) and anatta (there is no fixed self). Clinging to a false notion of a permanent self was the cause of suffering. The Buddhist teaching sought to show that everything arises in dependence upon conditions and that conditions are constantly changing.

Now, the term used for a permanently existing self is svabhava, and the Buddhist claim is that all things are 'empty' of this svabhava – they are conditioned and constantly changing. This is the specific meaning of 'emptiness' in Mahayana Buddhism – it is simply the logical outcome of the basic Buddhist view of conditioned existence.

In the earlier tradition, it was acknowledged that composite things (like selves) did not exist in their own right. We have seen that this was shown by analyzing things into their composite parts, called dharmas. Dharmas (or 'things') were the smallest units of reality and all composite entities were composed of them. The implication of this for the Sarvastivadins was that the dharmas were eternal, whereas the things that were composed of them were not. Nagarjuna challenged this – if everything was dependent upon conditions, then why should dharmas not also be dependent upon conditions? Why should they have self-existence? So dharmas were also shunyata (empty of inherent existence).

In other words

It's a matter of how radically you take the Buddhist idea of impermanence. For the Sarvastivadins, composite things are impermanent, but they are made up of permanently existing dharmas. For Nagarjuna, at an absolute level, everything is impermanent, everything has the quality of shunyata (emptiness). But remember too, that this is absolute, not conventional language. Conventionally, things are still described as existing.

Recognizing that everything is 'empty' does not mean that it is valueless. For Mahayana Buddhism it is quite the contrary – it is still real, nothing about it has changed, but by being recognized as 'empty' there is no point in trying to grasp and hold on to it, or expect it to be unchanging. Rather, that which is 'empty' will be expected to develop and change, to interact with us and with the rest its environment.

Comment

Shunyata prevents a person from asking 'What is the real "me"?'. You are exactly what you are – your thoughts, words and actions. You are what you are now as a result of what you have been in the past – your karma has produced its results. Equally, what you will be in the future will depend partly on choices you make now, and also on other factors over which you have no control, the conditions which will allow various situations and events to arise for you in the future.

You are therefore 'empty' – there is no eternal, fixed self that has somehow found itself trapped within this changing world. Like it or not, you are part of that process of change, and to pretend otherwise is to grasp at an illusion that will only lead to frustration and suffering.

This does not mean that nothing exists (which would be annihilationism), but that nothing exists eternally and in its own right. Everything exists only in relation to the conditions that bring it about; once those conditions cease, then it too will cease.

Western

Within the Philosophy of Mind, there has been what is called the problem of the 'elusive I'. The fact that I can speak of 'my body' and 'my mind', for example, implies that there is an 'I' that is over and above all these things. The problem, within Western philosophy, has been the elusive nature of such an 'I'. Buddhism enters this debate, simply by suggesting that the 'I' is elusive because it is an illusion. At most, it may serve as a conventional way of describing oneself. Although coming at the problem from a different position, this is not too far from the conclusions of Gilbert Ryle in *The Concept of Mind* (1949).

Some implications of shunyata

Nagarjuna came to the conclusion that ultimately there was not the slightest difference between nirvana and samsara (although at the level of conventional truth, the two are very different). Now this sounds radical, since traditionally Buddhism has been taken to be a method of overcoming the ever-changing world of samsara, with all the suffering that is involved in it, and enabling a person to come to a peaceful state of nirvana. What is the point of all this if they are actually identical?

What Nagarjuna was trying to put over was that if samsara has no inherent existence, if it cannot be a separate, defined and permanent thing, then samsara is not some separate entity over against another one called nirvana. But also, the state where the passions are calmed and all is bliss and insight, is not something that exists over against everything else – it is not a permanent 'thing'. Nirvana is simply the state of seeing the conditioned nature of the constant rushing to and fro involved in samsara. Nirvana is recognizing that everything is empty, and that nothing may be grasped and held.

Note: causation

Nagarjuna's philosophy may be applied to the problem of causation:

- Cause and effect cannot be the same (or nothing new would have been brought about).
- Cause and effect cannot be unconnected (or anything could cause just anything, which experience shows not to be the case – after all, the world is at least partly predictable).
- The effect cannot be part of the cause (or nothing new would have been caused).
- Thus, according to conventional thinking, for something to be caused, there has to be continuity, but there also has to be something new as well.
- Therefore conventional reasoning breaks down – it cannot explain the process of change.
- The answer lies in 'emptiness' – neither cause nor effect have separate permanent existence. Only in a conventional sense are they two separate and distinct entities requiring to be linked in some way.

Thus shunyata (emptiness) shows that problems about how one thing can be said to cause another are in fact no more than symptoms of our conventional thinking.

Comment

An old joke, from the days when there was a simple advert for a headache remedy which claimed 'Nothing works faster than A*****.' – to which the quip was 'Next time, try taking nothing.' The joke works through the mistaken reification of 'nothing'. Therefore beware of thinking that there is some entity called 'emptiness' that is at the base of everything – some invisible reality. Not so. The shunyata doctrine says that no such thing exists.

Yogacara philosophy

The other main school of Mahayana philosophy was developed by two brothers, Asanga and Vasubandhu, who lived in the fourth/fifth centuries CE, and (like the Madhyamaka school) it developed out of a system of interpreting the Mahayana sutras. It is generally referred to as Yogacara (the practice of yoga).

Both Yogacara and Madhyamaka schools agreed that the things that make up the world lack svabhava – in other words, that they do not exist in their own right, but are merely contingent, depending on the conditions that bring them about. This is hardly surprising, since it is basic to the whole Buddhist idea of interconnectedness.

Whereas Madhyamaka emphasized shunyata, claiming that things were 'empty' of inherent existence, Yogacara thought this had moved too far in the nihilist direction and attempted to restore the balance by coming at the issue of the transient nature of experience from a very different angle. It argued that the things we perceive as being in the world are in fact mental constructs; that what we experience is an interpretation imposed by our minds.

The Yogacara school of philosophy can be known by three other names, which between them show what it is about:

- *Cittamatra* = 'mind only'
- *Vijnanavada* = 'consciousness doctrine'
- *Vijnaptimatra* = 'perception only'.

In other words, Yogacara is what would be known in the West as an 'idealist' philosophy, since it takes as its starting point our mental interpretation of experience.

The reasoning behind the Yogacara approach can be presented quite simply:

- You can be mistaken about what you perceive. (For example, I suffer from Tinnitus. It sounds as if there is a waterfall to my left, and someone blowing a rather high pitched whistle. That is the reality of what I experience, but I do not keep looking over my left shoulder to check if either the waterfall or the whistle exist outside myself.)
- You may be dreaming. (Asanga, in his *Mahayanasamgraha*, argued that, when you dream, you are aware of a world of fantastic creatures, but they are merely in your mind. You

may see a mirage or hear an echo, mistaking it for the source of the sound. It is therefore possible to have 'real' experiences, but they do not necessarily correspond to anything in the external world.)

- You may lack a particular faculty. (For example, you may be colour blind, but that does not mean that the things you see actually lack colour.)
- Therefore, all you can know about is what you experience; you cannot get direct knowledge of anything external to that experience.

Western

There are parallels here with much 'idealism' in Western thought – although its main lines of development here came just over a millennium after Yogacara! The most obvious place to start with this is by looking at Kant, who effected a 'Copernican Revolution' within philosophy by suggesting that space, time and causality (in addition to the more obvious secondary qualities of colour and so on) were actually the result of the way in which the mind handled its data, rather than structures which we could perceive in the external world. What we see are things as we experience them – governed by our mental faculties – not things as they are in themselves.

On the other hand, you might argue that coherence and involuntariness are what suggest an external reality (after all, I have not chosen to see this particular thing, and I know that I have seen it every time I enter this room). But Yogacara counters this by suggesting that in a dream you do not control what you experience and the people in your dream appear to be consistent.

But what about the regularity of your experience? Does that not prove its external origin? Again, Vasubandhu argues that all experience is a sequence of events, and what we call 'true' perceptions are simply those that cohere with that sequence, false ones are those that do not fit with the sequence. Vasubandhu therefore points out that the claim that something is true or false, exists or not, does not depend on the knowledge of any external reality, but only on an assessment of whether that thing is compatible with the rest of our experience.

The Three Natures

We have mentioned the concept of svabhava (own being, or inherent and therefore independent and permanent existence) in looking at Madhyamaka philosophy. Yogacara uses this same term to describe three natures, or ways of understanding reality:

1 It is possible to believe that there are separate and independent objects out there. This it claims to be an illusion. This view is called *parikalpita-svabhava* (imagined own being). It is the conventional way of looking at the world.

2 There is the succession of perceptions and experiences that we have. This is termed *paratantra-svabhava* (interdependent own being). It is what a Buddhist is encouraged to be aware of all the time, and to recognize as arising in dependence on conditions and constantly liable to change.

3 But there is what Yogacara termed the *parinispanna-svabhava* (perfected own being) way of understanding reality. This is the awareness that there are no separately existing objects. Nothing much can be said about this, however, because it is the way in which an enlightened being would view the world, and the direct experience of an enlightened person cannot be put into words – and even if it could, it would not be understood by anyone who was not also enlightened!

Now, according to Yogacara, everyone actually experiences '2', but most interpret it mistakenly as '1'. Awareness of the conditioned nature of things, however, should ultimately lead to interpretation '3'.

Comment

The natural question to ask of Yogacara is this: 'If there are no external objects, what causes the sensations?' We may indeed mistake dreams for some external reality on occasions, but that is only because we habitually experience what we take to be external reality. And what are our senses for, if not to discover something that exists outside ourselves?

The answer given by Buddhism in general is that we are mistaken if we take an 'us and them' view of things – that the world consists of separate entities, each existing in its own right. That may be all right from a conventional point of view (and it is fairly essential in terms of the practicalities of day-to-day living) but actually, reality is interconnected and everything within it dependent upon the conditions that maintain it at every moment.

Perhaps we could summarize what Yogacara is trying to say in this way:

- My experience of this person is simply that – an experience.
- I cannot get back 'behind' that experience.
- I cannot say: 'There is a person out there whom I know quite apart from my experience of them.'
- What you experience is what there is. You can either accept it as a constantly changing flow of experience, or you can try to chop it up into separate entities – but to do that is to create an illusion of separateness.

Karma and the store consciousness

If there is only a flow of consciousness, with no continuity in terms of a permanent 'self', how is it that we recognize and remember things and behave in ways that others find predictable? Also, if everything is mental, how can karma operate? Vasubandu's answer to both of these dilemmas is given in the idea of an *alaya-vignana* (store consciousness).

Irrelevant note

You will remember the term *alaya* (meaning 'store place' or 'abode') once you know that the term for snow is *hima*. The Himalayas are 'the abode of snow'.

The stream of mental events you experience leave *bija* ('seeds') in this 'store consciousness'. These seeds are held in the store until eventually, when conditions are right for them, they mature and can then influence later events. This theory not only explains continuity of experience, but also provides a mechanism for the way in which karma works. You experience the results of past actions now, because those actions have influenced your store consciousness – and everything you have done in the past is stored up, influencing the present. Hence there can be a gap between a karmic event and its results, without the need to suggest a permanent ongoing self.

Western

Psychoanalysis, and the whole idea of the unconscious mind, can be explored as a parallel with Vasubandhu's ideas here. For modern psychology, events leave an imprint in the unconscious mind, remaining undetected until at a later stage in life they manifest in terms of a psychological problem – exactly the mechanism that Vasubandhu envisaged. His alaya-vignana is an early attempt to explain the operation of the unconscious mind. The key difference, however, is that – in Buddhism – karma is primarily concerned with a person's conscious action, whereas for Freud, the experiences stored in the unconscious often relate to what others have done to us, rather than what we have chosen to do.

Yogacara has no less that seven forms of consciousness. The first five correspond to each of the five senses. The sixth consciousness synthesizes the first five, producing mental impressions. The seventh and last consciousness is what he calls the *klistamanas* ('tainted mind') which is conventional self-consciousness. It leads to confusions about the self, to a sense of loss or pride. It is exactly the form of consciousness that Buddhism seeks to overcome, because it sees it as based on a false view of the self and of reality.

The Tathagatagarbha doctrine

Tathagata is a general term for the Buddha – 'one who has gone beyond'. *Garbha* means 'womb'. The *Tathagatagarbha* doctrine is the idea that every creature is the womb of a Buddha; that every creature has the potential to grow into Buddhahood. In a sense, this does not actually state anything that differs from the teaching of Siddhartha Gautama. After all, he taught the path that would lead to enlightenment, and the early scriptures give many examples of his followers becoming enlightened. Combined with the idea of re-becoming, it is clear that Buddhism sees all creatures as potentially able to come to a point at which they can be enlightened. Therefore, Buddhism holds that everyone is a potential Buddha. The distinctive feature of the tathagatagarbha doctrine is that we are *already* Buddhas, but we can't see it because of the illusory way in which we understand the world.

This has implications for Buddhist practice. So, for example, a Tibetan Buddhist may visualize himself or herself in the form of one of the Buddhas or Bodhisattvas. This is not seen as self-aggrandisement or fantasy. It is an attempt to get beyond the illusion of separateness and see one's true nature – Buddhahood. In the same way, Zen Buddhists of the Soto Zen tradition may argue that for the time during which one sits in meditation one *is* Buddha.

Comment

But – and this is crucial for any interpretation of Mahayana Buddhism – this does not mean that there is a permanent and self-existing inner self called the 'Buddha nature', waiting to be at one with some universal Buddha nature, for that would be exactly the same as the Hindu idea of an Atman becoming at one with Brahman. Rather, its implication is that enlightenment is the natural state, and illusion the unnatural. We all have the potential to see things as they really are, rather than living with illusion.

Misinterpreted, the 'Buddha nature' could (like the 'real self' of some New Age thinkers) become something to crave and cling to. And that of course, for a Buddhist, would be self-defeating!

The Trikaya doctrine

Buddha is a title, meaning 'enlightened one', and in its most straightforward use it is applied to Siddhartha Gautama. But Buddhism has rather enlarged its meaning in three ways:

First, it was believed that there had been and would be other enlightened beings. In the earliest traditions we find the idea of a future Buddha who would come to restore Buddhist teaching when it died out on Earth – the Buddha Maitreya. Within the Mahayana tradition this was extended further to include very many Buddhas, each with particular qualities or displaying a particular form of wisdom. This emphasized the idea that what Siddhartha Gautama achieved had universal significance, and was a potential for all (as we saw above in the idea of the 'Buddha nature').

Second, the Buddha is also reported as saying that 'he who sees the Dharma [the teaching, or truth] sees me'. Thus 'Buddha' became a term used, not just for someone who is enlightened, but for the truth which their enlightenment reveals. But also, third, in the course of meditation and visualization (particularly in the Tibetan tradition) there developed a whole range of images of Buddhas and Bodhisattvas (those beings who are destined to become Buddhas), with rich iconography and colour, each displaying aspects of enlightenment.

This led to a Mahayana teaching known as the Trikaya (three bodies). It claimed that there were three bodies of the Buddha:

- the *Nirmanakaya*: the Buddha revealed in earthly form (e.g. Siddhartha)
- the *Sambhogakaya*: Buddhas described in the Mahayana scriptures and visualized in devotional practices, and expressing graphically the qualities of enlightenment
- the *Dharmakaya*: ('teaching body' or 'truth body') the enlightened consciousness that is able to see the truth of things.

Comment

The first two of these are dependent upon the third. Siddhartha is only called Buddha at the point at which he becomes enlightened. Equally, the various images of the Sambhogakaya only make sense as aspects of the enlightened mind, and they have no reality or power except to the extent that they enable a person to get in touch with that particular quality and thus move in the direction of enlightenment.

Thus, provided it is not mistaken for some literal trinity of Buddhas, the Trikaya doctrine merely makes explicit what was implied originally in calling Siddhartha 'Buddha' – namely, that he was aware of the true nature of things, and that he displayed and taught the qualities implied by such awareness.

Western

It is tempting to seek parallels between the Christian concept of Trinity and the Buddhist Trikaya. At one level, however, they are utterly different, since Buddhism is atheistic and the Trikaya cannot therefore refer to divine beings in any way. From the standpoint of the philosophy of religion, there is a certain parallel in terms of the development of the two concepts:

In the Christian tradition, 'Father' can be taken to refer (via the act of creation) to the fundamental sense of structure and purpose within the universe – the ultimate reality, 'being itself'. 'Son' is a title given to Jesus, as expressing the belief that he is a unique revelation of God in human form, and 'Spirit' would then refer to the source of spiritual qualities that are experienced within the Christian community.

You could therefore argue that there are parallels between the Sambhogakaya and the Spirit, and between the Nirmanakaya and the Son, in terms of their function within an overall religious/philosophical framework. On the other hand, it needs to be clearly recognized that in Buddhism these refer to a process of spiritual development, whereas in Christianity they are taken to be independent spiritual realities, not aspects of human religious experience.

My guess, however, is that this is a discussion that is likely to generate more heat than light, for the two religions have arrived at superficially similar structures from very different philosophical presuppositions.

Cosmology

The multiplicity of world systems

At a focal point in the Lotus Sutra there is the most amazing image of many different world systems, spread out in the ten directions of space, and in each of these world systems there is a Buddha. The cosmology is vast and elaborate. This present world (called the *Saha* world – meaning 'the world in which one endures') is in one sense quite insignificant against this cosmic backdrop, but at the same time, the image suggests that all the other world systems and their Buddhas come together to acknowledge that the Buddha Shakyamuni has preached the true Dharma – the same Dharma that these other Buddhas have preached each in his own world system.

It is tempting to put all this rich imagery down to a tendency to elaborate and develop which we find throughout Buddhist (and other Indian) literature. But it would be wrong to interpret it simply as cosmological speculation. There is a tradition that the Buddha would not discuss whether the world had a beginning or not, since that would be unanswerable and at best a distraction – so cosmological speculation as such is not part of Buddhism. Rather, to understand the purpose of this material, we need to consider the effect it is intended to have upon the reader. The thrust of the image is that the present Buddha and world system is placed in a context – that it has a universal and eternal significance, in spite of its appearance within the world of change.

In other words
What appears to be cosmological speculation in Mahayana Buddhism may be accounted for by the need to:

- show the universal relevance of the Dharma, and
- show the relative insignificance of this present world system.

There is no sense that belief in other world systems is presented as a requirement of faith – that would be quite alien to the Buddhist approach.

Hua-yen (the interpenetration of all things)

Alongside the multiplicity of world systems, there is another important feature of Mahayana cosmology – the concept of *hua-yen*. This is related in some ways to the tathagatagarbha doctrine and partly to the basic Buddhist idea of 'conditioned co-production'. It may be broadly translated as 'the inter-penetration of all things', and as such is the basic Buddhist view of reality, but hua-yen has implications for understanding the Buddha-nature of each individual, since it claims that each individual is a manifestation of the universal Buddha principle, and hence has inherent value.

Comment
Notice again here that what might be taken to be cosmic speculation, is in reality simply a way of presenting the basic Buddhist vision of everything arising in dependence on conditions, and having no independent, inherent or permanent existence.

On the other hand, seeing the universe in terms of the interpenetration of all things has immense implications in terms of one's self-understanding, appreciation of the value of the transient, and one's moral orientation.

Western
Probably the nearest we come to hua-yen in the West is through mysticism, or through the writings of those involved with ecology – since it is within the appreciation of the interconnected nature of life within ecosystems that we touch on the significance of the hua-yen doctrine.

Within the vast arena of Mahayana literature there are other ways we could explore its fundamental vision of the nature of reality. One of these, for example, concerns the 'three spheres of reality' – *arupadhatu* (the formless sphere), the *rupadhatu* (the sphere of form) and the *kamadhatu* (the sphere of the senses). Another important approach, especially in terms of religious practice and meditation, is the Mahayana view of the five Buddhas, arranged within a mandala and each related to one of the skandhas. Here there is a graphic expression of a link between the components of the self and the fundamental features of the whole of reality.

Further developments of Mahayana Buddhism

In this chapter, and in Chapter 02, we have been looking at some basic features of Buddhist philosophy. However, Buddhism is a religion as well as a philosophy and some branches of Buddhism display traits of the former rather than the latter.

Tibetan Buddhism

Between the seventh and the eleventh centuries, Buddhists of different traditions spread their teachings within Tibet, coming from India, China and Central Asia. As time went on, the Chinese traditions were set aside in favour of the Indian and there developed a single organized system of teaching called *lam rim*, 'stages of the path'. This approach sees three traditions of Buddhist teaching as three vehicles (*triyana*), which lead on from one to the next in a graded progression. The classics of this approach are Atisha's *Lamp of the Path* and Gampopa's *Jewel Ornament of Liberation*.

The three stages are the Hinayana (the earliest Buddhist teachings, represented in modern times by the Theravada tradition), the Mahayana and the Vajrayana. This last is a Tantric approach to Buddhism and (since there are elements of Tantra in Hinduism as well as Buddhism) it will be considered separately in Chapter 07.

Buddhism in Japan

There are various forms of Buddhism that developed in Japan, each with its own particular emphasis. Tendai, for example, was promoted by Saicho (767–822) and accepts the validity of progressive revelations, the highest of which it claims is found in the Lotus Sutra. He seems to have promoted the idea that all forms of teaching may lead to enlightenment not because they were the same, but because all that was necessary was commitment to a form of *yana* or path.

Shingon Buddhism, was established by Kukai (774–835), known as Kobo Daishi – 'great teacher Kobo'. This is an esoteric form of Buddhism, in that it holds that the historical Buddha preached a limited dharma, but in reality there is another, hidden tradition, in which everyone can be enlightened and become a living Buddha. You develop spiritually until you achieve a point of seeing the whole universe as a manifestation of the cosmic Vairocana Buddha.

Pure Land Buddhism

This form of Buddhism speaks of the saving power of Amida Buddha, who rules over a pure land into which one may be born after death, depending on one's merits in this life. It arose during the tenth to fourteenth centuries, is associated particularly with Honen (1133–1212), and is based on the idea that Amida Buddha made a vow to save all beings, recognition of which, rather than any personal effort, is what is needed.

Honen thought that the world was in decline, and in such a period, it was practically impossible to gain enlightenment. The only answer then was to chant *nembutsu* (Namu Amida Butsu = Hail to Amida Buddha).

Shinran (1173–1262) took this one step further. He was married and insisted that monasticism was not central to Buddhist life. He also argued that secular life was not an obstacle to spiritual progress and that insistence on remaining sober and celibate was merely a sign of lack of trust. Gaining the Pure Land did not depend on moral goodness, but merely on trust in the power of Amida Buddha. Shinran took this position because (like Honen) he held that the world was in decline, and that people were fuelled by such blind passion that he could not imagine a way that relied on self-mastery and morality.

This is summed up in Shinran's Hymn on the Lost Age, which includes this verse:

> Because the power of the vow is without limits,
> Even our evil karma, so deep and heavy, is not burdensome;
> Because the Buddha's wisdom is without bounds,
> Even the bewildered and wayward are not abandoned.

> (Kyoto: Ryukoku Translation Centre: 1980)

For Shinran, Buddhism is summed up in the phrase *jinen honi* (*jinen* = 'things as they are'; *honi* = 'made to become through the dharma'). In other words, there is a point of naturalness that is prior to any reflection on human and other nature, or between oneself and others – a point at which one is and acts as part of a universe where everything is exactly as it is – nothing more, nothing less.

Comment

There are many parallels here. One could look at Zen (see Chapter 8), or at Taoism (Chapter 6). Buddhism becomes, in this view, almost synonymous with naturalness. But notice that you have here a conscious move away from reflection and analysis into what appears to be a 'faith' religion. It is very different from the philosophy of early Buddhism, and it is debatable whether it should be considered a philosophy at all.

Nichiren Buddhism is a particularly influential form of Japanese Buddhism, based on the *Saddharma Pundarika Sutra* (White Lotus Sutra) and with an emphasis on chanting as the basic spiritual activity. We shall not examine Nichiren Buddhism further, partly because it is concerned more with 'faith' than with philosophy, and partly because it shares the basic Mahayana philosophy that has already been outlined. There is one concept of Nichiren's that needs to be mentioned, however: the principle of *ichinen-sanzen*. This is the view that every moment of thought contains all world systems. Your mind is not limited to time and place. Just as, at enlightenment, one is thought to have immediate knowledge of everything; so, for Nichiren, at the moment at which you chant, you sum up everything that has ever happened in all world systems. The act of chanting '*Namu myo-ho renge-kyo*' ('Hail to the Lotus of the Perfect Truth') elevates the individual to a state of Buddhahood and oneness with the whole of cosmic reality.

Comment

Although having developed out of traditional Buddhist philosophy, it is interesting to see how close this comes to the traditional Hindu idea of the Atman becoming at one with Brahman. The self finds a greater self with which it is identified.

Note

With much of Eastern thought, as was said at the beginning of this book, there is a blending of what Westerners would separate into philosophy on the one hand and religion on the other. In this last section it has been important to mention some of the religious developments within the Mahayana tradition, although their exploration in terms of their religious significance is beyond the scope of this book.

On the other hand, there were two very distinctive directions taken within the Mahayana based on very different philosophical principles – Tantra and Zen. These we shall consider in Chapters 07 and 08.

Confucianism

In this chapter you will learn:
- the background to Chinese philosophical traditions
- the basic teachings of Confucius
- the nature of society and ethics in Confucian thought.

Background notes on Chinese thought

Chinese philosophy has a history that stretches back for more than two and a half millennia, and has been shaped by the blending of different traditions. Before the unification of China under the Ch'in Dynasty (from which the name 'China' comes) in 221 BCE, there were many different schools of philosophy; the principle ones being Confucianism and Taoism, both of which originated in the sixth century BCE. Of the others, we shall be considering the Yin/Yang school under Taoism (Chapter 06) and we will also be looking briefly at Mohism and Legalism in this chapter.

The thought of a people is shaped by its language and writing. To appreciate Chinese philosophy, it is therefore important to reflect on the nature of Chinese writing. In Chinese, a word gains its meaning largely from the context within which it is used. You can't tell the tense of a verb, for example, except by its context. What is more, Chinese characters are ideograms depicting whole concepts and those characters change as further ideas are added to them.

It is therefore a good written language in which to set a number of complex ideas next to one another, hinting at their relationship. It is not so easy to weld concepts into a logical argument in Chinese. One of the first impressions you receive when reading a traditional work of Chinese philosophy, such as the *Analects* of Confucius, is that you are presented with nuggets of wisdom, but not long arguments; you have advice for living well and harmoniously, but little explanation of the rationale behind such advice.

It is also important to recognize the very conservative nature of Chinese writing. It has changed very little since the earliest philosophy was written. Contrast this with the process of change that a Western reader has to deal with, looking at Greek terms and their meanings, whose English equivalents may themselves have been influenced by earlier Latin translations. A Chinese scholar examines and interprets characters which have remained almost unchanged in meaning since they were first written.

There are two particular features of Chinese thought, which might be summarized by the words 'harmony' and 'tradition'. In both Taoism and Confucianism we find the idea of the natural harmony and interconnectedness of everything, and wisdom comes by recognizing this and living harmoniously in the light of it. Unlike western thought, which has largely been based on a division between the world and God, with events in the former controlled by the Will of the latter, the Chinese have tended to look for spiritual inspiration from a sense of harmony within the world of experience. Even where terms like 'heaven' or 'fate' are used, these are more a description of the way the world is, rather than pointing beyond the world to some other reality.

The other feature, seen particularly in Confucianism, is the sense of tradition and stability. Filial obedience, and a reluctance to change anything done by the previous generation, are paramount. The cumulative wisdom of the past is taken and appreciated. This encourages social stability, in the sense of regulation and class structure.

This has proved a mixed blessing. In Chinese society, from the early fourteenth right up to the early twentieth century, the Civil Service examinations were based on Confucian thought, and thus we find philosophy being endorsed by society as a whole. On the other hand, with the coming of Communism, Confucianism was identified with the old feudal structures that had been overthrown and suffered as a result.

Finally, it should be appreciated that in Chinese thought there is a blending of what in the West would be separated into metaphysics, ethics, sociology, religion and politics. Reading the *Analects* of Confucius, you find a great mixture of advice on cultured living, personal qualities and political strategy, as well as a large number of quite inscrutable comments about individuals and situations.

Although from a modern perspective they appear to be religions, both Confucianism and Taoism are referred to simply as *chiao* (teachings). They both developed religious and cultic elements, but it is clear that they originated as philosophical systems, to be followed by 'schools' of teachers and by individuals.

Chronology

- Before the unification of China (in 221 BCE) you have what is often referred to as the 'classical' period of Chinese philosophy, with the emergence of a number of schools, including the broad traditions of Confucianism and Taoism.
- From the unification of China through until the tenth century CE, these traditions continue, but are blended with the increasingly popular Buddhism.

- From the tenth century, through until 1912, neo-Confucianism (which, as we shall see, was a form of Confucianism which had broadened and taken into itself a number ideas and attitudes which may have originated within the Taoist and Buddhist traditions, and had become more religious) became a key feature of Chinese culture, although existing alongside Buddhism and Taoism.
- From 1912 there is an influx of Western ideas, challenging traditional Chinese thought, particularly Marxism as interpreted within the work of Mao Tse-tung.

Comment

In this book, because it is possible to give an outline of only the main features of Chinese philosophy, we shall not deal with twentieth-century developments, since these reflect a partial acceptance of and reaction to Western thought. This is also made more complicated by the fact that they concern not just the ideas, but also the great social and political upheavals of the century, within which the ideas have been embodied. On the other hand, it is hoped that an appreciation of basic Taoist and Confucian philosophy may provide a useful key for interpreting the Chinese response to the West and to the events of the twentieth century.

Note on transliteration

There are many different ways of transliterating Chinese characters. Confucius may appear as K'ung Fu-Zi or Kong Fu-Zi. Zhu Xi and Chu Hsi are one and the same. Xun Zi may appear as Hsun Tsu. There may also be confusion between 'j' and 'r'. So, for example, Confucius may be seen as the founder of the 'ju' school or the 'ru' school, and a key concept 'jen' may equally appear as 'ren'.

In practice, the variations should be obvious from the context and an attempt at pronouncing each of them will generally reveal a common Chinese vocalization.

K'ung Fu-Tsu (551–479 BCE)

K'ung Ch'iu is usually known by the honorary title 'Fu-Tsu', which means 'Master'. In the sixteenth century, Jesuit missionaries in China latinized this as Confucius, which is why his teachings are now referred to as Confucianism. He is the founder of what is known as the Ru school of philosophy. *Ru* (or *ju*) means 'moralists' or 'scholars'.

Confucius sought the principles upon which a good society should be based and was concerned with what was involved in being genuinely human – humaneness (*jen* or *ren*). The result of contemplating *jen* was the formulation of a set of rules of etiquette (*li*). Putting these into practice constituted the moral life (*ch'i*).

A key feature to appreciate here is that Confucianism seeks to set out the principles that should govern right action and these are not based on a utilitarian assessment of situations. The 'gentleman' (and although applicable equally to men and women, the male gender tends to be used in the texts) does what he considers to be right, irrespective of the consequences such action may have for him.

Confucius' work can be summed up thus:

> The Master took four subjects for his teaching: culture, conduct, loyalty and good faith.
>
> (*Analects*, 7.25)

K'ung Fu-Tsu may have been born into an aristocratic family. He sought public office and became Minister of Justice in the province of Lu. Some accounts say that he was Chief Minister, but these may be the result of later exaggeration. His policies fell out of favour, and in 497 BCE he left Lu and for 13 years he travelled around the neighbouring states, trying to find other governments that would accept his ideas. He failed to do so, returned to Lu, and spent the remainder of his life teaching.

Confucius made a point of claiming that he was not expounding new ideas, but was simply handing on older traditions.

> The Master said: 'I transmit but do not create. Being fond of truth, I am an admirer of antiquity …'
>
> (*Analects*, 7.1)

This saying sets the tone for much Confucian thought, in which the wisdom of the past is revered.

Confucius taught from *The Book of Documents* (which records archives, mainly of Western Chou) and *The Book of Songs*, which he saw as illustrating an ideal age – that of the early Chou (Zhou) Dynasty (1027–266 BCE). In his day, various minor states were at odds with one another and he looked back to the early Chou as a time of strong leadership, harmony and peace. He therefore sought to re-establish the moral and social traditions of that time, particularly during the reigns of Kings Wen and Wu.

T'ien

Confucius spoke of the spiritual goal or purpose of the world as simply *T'ien* (heaven), and a ruler could therefore be called *T'ien Tsu* (Son of Heaven), since he had the responsibility for seeing that everything was correctly ordered.

Confucius regarded his teaching about personal qualities and social issues as being about T'ien, since he was teaching ways in which the individual person could bring his or her life into harmony with the universe as a whole. However, he did not believe that one could speculate about the nature of T'ien; one simply had to acknowledge it and get on with the task of living harmoniously.

Comment

The implication of this is that we live in a universe that has some sense of order, and therefore it makes sense to seek a way of behaving that reflects that order and structure. Once you understand the structure of the universe, then morality may be defined in terms of living in conformity with it – you follow 'heaven's way'. 'Way' is a translation of the word *Tao* (or *Dao*), which is a key term for both Confucianism and, of course, Taoism.

Western

There are interesting parallels here with the Natural Law approach to ethics set out by Aquinas, and with Aristotle's idea of things having a 'final cause', on which the Natural Law theory was based. For Confucius, 'heaven's way' is not a matter of personal preference, but is a given fact within the universe; it is not something to invent, but something to discover.

Both for Confucians and for those who accept Natural Law, morality is not to be assessed on pragmatic or utilitarian grounds, but is an expression of the fundamental structures and purpose of the whole universe.

One difference worth reflecting on, however, is that the 'final cause' in Aristotle appears to be fixed, in that each object or action has a purpose that is largely independent of its individual circumstances (e.g. the purpose of a knife is 'cutting', irrespective of what kind of cutting the knife is required to do). Within Confucianism, however, the keynote is not fixed purpose, but harmony. Purpose is therefore defined by context. In Taoism this is even more clearly the case, since the Tao is essentially movement, not a fixed essence. Whereas the West has a tendency to dissect experience into particular events and objects, Chinese thought tends to look at movement, direction and interconnectedness within the experienced world.

The *Analects* (*Lun-yu*)

The *Analects* is a compilation of moral and social teachings; a complete code of human conduct, with the aim of achieving a harmonious way of living. There is a great variety of styles in the work. Although generally ascribed to Confucius, some of the sayings may pre-date him, while others are later and concern his disciples. Many of them are clearly gathered from oral traditions, and start with the phrase 'The Master said:'.

Some sayings are of general application:

> 1.3 The Master said: 'Clever words and a plausible appearance have seldom turned out to be humane.'

This introduces the key term jen (humane). In a sense, everything in the *Analects* turns on this one question – 'What is it to be truly humane?' What is true human nature, and how should it be expressed?

Note

Jen (or ren), as it is used here, is very much a practical and external expression of qualities. Confucius divides people into three categories:

- *Sheng-ren* – a sage, who embodies and transmits wisdom;
- *Junzi* – a noble or 'gentleman' who strives to do what is right;
- *Xiao-ren* – a 'small man' who acts without reference to morality.

Jen enables a person to overcome selfishness and practise li. This is not just for the ruler but for everyone, and it is the natural orientation that one might have towards others.

In seeking this, tradition and social awareness are important:

> 1.2 ... filial piety and fraternal duty – surely they are the roots of humaness.

Confucius was concerned with the well-being of society, and he therefore promotes a general attitude of benevolence, though such benevolence is not offered universally, but clearly based on what is of most value and on family loyalty (a point that was criticized later by Mohism).

1.6 The Master said: 'Young men should be filial when at home and respectful to elders when away from home. They should be earnest and trustworthy. Although they should love the multitude far and wide, they should be intimate only with the humane. If they have any energy to spare after so doing, they should use it to study 'culture'.'

Comment

Notice how this verse introduces another key element in Confucian thought – culture. Education (which for Confucius meant the study of the classics, which included the collection of poetry used in royal rituals of the early Chou dynasty – *The Book of Songs* – along with *The Book of Rites* and *The Spring and Autumn Annals*, a collection of brief entries about the concerns of that time) was essentially a matter of exploring and assimilating traditional wisdom. For Confucius, the process of thinking was never to be separated from the cultural and historical matrix within which it took place.

For Confucius, it was never enough simply to think, one should also study. Indeed, he saw learning as necessary to prevent almost every other human quality from being spoiled by being taken to extremes:

17.7 If one loves humaneness but does not love learning, the consequence of this is folly; if one loves understanding but does not love learning, the consequence of this is unorthodoxy; if one loves good faith but does not love learning, the consequence of this is damaging behaviour; if one loves straightforwardness but does not love learning, the consequence of this is rudeness; if one loves courage but does not love learning, the consequence of this is rebelliousness; if one loves strength but does not love learning, the consequence of this is violence.

In other words, it is an appreciation of tradition and culture that acts to check the potential harm that can come from the exercise of otherwise positive qualities. Individual thought, assertiveness and courage are not good or bad in themselves, but they are dangerous without a sense of the culture within which they are exercised.

Of course, Confucius recognized that at each stage of life certain things are particularly likely to hinder the development of humaneness:

> 16.7 Master Kong said: 'There are three things which the gentleman guards against: in the time of his youth, when his vital powers have not yet settled down, he is on his guard in matters of sex; when he reaches the prime of life and his vital powers have just attained consistency, he is on his guard in matters of contention; and when he becomes old and his vital powers have declined, he is on his guard in matters of acquisition.'

In this verse, he uses the contrast between the 'gentleman' and the 'small man'. This is widely used as a way of highlighting the qualities that make for humaneness. For example:

> 2.14 The Master said: 'The gentleman has universal sympathies and is not partisan. The small man is partisan and does not have universal sympathies.'

> 7.37 The Master said: 'The gentleman is calm and peaceful; the small man is always emotional.'

> 13.26 The Master said: 'The gentleman is dignified but not arrogant. The small man is arrogant but not dignified.'

Generally speaking, his criterion for assessing individual action seems to be whether or not it benefits society as a whole. But this is not simply utilitarian, rather it is based on the view of the qualities that make a good ruler, and thus the qualities that should be promoted within society. He seeks to promote a balanced and open-minded view of oneself. For example:

> 4.14 ... 'One is not worried about not holding position; one is worried about how one may fit oneself for appointment. One is not worried that nobody knows one; one seeks to become fit to be known.'

> 6.18 The Master said: 'When substance prevails over refinement there is churlishness, and when refinement prevails over substance there is pedantry. Only if refinement and substance are properly balanced, does one become a gentleman.'

In dealing with society, a person should be even-handed and should act for the benefit of society as a whole, not for personal profit:

> 4.10 The Master said: 'In his attitude to the world the gentleman has no antagonisms and no favouritisms. What is right he sides with.'

> 4.12 ... 'If one acts with a view to profit, there will be much resentment.'

There are two key terms used in the *Analects* that need to be appreciated – li (rites) and jen (humaneness):

Jen (or ren)

Many passages in the *Analects* give definitions of jen, for example:

> 12.22 The Master said: 'It is to love others.'

> 13.19 The Master said: 'Courtesy in private life, reverence in handling business, loyalty in relationships with others. They should not be set aside, even if one visits barbarian tribes.'

> 17.5 Zizhang asked Master Kong about humaneness. Master Kong said: 'One who can bring about the practice of five things everywhere under Heaven has achieved humaneness.' When he begged to ask about them, he said: 'Courtesy, tolerance, good faith, diligence, and kindness.'

Li

Confucius considered that it was only by following a code of social etiquette that one could achieve humaneness. In this, he was following the tradition of the literature of the Chou Dynasty that he took as the basis of his teaching. Basically, it is ritual that balances life:

> 8.2 The Master said: 'If one is courteous but does without ritual, then one dissipates one's energies; if one is cautious but does without ritual, then one becomes timid; if one is bold but does without ritual, then one becomes reckless; if one is forthright but does without ritual, then one becomes rude.'

Knowing the correct thing to do in any situation (for example, in dealing with those who are in mourning), although it may appear formal and therefore devoid of spontaneity, aims to help shape a person's awareness, and therefore to increase his or her humaneness.

But one can only follow li if one knows one's proper place in the universal scheme of things. That involves what is called 'the rectification of names'. This is both an argument about the place of philosophy in society and a warning about misunderstanding concepts. In the *Analects*, it is put like this:

> 13.3 If names are not rectified, then words are not appropriate. If words are not appropriate, then deeds are not accomplished. If deeds are not accomplished, then the rites and music do not flourish. If the rites and music do not flourish, then punishments do not hit the mark. If punishments do not hit the mark, then the people have nowhere to put hand or foot. So when a gentleman names something, the name can definitely be used in speech; and when he says something, it can definitely be put into practice. In his utterances the gentleman is definitely not casual about anything.

In other words, one should think and speak precisely, in order not to be confused about what one (and others) should do.

Note

The 'Rectification of Names' issue was taken up later especially by Han Fei (280–233 BCE) of the Legalist tradition. He was concerned that concepts should relate to actualities and that there should be logical consistency in all claims. He gave the example of a man who wanted to sell a lance and shield, who argued that the shield could not be pierced by anything, but also that the lance was capable of piercing anything. Han Fei appropriately points out that the two claims cannot both be true. This example gave rise to the term *maodun* (contradiction) in Chinese, being made up of *mao* (lance) and *dun* (shield).

Confucius was concerned to promote hard work, courtesy between people and education. The teaching is practical and secular. So, for example, where there are religious rituals connected with those who have died, they are considered in terms of the effects they have on the living, rather than on any other-worldly beliefs. Notice also that, for Confucius, li allows for a social hierarchy. Each person's li is appropriate for his or her social position.

Western

Confucianism tends to take the same social valuation of action as modern Western sociology. All activity relates to social function and must be assessed on that basis.

Much of the teaching offers advice about what is worthwhile. Thus:

16.4 Master Kong said: 'There are three kinds of friendship which are beneficial and three kinds of friendship which are harmful. It is beneficial to make friends with the upright, to make friends with the sincere, and to make friends with those who have heard many things. It is harmful to make friends with the ingratiating, to make friends with those who are good at seeming pliant, and to make friends with those who have a ready tongue.'

16.5 Master Kong said: 'There are three kinds of pleasure which are beneficial and three kinds of pleasure which are harmful. It is beneficial to take pleasure in the proper arrangement of rites and music, to take pleasure in talking about the good points of other men, to take pleasure in having a large number of friends who are men of quality. It is harmful to take pleasure in the delights of showing off, to take pleasure in a self-indulgent lifestyle, and to take pleasure in the delights of feasting.'

Such advice, along with the precision involved in the 'rectification of names' (understanding concepts so that they can be put into practice), gives his teaching a moral tone. His ethics are seen in the qualities of the 'gentleman', in what he says about jen. However objectively the duties and rites are set out, it is important to realize that for Confucius (and later thinkers within this tradition) the essential thing is right motivation. You should not do what is right in order to gain respect or acclaim, but only because it follows li or is a natural expression of your cultivation of jen. His ethics is therefore closely linked with his basic view of the nature of humanity. Asked to sum up his teaching, Confucius gave what is known in the West as a form of the 'Golden Rule':

> 15.24 Zigong asked: 'Is there a single word such that one could practise it throughout life?' The Master said: 'Reciprocity, perhaps? Do not inflict on others what you yourself would not wish done to you.'

Two verses from the *Analects* sum up this early phase of Confucianism:

> 7.6 The Master said: 'Set your heart on the Way, base yourself on virtue, rely on humaneness, and take your relaxation in the arts.'

Underlying everything is the idea of fate (*ming*). There is a fundamental ordering of the cosmos and one cannot escape from what it presents. On the other hand, appreciating a sense of what is inevitable enables one to see what can be changed and cultivated. The last verse of the *Analects* sums up what is involved in following the Way:

> 20.3 The Master said: 'If one does not understand fate, one has no means of becoming a gentleman; if one does not understand the rites, one has no means of taking one's stand; if one does not understand words, one has no means of understanding people.'

Note on divination

Clearly, divination plays a significant part in Chinese thought, as we can see from the importance of the *I Ching* (*Book of Changes*). Divination is the prediction of the future on the basis of an awareness of the process of change here and now. But it is recognized that human beings have a part to play in the shaping of the future – indeed, knowing what one should do (and thus how one should influence the future) is the reason for seeking divination in the first place. Divination is therefore not the same thing as fate. The future is not fixed, but may be the object of wise forecasting.

Comment

In reflecting on the material in the *Analects* it is important to recognize in Confucius a natural harmony between heaven and earth. This distinction is not a mythological one – there is no separate world of 'heaven' which things on earth are advised to emulate, no separate world of God or the gods. Rather 'heaven' refers to an ideal or spiritual order, and 'earth' to the way things are in the here and now.

This is why Chinese philosophy integrates metaphysical ideas and moral and social concepts so easily. Heaven and earth may be very different in quality, but they are not two separate realms.

Authority?

What authority lay behind Confucius' teachings? Well, by his own admission, his teachings were not original. He saw himself as one who expounded traditional teachings, especially as they were reflected in the early Chou dynasty. His authority is the authority of tradition, and the appeal to it is backed up by the concept of a past golden age, contrasted with present chaos.

Comment

It is interesting to contrast Confucian and Taoist views on the source of valid knowledge. Lao Tsu said: 'Without going out of doors, one can know all that happens in the world; without looking out of one's window, one can grasp the law of heaven.' In other words, the basis of the Taoist approach is what the West would call idealism. You start with a concept, either apprehended intuitively or accepted as a result of logical argument, and observation or comment on actual societies, whether past or present, is made on the basis of the already established concepts. By contrast, Confucianism is based on the observation of actual societies and the acceptance of traditions that are passed down within them.

Critics of Confucius

Mo Tzu (479–380 BCE or 468–376 BCE)

Mo Tzu criticized the social and moral implications of Confucian thought, on the grounds that it encouraged particular concern for one's own family at the expense of a more universal feeling of goodwill. Mo Tzu claimed that such exclusive loyalty was the root of all evil and sought to replace it with a harmonious view of society based on *jianai* (respect) which leads to a utilitarian sense of benefit for all.

Whereas Confucius expected people to conform to the hierarchy, Mo Tzu wanted them simply to avoid those things that adversely affected others. Mo Tzu propounded a form of the golden rule, that one should love others as oneself. He thought that one should act to benefit society as a whole, and that this implied helping one another without distinction. He also believed that one should appoint as rulers only those who know and understand the common people. On a practical level Mo Tzu sought greater frugality in general, and in particular criticized the resources that were lavished on funeral rites. The Confucian response to this complaint was to claim that to have no sovereign and no father was to revert to being like birds and beasts, and that one must love those to whom one is nearest before one can develop love for those far off.

Mo Tzu also criticized Confucius for not believing in gods and spirits, for wasting money on ceremonies and for supporting the hierarchy. He wanted to set aside tradition and authority and start looking at society on the basis of reason. He seems to have had some idea of a deity – with a purpose and a will – expressed in the perceived sense of order in the universe. He argued that all are equal in the eyes of heaven – and therefore that one should love all equally. Mencius (see page 140) was later to say that this outraged all human feelings.

Mo Tzu argued that people understand what is to their benefit and what to their harm. Therefore the right thing to do is that which is required by the common good. Consequently, he held that people should rise in society depending on their merits, not on their ancestry. He held that the common good, and the agreement of all to that common good, should be the ruling principles of society.

Comment

In terms of political philosophy, Mo Tzu introduced some important principles, aimed at a practical mean between the extremes of Confucian traditionalism and Taoist individualism. He establishes here a basis for democracy, for a free market economy and for utilitarianism. The essential feature of his thinking is the conviction that individuals do actually know what is best for them, and do not have to discover it through publicly accepted traditions.

For Mohists (the term used for those who follow Mo Tzu's philosophy) the highest good was to give of oneself for the benefit of all. They argued for simplicity in living, and were totally opposed to war and aggression of any kind. They were prepared to defend a city against attackers, and if necessary they were prepared to give their lives in doing so, but would not approve of any offensive action.

Western

The approach to ethics taken by Mo Tzu has parallels with the Christian principle of self-giving love, offered to all equally, on the basis that one should love others as one loves oneself. Also, his ethical theory is what we would call utilitarian (see Western utilitarianism in the works of Jeremy Bentham and John Stuart Mill), namely, the principle that one should seek the greatest good for the greatest number of people.

Of course, Confucius (and later Mencius) would have said that such an approach was naïve, and did not fit the universal experience of preference for friends, family and those of like disposition and social status – in other words, that human beings are not naturally utilitarian.

As well as making these important moral and political points, Mo Tzu also had some very clear views on epistemology (the theory of knowledge). In order to be confident in accepting the truth of a belief, Mo Tzu recommended that one should do three things:

1 check the source of that belief
2 examine the situation in which that belief applies and
3 test it out to see if the belief is practical.

Western

One could almost imagine David Hume taking this approach; indeed, it is not far removed from his own examination of evidence. For example, in the case of the claim that a miracle had taken place, Hume wants any evidence to be assessed in terms of its conformity with the rest of experience and also in terms of the reliability of the person who makes a particular claim – in case it is more likely that a person was mistaken than that an event took place.

Comment

Notice in general how Mo Tzu reflects the Eastern approach to philosophy, which tends to blend epistemology, metaphysics and morals. What you understand to be true depends on the nature of reality, and that is assessed by testing out a belief in practical situations. Belief is a very practical and social matter.

Confucius had approved of the idea of destiny or fate (see page 134). He believed that one should recognize what cannot be changed, in order to enable one to channel one's energies more effectively into what can be changed. In this sense, fate was a guide to action. Mo Tzu, however, was opposed to the idea of fate. He thought that any belief in fate would encourage people to be lazy, for they would see no point in making an effort to improve something that was inevitable. Also, he argued that morality should be encouraged by the use of rewards and punishments, and people should be made aware that they have both the possibility and duty to behave morally. This approach contrasted with both Confucius and later Mencius, for whom morality should be its own reward.

Yang Chu

Yang Chu was a later critic of Confucian thought (in this case, as expounded by Mencius). We only know of him through the comments of his opponents, since none of his writings have survived, but apparently he argued that the age of the city state was past and that people needed now to look to themselves and the cultivation of their own integrity. One should therefore refuse to become involved in material things and should not take one's social position or the wishes of other people as a basis for action. Rather, one should pursue one's own interests and pleasure and assume that others will do likewise. In other words, in Western terms, he was an individualistic hedonist.

The legalist school

For Confucius, the li of the early Zhou dynasty was basic to his view of morality and society. Moral education was possible and comprised cultivating a person's ren, and the consequent establishment of yi (virtue). Although critical of this in many respects (see above) Mo Tzu also held that it was possible to educate people morally, with the help of rewards and punishments. By contrast, Taoism did not attempt to teach social ethics, but rather encouraged individual self-expression and naturalness.

In contrast to all these positions, the Legalists (e.g. Han Fei 280–233 BCE) gave up any attempt to cultivate moral sensitivity. They argued that the only basis of a good society was the rule of law, and that people did not need to develop their own morality, merely the ability to obey the laws that were established.

They argued that each individual acts basically for himself or herself. In order for society to work, this self-interest has to be curbed, recognizing that everyone has some weaknesses and is therefore unlikely to work for the benefit of society as a whole without the imposition of rules. Such rules should be based on *fa*, the principle of justice.

In other words, morality is taken out of the sphere of personal development and the ideal human nature, and is placed squarely in terms of the needs of society and the structures that will enable it to work. Legalists looked at society and then examined how individuals could fit into it.

Comment

A key philosophical issue here is the extent to which society can be said to exist over and above the individuals that make it up, and therefore whether you can use an idea of society to provide the basis for ethical action. Confucianism and Legalism see social structures and inequalities as a given fact, and allow them to determine what each individual should do. Social harmony comes at the price of social conformity.

By contrast Mohism sees a universal principle (in this case equal treatment for all) as providing the norm and therefore determining how society should be organized. Mo Tzu promotes that norm even if it seems to go against natural inclinations and observed facts of human behaviour.

Yang Chu, faced with the dilemmas of either applying norms to transform society, or accepting society's inequalities, opts out completely and takes an individualistic and hedonist approach.

We shall see also how different this is from the Taoist approach, in which everything is based initially on the individual and his or her living at one with the Tao.

The fundamental question here is 'Is society natural?' If it is, then its inequalities and structures are an inevitable development of human nature and should be accepted as such. If it is not, then we can expect individuals to criticize the norms of society and either provide individual or global principles of action by which existing societies can be judged.

Western

Is it possible for people to get together and set aside their own particular needs and views, in order to decide on a set of rules that will benefit the whole of society? This is the issue that underlies much of this debate from the early Chinese schools. In modern Western philosophy, Rawls' important work *A Theory of Justice* examines this situation.

Developments of the ru school

Confucius had combined jen (humanity) with li (etiquette or propriety). A person should cultivate the inner passions and energies (*de*) in a way that was appropriate for his or her social position. This maintains social stability, since one's li is given by one's existing social position.

Two thinkers in particular are important for the later development of Confucianism. His ideas of jen were elaborated by Mencius, who further developed a system of moral self-cultivation, and the idea of li was expounded by Hsun Tzu into a set of objective social norms.

Mencius (Meng K'o or Meng Tzu, 390–305 BCE)

Whereas the teachings of Confucius, as they have come down to us, take the form of strings of aphorisms and images, each giving particular insights into his understanding of the nature of reality and the appropriate human response to it, Mencius offers a rather more coherent interpretation, although *The Book of Mencius*, which is an important text for Confucianism, also contains many anecdotes.

Mencius was concerned with social justice and that the *min* (the common people) get what they deserve from the *jen* (the aristocracy). The well-being of the common people is the criterion by which a ruler is to be judged. Mencius was concerned above all with establishing political and social stability. In his view, the world needed to be unified and such unity could only come about with the aid of clear principles.

Much of his teaching places emphasis on the practical. On work, he says:

> A constant mind without a constant livelihood is impossible.
>
> (*Mencius*, 3a:5)

and on government, its task is:

> ... to produce the necessities of life in sufficient quantity.
>
> (Mencius, 7b:12)

Mencius believed that everyone is born good and only subsequently learns to do what is evil. His example to illustrate this is the natural response that everyone would have to save a child who is in immediate danger of falling into a well. In fact, he thought that there were four things that pointed to innate goodness: a natural feeling of compassion; a sense of shame; courtesy; and a sense of right and wrong.

Developing that innate goodness is central:

> To preserve one's mind and nourish one's nature is the way to serve heaven.
>
> (Mencius, VII, A, 1)

Jen brings about **te** (power), which has the sense of authority rather than physical force. A ruler should govern by *wang* (true kingship) rather than *pa* (physical force); in other words, one should govern through superior virtue.

Mencius debated human nature and also human fate, about which Confucius had said nothing. Mencius held that, although human nature (*hsing*) was essentially good, it needed to be nurtured. A person's character is determined by hsing (nature) and *hsin* (mind), but it is *ming* (fate) that determines exactly what will happen to that person. People cannot change their fate, for it is in the hands of heaven.

He held that the basic substance (or energy) of the universe was ch'i, and that some ch'i was heavy and some more refined and subtle. Human beings were a mixture of the heavy and the subtle and the recognition of this gives the possibility of self development in line with the natural harmony of the universe. We shall see later how these ideas came to be further developed within neo-Confucian philosophy.

Hsun Tzu (Xun Zi, 312 (or 325 or 289)–238 BCE)

By contrast with Mencius, the other main philosopher of the Ru school, Hsun Tzu, was an atheist and rationalist. For Hsun Tzu, heaven is impersonal, and it is identified with nature and the natural process.

Comment

In a way, this identification of 'heaven' with the natural process brings the Confucianism of Hsun Tzu nearer to Taoism, since, unlike Confucius who sees 'the will of heaven' as in some way an external, ideal structure to which individual people and events should conform, Hsun Tzu finds his guidelines only within the natural process.

Unlike Mencius, he held that humans were actually born with a naturally selfish hsing (nature) and had to be educated to become good; human nature needed to be tamed and guarded by li (conventional etiquette). So li, the rites of early religion which had become a code of conduct for Confucius, was seen by Hsun Tzu as a way of controlling the lives of those who had not yet been fully tutored into goodness. Li therefore became a training device for social control.

His key theme was self-improvement through study, and consequently he saw the proper function of an educated man as to govern.

For Hsun Tzu, the human mind is central. He held a totally rationalist and humanistic view, and was against superstition of any sort. If humans are born selfish, that is the way life is, and he does not seek to explain it away, rather he tries, through education, to enable individuals and society to rise above their natural state.

Notes

These three early philosophers – Confucius, Mencius and Hsun Tzu – form the basis of what was later to be known generally as 'Confucianism', although – as we shall see – there were later developments.

During the last couple of centuries BCE, Confucianism accepted ceremonies, and in this sense started in the direction of becoming more like a religion than a moral and social philosophy, which it had certainly been under its founder. At the same time, Confucian thought became more influenced by the important Chinese description of balance within nature in the form of the Yin and the Yang.

The Yin represents darkness, passivity and the feminine principle. The Yang represents light, activity and the masculine principle. Life requires both and the one should balance the other. This balance of Yin and Yang is particularly important within the Taoist tradition and a description of it is given on page 162. But it should be noted that Yin/Yang is a view of nature that really almost constitutes a separate school of philosophy and it certainly influenced Confucianism as well as Taoism.

Neo-Confucianism

Although during the Han dynasty (202 BCE–220 CE), Confucianism had briefly been accepted as the state cult, the major change took place with the Sun dynasty (960–1279) during which it became the official cult. By this time it had been influenced by Taoism, Buddhism and Yin/Yang philosophy, and the result is generally referred to as neo-Confucianism.

Chu Hsi (Zhu Xi) 1130–1200

Chu Hsi started out as a student of Buddhism, but he could not accept the Buddhist idea of anatta (no fixed self). He therefore turned to the Confucian tradition and became the main exponent of what is called neo-Confucianism. His teachings were accepted as orthodox during the long period of the Ming and Quing dynasties (fourteenth to twentieth centuries), and this form of Confucianism was really influential in shaping China's social fabric right up until the Communist takeover in 1949.

Four books form the canon of neo-Confucianism: *Lun Yu* (The Analects of Confucius), *Meng Tzu* (the book of Mencius), *Ta Hsuch* (the Great Learning) and *Chung Yung* (the Doctrine of the Mean).

Ultimate principles

The Confucianism of Chu Hsi is far more metaphysical than the earlier tradition. He linked human conduct and tradition with a set of ultimate principles and in doing so gave new meaning to some basic Confucian terms. In early Confucianism, Li was the term used for the principle of moral behaviour, which can perhaps best be translated as 'doing what is right and appropriate'. For Chu Hsi, however, the term Li is used for what might be called 'the great ultimate'.

Li is the ultimate principle behind everything; eternal, unchanging and good. The li of everything is its true nature, it is the reason it is as it is. It therefore includes the earlier meaning of 'right order or behaviour' but now involves much more. But nothing can be pure li, it needs a physical basis, the actual stuff out of which it is made. That physical element Chu Hsi called ch'i. Thus the ultimate principle (li) is expressed within everything through the ever-changing material force (ch'i), which is the energy and matter of the cosmos.

The hsing (nature) of human beings is the expression of the li within them. Individuals do not always understand their li, however, because their minds are clouded through the dulling effect of impure ch'i, and as a result their natures, although basically good, may be distorted. The process of self-cultivation is one of shedding the distorting effects of ch'i to reveal the underlying li.

Western

There appears to be a basic dualism here, with the ultimate principle on the one hand and matter on the other, but it is not the same as the Western mind/matter dualism. Ch'i produces both mind and matter. It is safer to keep away from Western dualistic notions in looking at neo-Confucianism, and simply think of li and ch'i as 'principle of reality' and 'actual expression of reality'.

Ch'i, as the material force of the universe, integrates to produce life and disintegrates to produce death. Since ch'i produces the mind and consciousness as well as the body, these too arise as a result of the integration of force, and cease to be once disintegration takes place. All of life and death is therefore a direct expression of ch'i.

Yin/Yang philosophy is integrated into the general metaphysical scheme, since Yin/Yang is the vehicle for change. Both these passive and active aspects of life are expressions of li (the ultimate principle) and come about through ch'i (material force).

As always in Eastern Philosophy, metaphysics leads on to matters of morality. But there is a basic problem for Chu Hsi:

- If everything is an expression of li, and if li is fundamentally good then where does evil come from?

His answer was to hold that, although human nature is fundamentally good, it can be influenced by the dulling effect of material forces. There is no positive force of evil, but rather a range of impurities within material form. Another way of expounding the same thing is in terms of balance and imbalance. When there is natural balance and harmony, the li of the cosmos is reflected and all is well. When there is imbalance, brought about by the density of material forces, then the li is obscured and the result is evil.

Chu Hsi followed the original terminology of Confucius and went on to say that the unhindered operation of li through an individual was shown as jen – right and noble conduct.

Chu Hsi gives a positive role to individuals in generating ren. Evil is overcome by knowledge, in that a person needs to investigate things and see the ways in which material forces are obscuring the basic li, and thus overcome them. It is therefore possible to cultivate an awareness of the fundamental principle within things (li), and this naturally leads to the production of ren.

Tai Ch'i (the Supreme Ultimate)

In neo-Confucianism li does not just refer to external behaviour, but is a principle of reason which exists eternally in everything. This gives rise to a further term – *Tai Ch'i* – which is the li of heaven and earth. There is therefore a Confucian cosmology: at its starting point is Tai Ch'i, from this there arises ch'i, which is the material basis of things. The ch'i gives rise to the *Yang* (movement) and the *Yin* (quiescence), representing the ongoing process of change and balance, and these in turn give rise to the five elements – water, fire, wood, metal and earth – of which everything is composed.

In one sense, however, these elements are not merely physical, they refer to dispositions within everything. Thus the 'five powers' theory of nature expounds the five natural processes in a way that enables them to be related to human activity and dispositions:

- water – has the quality of flowing down
- fire – has the quality of flaming up
- wood – has the quality of growing either bent or straight
- metal – has the quality of alteration
- earth – has the quality of allowing itself to be cultivated.

This is all part of the natural integration of the Chinese view of life – the five powers are symbols of processes which bind human beings to the rest of the natural order.

Neo-Confucianism developed many different schools, each with particular emphases. One thinker who deserves special mention is Wang Yang-Ming (1472–1529). Self-cultivation is at the heart of Confucianism, and the way in which one is to set about this is therefore of great importance. Chu Hsi – as one might imagine from the way in which he set out the normative canon of scriptures – considered that one ought to study the classics as a means of self-cultivation. This became the standard view and the norm for entry into the Civil Service was just such knowledge. Wang Yang-Ming, however, emphasized the importance of reflecting on one's own actions and thoughts, becoming vigilant for signs of selfishness and other distorting factors.

Comment

Watching the mind at work as a method of self-cultivation has many parallels within the Buddhist tradition, where 'mindfulness' has always been a key feature, and it was the Ch'an tradition of Buddhism that had a particularly important impact in China. It is clear that much neo-Confucianism was influenced by Taoist and Buddhist thought, and from time to time there were attempts on the part of Confucians to distance themselves from the resulting metaphysics and get back to a study of the classic texts.

Western

For neo-Confucianism, morality reflects a natural balance within the cosmos. There are interesting Western parallels to this, particularly in the pre-Socratic philosophies of ancient Greece. One might explore the ideas of Heraclitus, who – in a world where everything is in a constant state of change – sought the 'logos' or principle behind everything and the natural equilibrium of things. Equally, Pythagoras spoke of moral qualities in terms of finding an expression of heavenly harmony within the human soul. This approach is fundamental also to Stoic philosophy.

In other words

- Neo-Confucianism is about becoming harmoniously integrated with the whole cosmos
- some parts (e.g. Yin/Yang) sound Taoist
- some parts (e.g. investigation of conditions) sound Buddhist
- but they were integrated into a single overall philosophy which has been immensely influential within Chinese thought and culture.

The self and society

Principles of conduct

Li finds its expression in the five different kinds of relationships: sovereign/subject; father/son; husband/wife; elder/younger brother; friend/friend. But Confucius also distinguished between two different categories of people – *Junzi* (prince, or ruler) and *Xiao-ren* (common person). This distinction was not simply one of social position, but was thought of as distinguishing between those who lived by superior or inferior moral standards. The moral requirements placed upon the ruler being superior to those expected of the common man.

Western

One could explore interesting parallels here with Plato's quest for justice in *The Republic*, between what is expected of the Guardians in his state and Confucius' junzi.

But li is an outward expression of an inner quality, ren, which is warmheartedness or love. The person who is filled with jen towards all, will automatically express that in li, doing what is right towards them. Although one's yi (duty) lies in performing li, that does not imply that everything is formal or mechanical – at its best, it reflects the cultivation of inner quality and integrity of action.

Confucius thought that a ruler should not govern by threats or force:

> If you govern them by regulations and keep them in order by punishments, the people will avoid trouble but have no sense of shame. If you govern them by moral influence, and keep them in order by a code of manners, they will have a sense of shame and will come to you of their own accord.

> (*Analects*, ii;3).

However, Mencius argued that people had a right to rebel against a ruler if he behaved unjustly. This could be done on the basis of the 'rectification of names' – on the grounds that the ruler was not behaving as a ruler, and therefore should not be considered to be a ruler.

It is important to see the place of destiny within the Confucian moral system. Unlike Buddhism, which saw events as the working out of an individual's karma, Confucianism sees events as decided by destiny, not as a result of moral goodness or lack of it. Therefore, Confucian thought encourages a person to choose what to do single-mindedly, without taking consequences into account. (This, of course, had been opposed as unrealistic by Mo Tzu; see page 135.)

In assessing conduct, and what individuals might or might not be expected to do, a basic question remains: 'Is human nature fundamentally good or bad?' Confucius refused to give an answer to this. Mencius, of course, held that we are all naturally good. Although both the negative assessment of Hsun Tzu and the positive one of Mencius existed for a long time within Confucianism, in the end it was the positive view that became Confucian orthodoxy.

Thus the movement from nature to social training can be summed up in the opening of the chapter on 'The Doctrine of the Mean' from the *Book of Rites*:

> That which is decreed by heaven is what is meant by 'nature'; to follow his nature is what is meant by the 'Way'; cultivation of the Way is what is meant by 'education'.

Rituals

Rites, or the norms of social etiquette (li) aim at setting down a framework for society and defining civilized human behaviour. For example, there are rites in connection with paying respect to one's ancestors, thereby strengthening family ties. Confucius generally believed that a state would prosper if everyone performed the appropriate rites correctly. As we have seen, the concept of li was later broadened and it became a term for the nature of things in themselves.

The six arts

These are: ceremonies (li), music, chariot driving, archery, writing and arithmetic. They come from a period before Confucius and are found in the classic texts that formed the basis of Chinese culture.

The first of these has been described already; it is very broad and covers all rules of civilized behaviour. The state is thought to thrive if rites are followed appropriately, for they are the external expression of a good inner attitude towards life.

Music had a particularly important role in Confucian thought:

> Education begins with the Odes, is confirmed by practice of the rites and is completed by music.

> (*Analects*, viii:8)

Music was thought to operate on a person from within, unlike the rites, which operated externally and only reflected inner attitudes. Music was therefore seen as a force for harmonizing and levelling the emotions. Hsun Tzu said that those who listen to music are filled with a sense of harmonious reverence. When rulers and ministers, members of a family, or the young and old listen to music together, the result is social harmony and the leading of people into a single Way (Tao). In other words, he endorses the idea of music as an instrument of social control and civilization.

Comment

Notice here the balance between internal attitude and external performance. External rites both influence and give expression to inner attitudes. Equally, music, which operates on the emotions, can be used in order to achieve external social cohesion. This would seem to be typical of Chinese thought generally – that the goal of wisdom is to harmonize the inner and outer aspects of reality.

The five cardinal virtues

These have be described already, but they are gathered here to show the balance of qualities that is sought within Confucian philosophy:

- *jen* (*ren*) (sympathy towards others; noble, civilized – it is a very general quality of goodness. It finds expression in five qualities: politeness, liberality, good faith, diligence, generosity; *Analects*, xvii:6): Jen is wanting for others also what one want's for oneself – plus coming to appreciate the needs of others. Mencius insisted that this altruism must be completely disinterested: you should do what is right for its own sake, not for the sake of your reputation, or to be praised.

- *yi* (duty – putting jen into practice).
- *li* (the rites that determine good manners; the Book of Rites has three hundred major and three thousand minor rules of behaviour.): notice how this concept has broadened out, first to include all correct activity, and later – in neo-Confucianism – to be a metaphysical principle underlying the universe.
- *chih* (wisdom; the sense of right and wrong).
- *hsin* (trustworthiness).

Sexuality in Confucian thought

Generally speaking, the only valid use of sex according to Confucian thought is the conception of children, and particularly of sons who will be able to honour and make sacrifices to their father after his death. There is a sense that male energy is dissipated through sexual union (there are parallels here with Taoism; see page 176), and that men may be worn out both physically and morally by too much sex. Indeed, sexual excess on the part of a ruler is given as a valid reason to take from him the right to rule.

Comment

In general, sexuality is seen very much from a male perspective in Confucian writings. This is perhaps understandable, given the social situation at the time of early Confucian philosophy. On the other hand, one might have expected the neo-Confucian ideas of cosmic balance and harmony to have been reflected in a similar male/female balance within sexuality.

Ancestors

The family is central to Confucian ethics and there is great respect for those who are old. Beyond death, respect is paid to ancestors and one should act as though they were still alive, doing nothing which would offend them. Like many features of Confucianism, what appears to be a metaphysical belief (that the ancestors are still alive in some way, watching over the family), is actually justified in terms of social cohesion – paying respect to dead ancestors reinforcing the sense of identity and the coherence of the family group. It should not be assumed that the object of that respect is believed to continue to exist after death. Confucius himself was dismissive of questions about death:

> Until you understand life, how can you understand death?
>
> (Analects, xi:11)

In the neo-Confucian period, Chu Hsi believed that consciousness ended with death. On the other hand, there was also the belief that when sacrifices are made to an ancestor, that person's spirit reassembles during the time of the offering and then disperses again afterwards.

Essential goodness of the self

We have already noted the conflicting views of Mencius and Hsun Tzu on this. Mencius held that people were naturally good, while Hsun Tzu held that they were naturally evil and needed to be trained in goodness, and that society needed laws and guidance to restrict what people might be inclined to do. Good conduct (li) for Hsun Tzu was therefore conventional rather than innate.

Comment

This has implications for education. In Mencius' view, education is a matter of drawing out what is already in people. In terms of morality, they already know what is right and need only the opportunity to reflect and act on it. By contrast, Hsun Tzu's view is that morality needs to be instilled in people for the good of society. And, of course, Taoism would take a view closer to that of Mencius.

There is a fundamental philosophical problem raised here. Is there (as Confucius implied in calling his moral system 'heaven's way' and in the concept of li) a fundamentally moral structure to the universe? If there is, then morality needs to conform to it in order for people to live according to their natures. It would also imply that morality is fixed, since fundamental reality does not change with circumstances. Or is morality socially constructed, an attempt to apply reason to unreasonable and destructive human desires, and therefore changeable to suit different social circumstances?

Western

One could explore parallels between the Mencius/Hsun Tzu debate and the discussion in Western ethical theory between those who take a Natural Law approach (and who therefore accept the principle that there are things that are absolutely wrong irrespective of the wishes of those concerned, simply because they violate the essential purpose of the action in question) and utilitarians, and those who take a relativist approach to ethics, for whom the happiness and wishes of those concerned, and of society as a whole, determines what one ought to do.

Social change and the natural order

Neo-Confucianism developed alongside Taoism and Buddhism, but its attitude to society was fundamentally different from those other traditions. There was an important sense in which Confucianism wanted to develop and improve society – and whether morality was to be revealed or instilled, there was no doubt that the good of the individual was to be seen in terms of his or her contribution to the overall good of society.

By contrast, both Taoism and Buddhism tended to start with the individual and the desire for individual spiritual progress. Indeed, both traditions tend to revel in the most eccentric of behaviour at times, in order to break down conventional thinking.

In other words

At risk of over-simplification, one may say that neo-Confucianism saw its task as improving society and thereby helping individuals; Buddhism and Taoism as improving individuals and thereby helping society.

There was another side to Confucianism, however. If the li of relationships is fixed, then changes in the social order violate natural law. Therefore, although Confucianism was always concerned with social well-being, it was a well-being that arose simply as a result of the application of already established relationships. As time went on, therefore, Confucianism became increasingly seen as an obstacle, resisting social change.

For a Taoist or Buddhist the justification for social change would seem to be the degree to which it allows individuals within that society to develop and express themselves. For a Confucian, social relationships are already defined and established. Any change which does not conform to those relationships, even if it allows individuals to express their own personalities, is seen as being, in the long run, a threat to harmonious society.

> **Western**
>
> Although Confucianism has a problem with social change, it does not in principle deny the reality of change. In Chinese thought, there is no separate 'eternal' realm that is real, in contrast to the unreality of everyday experience. By contrast, in Greek thought, the real is by nature changeless. Thus for Plato particularly, the 'Forms' are eternal realities of which particular things are imperfect copies. Chinese thought does not see things that way at all.

Confucianism and the Chinese Republic

Confucianism is not 'other worldly'; but concerned with a tradition of wisdom that has developed in terms of human conduct. For this reason, it has been closely associated with the culture within which it developed, reinforced by the fact that neo-Confucian texts were at the heart of the Chinese Civil Service.

After the ending of the last (Ch'ing) dynasty and the formation of the Chinese Republic in 1912, Confucianism lost the social and political basis that had supported it, and its influence diminished rapidly. It quickly became identified with Chinese feudalism, particularly in the way that its concepts of filial piety and loyalty had reinforced regimes, and a whole way of life, that was then being seen as repressive. Nevertheless, many of the moral qualities instilled by centuries of Confucianism continued to be followed by individuals.

On the other hand, Mencius had insisted that the people's welfare should take precedence over that of the ruler, and that they had the right to replace a ruler if he did not prove to be just. This feature of Confucian teaching was used to justify social change in the early twentieth century. Overall, however, the arrival of communism and the rejection of social hierarchy put an end to Confucianism as a working basis for society.

Confucian ethics, particularly in connection with hard work and family loyalty, may have aided the rise of the commercial and industrial economies of the Far East. But for many, the potential of Confucianism in modern times is mainly in terms of the benefits for individuals in a philosophy that encourages times of quiet, moral reflection.

There has been renewed interest in Confucianism, but mainly in terms of the preservation of Chinese culture and a rejection of Westernization. In particular, it has been emphasized that although Confucianism is a philosophy of life which includes political views, it does not want a return to the old social order.

06

Taoism

In this chapter you will learn:

- the teachings of Lao Tzu
- the developments within Taoism
- the Taoist view of living in harmony.

Background

Before examining Taoism, it is important to remember its context, in terms of the various Chinese philosophies, recapitulating what was said at the opening of the chapter on Confucianism. Prior to the unification of China in the third century BCE there were a number of different philosophical schools, including:

- Taoism
- Confucianism
- the Yin-Yang school
- Mohism
- the Legalist School (Pa Chia) and
- the School of Names (Ming Chia).

Although they did not all survive as independent schools of thought, they influenced one another. Confucianism and Taoism, the two principal traditions, were by no means fixed. As we saw with Confucianism, and will see again in Taoism, there were quite radical changes brought about by subsequent interpretations and application of their basic ideas.

With the introduction of Buddhism into China there was a further blending of thought. Buddhism adapted itself to fit into the Chinese culture and in turn it influenced the existing philosophies. What emerged from this was a triple tradition, comprising Confucianism (in the form that is generally referred to as neo-Confucianism), Taoism (in both its religious and philosophical forms) and Buddhism.

As we shall see, Taoism is very different from Confucianism, in that it is based on the individual and tends to reject the impositions of organized society. Within China, both traditions have embedded themselves into the general consciousness in such a way that people may accept both, but apply them to different aspects of their lives. In terms of the personal balance of one's life, Taoist teachings may be followed, but in terms of social etiquette, one becomes a Confucian. And indeed, in the face of suffering, one may respond as a Mahayana Buddhist. In the Chinese consciousness, boundaries between these are largely unnecessary, for each contributes to the overall wisdom with which life may be encountered and interpreted.

In general, it would be true to say that these traditions did not demand exclusive loyalty. The Chinese were happy to accept a blend of all three, taking from each tradition what was most appropriate for their particular social or personal circumstances.

Lao Tzu

If Taoism can be said to have a founder, it is Lao Tzu. But that means 'old master', and it is therefore an honorary title rather than a name. There is a tradition that he was an older contemporary of Confucius in the sixth century BCE, but in fact he may have been a considerably more ancient figure. It is also clear that the *Tao Te Ching*, the work that contains his teachings, is in fact a compilation of sayings that have been gathered, perhaps over a considerable period of time, some being ascribed to Lao Tzu, others to his disciples. In any case, what matters is not the individual, but the tradition of teaching that his name stands for.

The *Tao Te Ching* is essentially a collection of aphorisms, arranged by subject. Three words that make up the title:

- *Tao* means 'way'
- *Te* means 'power'
- *Ching* can mean 'essence', but here it means a work of authority – perhaps 'authoritative handbook' or 'classic' is the best translation – something which deals with the essence of the subject.

So one might translate the title as 'Authoritative Handbook on the Way and its Power'.

Key concepts in Taoism

The Tao

Tao (or *Dao*) means 'path' or 'way', and it refers to the natural way things are. The aim of Taoism is to help individuals to be aware of and live in unity with the Tao, characterized by behaviour that is natural, spontaneous and in a harmonious balance.

But before examining the individual's response to the Tao, let us first of all look at the way in which Taoists view the world, for the Tao is seen as the principle of creation and the source from which everything arises.

The Tao is thought of as so fundamental that it is beyond description. In the famous opening statement of the *Tao Te Ching*:

> The Tao that can be talked about is not the true Tao.

And Chapter 42 gives what amounts to the Taoist sequence of creation:

> The Tao
> gives birth to the One;
> The One
> gives birth to the two,
> The Two
> give birth to the three;
> The Three give birth to every living thing.
> All things are held in yin, and carry yang:
> And they are held together in the Ch'i
> of teeming energy.

(trans: Element Books 1993)

We shall look at individual aspects of this a little later.

Western

If the Tao is thought of as creative, it should not be identified with the Western idea of a creator God, a being who is in some way independent of and external to his creation. Rather, the Tao is the spontaneously creative foundation or basis of everything.

The Tao is described as the 'origin and mother of the Ten Thousand Things', a standard phrase to indicate everything that exists. It is said to achieve everything without force; it gives life without thereby possessing the things it has created. It is the very essence of naturalness. It is that by which all things become what they are. It is boundless, and it produces the constant flow of ordinary, limited things.

One popular simile used to describe the Tao is water. Water is soft and pliable, but it can exert great force and will eventually wear away even the hardest rock. To follow the Tao is to find a natural way of achieving one's end which may require similar qualities.

Another image used by Lao Tzu to describe the Tao is that of a pair of bellows. Once they are being pumped, bellows can provide a constant supply of air, and yet they themselves are empty. They are not diminished by the air coming from them, nor is the air part of them – but there would be no air pumped without them.

The Tao cannot be described as 'a being', but more 'non-being'. It is that out of which beings emerge. In this respect it is like the Buddhist concept of shunyata (nothingness). Tao is universal and all-pervading, it is also indestructible.

In terms of metaphysics, the Tao represents a silent background out of which things emerge and into which they move again. It is not a separately existing thing, but the ground of the coming and going of all existence.

According to Taoist philosophy, rest is prior to motion, and stillness is prior to action; therefore the Tao is basic to everything. The Tao, although motionless in itself, offers the basis for all other movement. In this sense, the Tao is that which is absolutely natural.

Western

Here we have a parallel with the unmoved mover and uncaused cause of Aristotle and Aquinas. The Tao acts as exactly the unmoved and uncaused basis of everything. The only crucial difference is that whereas Western thinkers went on to say that this uncaused cause was 'God' and therefore set over against created things, within Taoism (and other Eastern philosophies) the source of life is not set over against individual beings, but is their true nature. Becoming aware of the Tao is also to become aware of oneself, just as for Mahayana Buddhists there is awareness of one's own Buddha nature. The Western equivalent of this is panentheism (God in everything, but not simply to be identified with everything, which would be pantheism).

Even then, it is important to recognize that Tao is not something that can be grasped with the intellect (that was the essential thing to recognize in that opening sentence of the *Tao Te Ching*). One may become aware of it, but not define it.

Te

Tao is essentially unknowable and yet is said to bring everything about. What can be seen, however, is *Te*, which means 'power'. This represents the presence of Tao within individual things; the energy of Tao at work in the world.

For Taoism, this is not merely a statement about metaphysics – about the general principles that determine how the world is; it is also practical. If a person or thing is following its Tao (in other words, if it is acting naturally) then it will be filled with power (Te). This is not thought of as a coercive power, seeking to force change in the world, for that would be contrary to the fundamental insights of Taoism, but a natural power in which something acts to its full potential. To use the analogy of water – if Tao is like the compliance of flowing water, then Te represents that force that such water can have; the impact in a particular place of the flow of Tao.

Ch'i and ming

The word *ch'i* literally means 'breath', and refers to the spirit, energy or life-force within everything. It is seen as the origin of the universe, but that comes from something more fundamental, the single Tao, the ultimate reality.

The ideal state is one in which a person returns to the Tao, the ultimate source of oneself in a way that gives total satisfaction and naturalness. For a person at one with the Tao there is no need for any struggle or artificial goals. This ideal state is termed *ming* (enlightenment); it is the state in which one sees the eternal law (ch'ang), that which is permanent and yet causes the constant flow and change of everything else.

Comment

In many ways, the Taoist idea of ming is like Buddhist enlightenment. Both are the point at which a person becomes aware of that which lies beneath the changes of life and which directs the process of change.

Change and the Tao

Taoism holds that everything is in a constant state of flux, but that flux is balanced by the Tao. Chinese thought has always recognized that the ultimate is not something fixed but a process of flow and change. An ancient classic text exploring this is the *I Ching*. ('I' is 'change' and 'Ching' means either 'authoritative text' or 'handbook'.) So the *I Ching* can perhaps best be described as a handbook for divination, a way of interpreting and predicting events and assessing the appropriateness of courses of action on the basis of those predictions. It engages with the individual using it, so that (rather like astrology) the individual must contribute an element of interpretation if it is to be used wisely.

Like Buddhism, Taoism sees everything as changing and impermanent. The only thing that is permanent is *ch'ang* – the eternal principle or law which governs that process.

In other words
The only permanent feature of life is change.

When everything is changing, the temptation is to look beyond the change to find something that is permanent, perhaps in terms of some eventual outcome. But once this happens, a person ceases to be aware of what is happening in the present moment, and there is a tendency for the present to be interpreted in terms of the past (its origin) or future (its goal). By contrast, Taoism (like Buddhism) insists that one should focus on the reality of the present moment. Chuang Tzu (in Chapter 14 of his book of the same name) commented:

> If people could follow the ancient way, then they would be masters of the moment.

Here is another important feature of Taoist thought. The world is as it is, and if there is any perfection, it is the perfection of what is, not what we imagine it should be. But if that is the case, then any attempt to change the world is an attempt to make it less perfect. To find perfection, we have simply to rest in that which is natural. Returning to perfection is a movement from the unnatural to the natural.

In other words
The enemy of human perfection is the unnatural, which includes the forced, the premeditated and the socially prescribed.

Western
Within a Western Judaeo-Christian tradition, the world is fallen, it is a place where being natural is to be in a state of sin. The best hope of redemption is to be restored to the state that Adam found himself in before the Fall. (One of the more delightful responses to this conviction was the Adamite sect, a Christian denomination in the seventeenth century who worshipped naked in order to recreate the conditions in which Adam originally found himself.)

From the Western perspective, to be natural is to be fallen, and some of the most powerful aspects of naturalness, like sexuality and aggression, need to be restrained severely and allowed to operate only within narrowly prescribed parameters.

Taoism is quite the reverse. It seeks to be rid of that which is rational or socially prescribed and restrictive, and to return to the Tao, the natural balance of nature.

Yin and Yang

In the creative process by which the Tao is said to bring forth the multiplicity of things (as described in the quotation from the *Tao Te Ching* given above), there is reference to 'The Two', a first differentiation in the movement from the one to the many. This is a reference to *Yin* and *Yang*, a pair of concepts that are found in both Taoist and Confucian thought, and (as we saw earlier) may actually be considered to be the basis of a school of philosophy in its own right.

The idea of Yin and Yang is probably very ancient, but its first systematic formulation was set out by Tsou Yen in the fourth century BCE. It is also set out in the *Shih-I*, a commentary on the *I Ching*, written in the third century BCE.

Yin (dark/female) and Yang (light/male) were regarded as the two universal energies, which combined with the five elements to form the basis of everything. Just as the Tao restores balance, so Yin and Yang, the female and male, need to be balanced. In fact, like the sunny and shady sides of a mountain (from which image we get the terms 'Yin' and 'Yang') they are quite inseparable and imply one another. Life cannot be all sunshine, nor will it be all shadow; to think otherwise is to be immature.

Comment

A quest for a life of unremitting sunshine is doomed and inevitably leads to disappointment, and so is the attempt to be 100 per cent male or female. This is central to Taoism: a sense of balance; a natural correction when an extreme is reached.

The T'ai-chi-t'u is 'the symbol of the supreme ultimate':

The dark area represents the Yin and the light the Yang. Notice that each defines the other. You cannot have Yin without Yang or vice versa. Notice also how one flows into the other in perfect balance. There is also a small seed of each of them within the heart of the other. This represents the continual flow of male/female, light/dark within everything, recognizing that in the heart of the female there is a male side, and a female side in the heart of the male.

Notice also that there is constant movement in the symbol. There is no point of static balance, only of balanced flow. This balance of the Yin and Yang aspects of life is very influential in all aspects of Chinese thought and culture, but it is not an exclusive philosophy and it is compatible with other religions.

In examining Buddhism, with its acceptance of the universal phenomenon of dukkha (suffering or unsatisfactoriness), we saw that the philosophy was not negative or pessimistic, but merely sought to be realistic. So also the Yin/Yang balance is not offered in some fatalistic way, but is simply offered as a realistic assessment of the way things are. To pretend that you can live life without shadow, or that the shadow is some accident that has happened in a world designed to be all light, is fundamentally alien to Eastern thought as a whole. The balance of growth and diminishment, happiness and sadness, gain and loss is an essential feature of life. From this perspective, wisdom consists of seeing it, living in harmony with it, and thereby finding a happiness that is not dependent upon permanent sunshine.

Western

In the West, there has been a tendency to define how life should be, and then struggle with the fact that life does not conform to such a definition. Typical of this is the 'problem of evil', where belief in a good and loving creator is challenged by the fact of suffering and death. In the East, as exemplified by the blending of Yin and Yang, there is a recognition that in reality life is always a balance between opposing energies. See also, for example, the Hindu concept of the god Shiva as both creator and destroyer, or the Buddhist 'Wheel of Life', where the craving for life is depicted as a process held within the jaws of death. Yin and yang, distinct but inseparable, express the natural flow of the Tao.

There is another important feature of the Yin/Yang balance in life: Yin represents inactivity, rest and reflection; Yang represents activity and creativity. The ideal is to balance these two features of life. Taoist philosophy suggests that you cannot act effectively without periods of quiet reflection, but equally such periods of inactive reflection lead naturally into taking skilful action.

This balance is not merely a feature of lifestyle, but reflects the very basic feature of the Tao, that it restores balance. When anything reaches one extreme, it starts to swing back to the opposite. There is therefore a constant movement from activity to inactivity and back again.

A person's identity is also related to Yin and Yang. Whether male or female, we have both yin and yang aspects, and this produces a process of change and apparent contradiction which cannot be resolved. But it is important to realize that for Taoism it would be wrong to attempt to resolve this particular struggle, for it is simply our particular manifestation of the Yin/Yang movement within everything.

We do not have a fixed identity – that is the central feature of philosophical Taoism's approach to the self. We are what we are through a natural process of change. At no point do we arrive at a true or authentic self. As with the universe, the only thing that is fixed within the self is the process of change itself.

Western

Notice how radically different this is from Western thought. For Plato, there are ideal forms of which individual things are but imperfect copies. Within the monotheistic religions, there is a single, good, omnipotent creator God, and whatever is imperfect or changeable has to be explained in terms of a voluntary limitation of his creative power, or the existence of a separate evil power – giving rise to 'the problem of evil'. Your true self will one day be revealed, either because you are essentially eternal, merely trapped within the material world (as was held by many western gnostic groups), or because God will eventually raise you to a new life in heaven, where your true nature will be displayed through a process of judgment, with eternal rewards or punishments to follow.

Taoism is so different from all this. Like Buddhism, there is no fixed self; there is no single essence that is you. Rather, you are the dynamic process by which different elements, both Yin and Yang, are blending and flowing on, the one never displacing the other.

The Taoist equivalent of the 'eternal' judgment of Western thought is the recognition that beneath the duality of Yin and Yang there is the basic life force, the Ch'i, and that beneath that there is the Tao, the creative origin of everything. Mystical awareness of the Tao puts the whole process of change into perspective – but it does not stop it.

Chuang Tzu (369–286 BCE)

At about the same time that the ideas of Confucius were being set down in a systematic and logical form by his disciple Mencius (see page 140), the work of Lao Tzu was being given a similar treatment by Chuang Tzu. In the book which bears his name, he gave a careful exposition of what we now refer to as 'philosophical' Taoism. Of the 33 chapters in that book, the first seven are by Chuang Tzu himself and the others by his disciples.

Much of what has already been said about acting naturally, was expounded most clearly by Chuang Tzu. In particular we see him using the term **li** (principle) to explain the operation of the Tao in continually transforming things.

Comment

Notice that Chuang Tzu uses the term *li* for 'principle'. This is not the same as Confucius' use of the word *li*, which referred to the ordering of society. The Taoist *li* is the ordering of the whole of reality and is thus much closer to the later use of *li* by Chu Hsi in neo-Confucianism.

Whereas Lao Tzu had expressed ideas of the Tao using images, Chuang Tzu tried to express it through philosophy. He was well aware of the limitations of language, however:

The fish trap exists because of the fish; once you've caught the fish, you can forget the trap … Words exist because of meaning; once you've gotten the meaning, you can forget the words. Where can I find a man who has forgotten words so that I can have a word with him?

(*Chuang Tzu*, trans. Watson, 1968)

One particularly important concept expounded by Chuang Tzu was an approach to life and ethics called *wu wei* (non-action). This lies behind both Taoist spirituality and also the practical and material expressions of the Taoist vision of what constitutes the natural balance of activity, and will be considered in the next section.

Living in harmony

According to Taoism, both the universe as a whole and each individual share three life-forces: *shen* (spirit), *qi* (breath) and *jing* (vital essence). In meditation a person tries to join the microcosm (self) to the macrocosm (world). In order to do this, it is necessary to get rid of all dualistic concepts like subject and object, so that one may sense oneself as being in a unity with everything. Thus, the basis of Taoist meditation is what is generally termed mysticism. The mystical unity of all things is not something that can be rationally explained, it is to be directly experienced. And that, of course, is very much in line with the basic position of Taoism, where the Tao that can be spoken about is not the true Tao. What is known through meditation is not the same as the attempt to describe it.

Comment

In Taoist thought, the whole universe is found within each individual. Meditation is the method by which Taoists become aware of this. Living in a way that follows the Tao is therefore not something alien to the individual, nor does it involve a loss of the self. Rather, by allowing the self to live consciously in harmony with the universe, Taoists believe that one is also being true to one's own nature.

Western

The great divide between the thinking self and the external material world, so widespread in Western thought (a dualism particularly associated with Descartes), does not feature in the same way in Eastern Philosophy. In Western thought, with the constant temptation to define the self over against the world, mysticism might be seen as a way of 'losing' the self in some undifferentiated other. In the East it is seen differently. Whether we are considering Taoism or Buddhism, the self arises out of and finds its natural expression within the 'all'. It does not have an inherently separate existence.

If everything is in a state of constant change, then to hold to a fixed self is a painful illusion, and one that is doomed to failure. Sooner or later the reality of change prevails. Central to Taoism, however, is the acceptance of change, and an individual is therefore encouraged to strive to allow the natural process of change to take place, so that he or she can consciously become part of the flow of the Tao.

Comment

In Taoism, meditation does not aim to bring a person to a place of peace, free from further change. Rather, it develops an attitude that allows a person to change in a natural way.

Feng Shui

If meditation is the internal means of living in harmony, then the most obvious external one is Feng Shui. The literal translation of this term is 'wind and water', the natural elements that shape the landscape. Feng Shui is a theory about the movement of the ch'i (life force) throughout the environment. To understand

Feng Shui is to know how to design your environment in such a way that you take account of the natural flow of energy and are therefore able to benefit from it.

The design and orientation of a building, even its furnishings, can affect the flow of ch'i. Parts of a building are related to parts of the lives of people who live in it, and a Feng Shui consultant can advise on how to make the living space positive and life enhancing. Basic rules are applied, but the result of good Feng Shui is that a place can feel homely, or offer a natural welcome.

In terms of the basic philosophy behind it, what Feng Shui is doing is to bring those artificially constructed aspects of life into a natural balance. A house that is balanced and correctly arranged, it is claimed, will give out positive energy and become more naturally attractive to those who enter it.

Comment

Feng Shui is a good example of the way in which traditional Eastern Philosophy is not divorced from other aspects of life, or restricted to the area of academic enquiry. Here we have a very practical technique, claiming to improve the quality and energy available in one's life, which is directly the result of applying fundamental metaphysical concepts.

Non-action and non-ethics

The key term for a Taoist approach to the evaluation of action is wu wei. This means 'non-action', but it does not mean total inactivity. Rather, it is action that is undertaken on two principles:

- no effort is to be wasted, and
- nothing should be done that is against nature.

Wu wei might be translated as 'spontaneous' or 'natural' action. It is the sort of action that is done intuitively, not as a result of premeditation. It displays the skills of a child, who will see and act quite naturally, without giving thought to the appropriateness or consequences of what he or she is doing. It is action that is based on reality, not on fantasy.

In other words

We often act against our nature, in order to promote an idea or principle to which we feel we ought to conform. In this, we may be inwardly torn, our emotions wanting one thing, our rational mind demanding another, our conscience prompting yet another course of action. Our action is neither effective nor natural, but is the result of a compromise between warring priorities. By contrast, wu wei is spontaneous and natural. It is that moment when we don't stop and ask if the action is right, we just find ourselves doing it.

Chuang Tzu argued that one should only act when that action can be effective. If there is nothing that can be done, then one should do nothing. He saw wu wei as the key to successful living. In Chapter 3 of the *Chuang Tzu*, he gives as an example of wu wei the case of a butcher whose knife remains sharp for a long time although he is constantly carving up animals. The reason for this is that he is so skilled that he never cuts into bone or ligament, but allows the knife to slice through natural cavities with maximum efficiency.

Examples

For vegetarians and others who might not welcome Chuang Tzu's example, let us take two others:

1 Watch a learner drive a car. He or she is constantly thinking about when to change gear, how to be positioned on the road, where the indicator switch is located, how slowly to take the foot off the clutch, where the brake is kept. While the learning process is in its infancy, each action is made as a result of remembering a rule and applying it, having first located the required instrument. Then watch an experienced driver. He or she does not consciously monitor all the various controls, but acts instinctively. Faced with a sharp bend or an accident ahead, there is no time to think 'I need to slow down, and to do that I must press this middle pedal with my foot' – the driver slams on the brakes instinctively.

2 Ballroom dancing. Need I say more?

Wu wei is the skill that makes everything look easy. It is the art of completely unselfconscious action. Wu wei is being confident and spontaneous. Wu wei happens when one is able to set aside the conscious effort of remembering how to do something. Wu wei is your unconscious mind working so quickly and effectively that your conscious mind does not have time to catch up and so learns to trust what happens.

Comment

Perhaps now it is clear why the heading of this section includes 'non-ethics'. Ethics implies the rational assessment of action and the ways by which it may be assessed. Mostly, ethics is done after an action has taken place – assessing whether (and on what grounds) it might be judged right or wrong.

But ethical considerations are also weighed up by those contemplating action. Legal, social and religious rules come to bear on a person's conscience. In struggling to know what would be the right thing to do, a person is in a moral dilemma. Ethics is the study of such moral dilemmas, whether pre- or post-action.

- Taoists don't favour ethics in this sense. If one acts spontaneously, one does not stop to weigh the consequences or take account of the rules.
- Ethics is the study of what happens when one is out of touch with the Tao.

It is worth noting the fundamental difference in approach between Confucianism and Taoism on the matter of ethics. Confucianism is always ready to intervene in life, to prescribe certain courses of action, to define how one should behave. In other words, there are actions that should be performed for the good of society, even if they are totally contrary to the natural inclinations of the people concerned. By contrast, Taoism will have none of this. Such intervention fails to perceive the natural ordering of the Tao.

Life throws up similar problems for everyone, but Taoist philosophy suggests that, by being natural, one can minimize the damage they cause. Chuang Tzu, in an example that illustrates his wit, comments on the fact that a drunk can fall from a carriage without hurting himself, whereas someone who is sober would be injured by the same fall. The reason he gives is that the drunk is 'united', his body is reacting naturally, whereas the sober man, perceiving danger, tenses himself and thus makes himself vulnerable.

Individualism

The self, for Taoism, is a direct expression of a person's Te (power), which is the energy of the Tao in him or her. The aim of a Taoist is to achieve a unification of everything within the self, and this is to be done by returning to the source of oneself – the Tao.

Notice that this is focused on the individual, not on society. In looking at Confucianism, we saw that the correct way to behave was to accept the li, the etiquette accepted by society and given by tradition. By contrast, Taoism starts with each individual. The great debate between Taoist and Confucian approaches to life is between the natural and the artificial, the spontaneous and the imposed.

Thus Chuang Tzu insisted that one should not introduce any external motive into action – whether in the form of social approval or the anticipation of praise or blame. That does not imply that one's action will necessarily be to the detriment of others, or that it should not take them into account, simply that the effect on others should not be the primary reason for taking that action.

Comment

Mo Tzu, a critic of the Confucian philosopher Mencius, promoted universal love, and criticized Confucian thinkers for accepting a natural scale by which one paid greater respect and love for one's own relatives and friends than to those who were deemed worthy of that love. At the opposite extreme, Yang Chu, an older Taoist thinker, claimed that it would be wrong for him to take any action that would harm himself, even if the whole of the world would benefit as a result, since the two basic aims of life were to keep oneself away from harm and to live for as long as possible. To what extent that view can be taken as the only logical conclusion to be drawn from applying Taoist principles, is a matter of debate.

Chuang Tzu takes the position that nothing is inherently good or bad, but that it depends on the circumstances and the people concerned. This does not mean that moral rules have absolutely no place within Taoism, but rather that there comes a point at which one has to be prepared to go beyond all moral rules. He points out (in Chapter 2 of the *Chuang Tzu*) that, where two people disagree, it is quite impossible to get fair and absolute arbitration, for whoever is brought in to arbitrate is bound to take one side or the other and will have a view of his or her own.

In other words, in matters of moral choice, there is no absolute that can be brought to bear on the process of decision making or evaluation – everything and everyone has a particular viewpoint.

Natural spontaneity and simplicity

Like flowing water, one should take the line of least resistance. The Taoist ideal is therefore to live in simplicity, free from all desires and ambitions. But freedom from desire may seem to be threatened by education, for increased knowledge tends to lead to an increase in desires and ambitions. For this reason, there developed a strand of Taoist thinking that resisted intellectual progress and education.

One's natural simplicity is called *p'u*, and it is characterized by wu wei, spontaneous action. This reflects a natural harmony. The naturalness of wu wei produces both simplicity and integrity – it is action in which the whole, undivided self is engaged. The unconscious mind directs it even before the conscious mind has had time to rationalize about it.

Comment
Taoism seems to be striving for a kind of free-flowing natural integrity that is too often lost with childhood.

This simplicity and naturalness leads to an awareness of all living things and of the place of humankind within nature. Rather like Buddhism, this encourages empathy for other species. It was Chuang Tzu who dreamed that he was a butterfly and, on awaking, posed the interesting question:

> How do I know that I was a man dreaming that I was a butterfly, or that I am now a butterfly dreaming that I am a man?

Chuang Tzu's work had a great impact on Buddhism when it arrived in China, since it shared Buddhism's quest for an immediate awareness of 'no-self', losing what we conventionally call ourselves within a larger perspective. It was also influential in terms of Chinese landscape painting and poetry. Knowing exactly the right and natural place for something within a landscape, or giving a very simple poetic evocation of an experience – these come from a sensitivity towards the natural that Chuang Tzu encouraged. Within Chinese art there are many aspects of balance. In landscape painting, for example, there needs to be a balance between mountains (Yang) and water (Yin). Sometimes the artist will deliberately give the impression of the constant changes within the landscape, for example, rocks are seen to crack from the pressure of tree roots. In particular, people and dwellings are generally small within the overall landscape and placed with care. They are placed (as in Feng Shui) to reflect the right balance and flow of energy. In general there should be an overall, harmonious sense of flow and change.

Taoism extends into all aspects of life, just as Feng Shui considers the artificial environment and attempts to bring it into line with the natural energies of the ch'i, so a consideration of Yin and Yang influences Chinese cooking. Some foods (e.g. meats) are considered to be Yang and others (e.g. vegetables) are Yin. Within a dish, or certainly within a meal, there needs to be a natural balance of Yin and Yang. Hence one would serve beef (Yang) with nuts (Yin), and with a meal involving meat, one would choose a Yin drink (e.g. tea) rather than a Yang (e.g. alcohol).

In the West, probably the best known of all Taoist practices is T'ai Ch'i. This uses a sequence of carefully balanced movements, performed in order to balance the Yin and the Yang, leading to an enhanced sense of poise, balance and harmony. It is a most visible expression of what Taoism is about, for the person who has learned the sequence of movements can be absorbed in their performance without conscious thought, but allowing a natural flow of physical and emotional energy. It originated in the fourteenth century, and is practised by many people who experience its benefits without knowing anything of the Taoist theory that underlies it.

Comment

Here we have culture that deliberately strives to reflect its underlying philosophy. It is not a matter simply of social convention, nor is it an ethic produced as a result of underlying principles; rather, it is the attempt to reflect metaphysics (in the sense of the underlying structure and meaning of reality) in everyday life and thereby make naturalness and integrity possible.

Minimalist politics

A major theme of the *Tao Te Ching* is its critique of the artificiality of human culture and social life. It argues that government should not interfere with the natural process. Lao Tzu sought something that was deeper and more natural than the social and political reality he encountered around him.

Since it takes the individual as its starting point, Taoism sees the organizations and imposed rules of society as there to frustrate people's natural desires and abilities. As an ideal, the state should therefore interfere as little as possible in people's lives. The principle that a ruler should do as little as possible was probably taken largely in response to the observation that rulers tend to act in their own interests, rather than in those of their subjects.

Western

The most obvious Western parallel here is with anarchism. See, for example, the nineteenth-century anarchist Proudhon, or even Leo Tolstoy.

Religious Taoism

There are two very different forms of Taoism: philosophical and religious. Religious Taoism developed from about the second century CE and it included rituals, temples and priests. Unlike the earlier philosophical Taoism, this became fundamentally a quest for healing and immortality, so that the principal concern of Taoists became retaining and enhancing the vital forces within the self in order to prolong life.

Here we shall examine just two features of religious Taoism – its views on immortality and on sexuality. Both serve to illustrate the very different philosophical basis being used.

Immortality

There are two very different attitudes to death within Taoism. In the earlier philosophical Taoism, death is seen as natural, and the fear of it misguided. Chuang Tzu (in Chapter 2 of his work) said:

How do I know that loving life is not a delusion? How do I know that, in hating death, I am not like a man who, having left home in his youth, has forgotten the way back?

(trans. A. C. Graham, *Chuang-Tzu: the Inner Chapters*, Mandala, 1986)

By contrast, the main preoccupation with religious Taoism was with the prolongation of life. In particular, they sought it through internal alchemy. The quest was to become an 'immortal' (*hsien*), a mark of which was to display magical powers, including the ability to fly.

Curiously, the quest for immortality did not involve an attempt to regain youth. Those heading for immortality continue to age – so that the 'immortals' are portrayed as being extremely old.

Awareness of breathing, as a form of meditation, has a long history, both within Taoism and Buddhism, but there developed in the twelfth century a Taoist school call 'The Way of Realization of Truth' which placed particular emphasis on awareness of breathing. It was believed that the air was the physical basis of the universe and that it contained 'fine parts' which could be accumulated within the body, thus prolonging life. But it was also believed that a person had only a certain fixed number of breaths in this life, so that the faster a person breathed the sooner they would die, and conversely, retaining the breath for as long as possible would prolong life. This led to the practice of embryonic breathing (in other words, breathing like the embryo in the womb), which in practice requires the breath to be held for as long as possible.

We see here a basic, quantitative assessment of the ch'i: there is only a fixed amount of breath, and one needs to take care to conserve it. Notice how very different this is from the natural flowing of energy in earlier Taoism.

Rude comment

In the rather literal approach taken by religious Taoism, the fixed amount of breath you are believed to have been given at birth has an unfortunate consequence. Not only does each breath through the mouth or nostrils go to exhaust one's supply of ch'i, but the passing of wind in the other direction will also shorten one's life! Perhaps this is one occasion where the generally individualistic approach of Taoism is at one with the Confucian emphasis on social etiquette!

Sexuality

As early as the *I Ching*, we have a basic sexual polarity in nature. Heaven is seen as male and earth as female. Clearly, sexuality is bound to play an important role within Taoism. Yin and yang, the very basic dual form of creative energy, represents female and male. Neither can exist without the other. Therefore, logically, one would have thought that the sexual act between heterosexual partners is likely to be of great benefit in helping men and women to realize the Tao – part of the natural flow and balance of life, as promoted by philosophical Taoism. We know that Chuang Tzu, for example, was a married man, and that certainly did not count against him. Clearly, the whole basis of philosophical Taoism, therefore, was such that family life and sexuality could be seen as natural, in contrast with the Buddhist encouragement of monasticism.

When we turn to the later religious Taoism, however, we find that sexual intercourse created problems. In the quest for immortality, it was essential to conserve ch'i energy, and it was feared that, in the sexual act, the woman would drain her partner of his basic Yang (the masculine aspect of the ch'i) which he needed to stay alive. It was thought that the emission of semen during intercourse involved a leaking away of a man's ch'i. On the other hand, sexual stimulation itself was good for producing yang, and thus maintaining ch'i.

Religious Taoism, with its very literal view about the need to preserve ch'i, and the priority given to extending life, therefore had a real problem with sexuality. How could the stimulation of Yang be maintained without the resulting threat to a man's ch'i? Within some Taoist circles, the way of overcoming this problem was by *coitus reservatus*. The man produces Yang essence through becoming sexually aroused, but then he stops short of emission and reabsorbs the semen into his body, avoiding a loss of ch'i. This, it seemed, offered men the best of both worlds!

Within one particular Taoist society, founded in the second century CE and named 'The Five Bushels of Rice Society' after its alleged entry requirement, this was taken one step further with the practice of communal sex. To maximize the possibility of enhancing yet retaining Yang the maximum ch'i, it was argued that a man should have sex as often as possible, whilst retaining his semen. Hence, it became the custom to arrange for situations where men could enjoy frequent penetration of various partners but without emission. This was never widely accepted as part of Taoism, and it was clearly organized for the benefit of men rather than women. Nevertheless, it is interesting to see the logic that brought them to this point. Religious Taoism had become in some of these groups a matter of the preservation and maintenance of the vital essence at all costs. Their quest was for long life, and – ultimately – for immortality.

Nevertheless, setting aside the extremes to which this approach was taken, and the difference between the views of philosophical and religious Taoism in this respect, it is still the case that sexuality was generally regarded as a positive and natural thing.

In other words

Sexual intercourse highlights the fundamental difference between philosophical and religious Taoism:

- For philosophical Taoism sexuality is natural, with a flowing between Yin and Yang;
- For religious Taoism, there is a quest to conserve and hold on to the life essence.

Whether it is the conservation of semen or the conservation of breath, religious Taoism seems to be very far removed from the earlier tradition. Whereas death is natural for philosophical Taoism, in the later religious Taoism it is the enemy, to be staved off by all means, however unnatural they may seem.

Taoism and other philosophies

It is important to recognize the very fluid situation in China with regard to different religious and philosophical systems. We noted at the beginning of this chapter that, prior to the unification of China in the second century BCE, there were a number of different schools of thought. This continued to be the case. With the arrival of Buddhism, the three major philosophies – Taoism, Confucianism and Buddhism – coexisted and cross-fertilized to a considerable degree.

In particular it is important to recognize that Taoism provided a complementary philosophy to Confucianism. Confucianism continued to be largely concerned with people in their social context, with society as a whole and how it should be organized. Taoism is far more concerned with the way in which individuals understand their life with its changes. Social, political and cultural things follow from this, as we have seen, but they are a secondary consequence of Taoism, rather than its main concern.

Although the fundamental arguments are presented quite differently, the Taoist sense of constant flux, and the denial of a fixed personal identity, found parallels in Buddhism. During the last two thousand years, in varying degrees at different times, all three main philosophies have influenced Chinese thought and culture, and they have also, in doing so, influenced one another.

07

Tantra

In this chapter you will learn:
- the background of Hindu and Buddhist Tantra
- the theory behind Tantric sexuality
- the part played by imagination and emotion in Tantra.

Background

Tantra is the term used to describe a movement that developed within both the Hindu and Buddhist traditions, concerned with the use of images and rituals as a means of utilizing the energy generated by the emotions and sexuality in the quest for spiritual liberation and insight.

At one level Tantra may appear to be little more than magic and the crude attempt to manipulate the external world by means of ritual, at another it can be examined in terms of the psychological implications of the images and values exhibited within its practices. Much Tantric literature is concerned, directly or indirectly, with sex – a topic that often invites a superficial or sensationalist approach.

We may explore the implications of Tantric practices and the presuppositions of Tantric writers, but we are unlikely to find any rational exposition in tantric texts of what Tantra is or how it relates to an overall understanding of life. So, when we approach Tantra in a book on Eastern Philosophy, the first question to ask is 'Can Tantra possibly be considered a philosophy?'

Philosophy is sometimes concerned with a limited range of intellectual questions, but equally it may set out to formulate an overall understanding of life and its meaning. In looking at Eastern Philosophy, we have found that the latter task predominates, and it may include those things that lead to an awareness of reality and a way of sustaining that awareness in the face of the general tendency to become immersed in the mundane and the limited. Without doubt, Tantra should be understood as a method of achieving such awareness, a method which – although not intellectual – is based on presuppositions and intuitions that are worth exploring and setting within an overall philosophical framework.

Within the Indian tradition, meditation, wisdom, morality and devotion are considered to be 'ways of release' – ways of achieving the state of freedom, insight and bliss that is called *moksha* or *nirvana*. The problem is that all such ways require a great deal of time and effort. Hence the ascetic tradition, in which a person on a spiritual quest leaves home and family in order to spend a life of simplicity and meditation.

However, Tantra offered a means by which – under the direction of a spiritual guide (a *guru*) – people sought to speed up the process of spiritual development by harnessing emotional and sexual energy and by the use of the imagination alongside the intellect. Tantra is a broad tradition which embraces everything from the gestures used in Tibetan Buddhism, to the esoteric quest to gain spiritual benefit from sexual intercourse and the deliberate breaking of taboos.

Now, whereas the method used may not be considered philosophy, it would seem quite appropriate for philosophy to explore the implications of using emotion and imagination in this way. What is more, the integration of intellect and emotion may have implications for an overall understanding of the self in relation to reality as a whole. It may well serve to set the purely intellectual approach to philosophical problems within a broader human context. For this alone, it deserves a place within a book on Eastern Philosophy.

In other words

Just as you cannot have ethics without people actually making moral choices, so you cannot understand the contribution of emotions and imagination without entering into the process by which people find their perceptions changed as a result of them. Also, if an understanding of life is shaped by imagination or emotions, then that in itself says something important about our understanding of life! Tantric philosophy is never going to be crisp, clean or straightforward, but it is likely to be very rich and very instructive about the human condition.

The origins of Tantra cannot be determined with any precision, but some things that featured in later Tantra (specifically the use of Mantras) were known in India from about the second century CE. Many Tantric texts take the form of dialogues between the Hindu god Shiva and his consort Shakti, although 'Shakti' developed into a more general term for the feminine power within divinity. The potency of Shiva and Shakti had long been represented within Hinduism by the sexual symbols of the lingum and the yoni, and the image of Shiva goes back to the very earliest strand of Hinduism, so there are very ancient elements within what was later to be the sexual imagery of Tantra.

On the other hand, it is quite likely that Tantra developed during the second and third centuries CE within Mahayana Buddhist circles, and that Hindu practice was subsequently influenced by it and linked it to the already established sexual iconography of the worship of Shiva. We also know (see for example the introduction to Buddhist Tantra in A. Skilton, *A Brief History of Buddhism*) that Tantra went through different phases, from the earliest evidence of the use of mantras (sacred chants), through a period when it was studied in Buddhist universities and practised within the monastic community, to a later phase when there were individual, itinerant Tantric teachers, often accompanied by lower caste partners with whom they could perform the Tantric rites.

All we can say with some certainty, however, is that Tantra developed progressively in India within both Buddhist and Hindu religious traditions.

The secret tradition

Tantra has generally been kept secret, and those who try to read Tantric texts will find in them little that makes immediate sense. They appear sometimes to be stage instructions for a play, with cryptic hints at action and with words that have no meaning.

This secrecy is partly because of the potential for mis-understanding the motives of those more extreme practitioners of Tantra who enjoyed (whether literally or imaginatively) sex as part of their practice, but more generally because it was believed that one could only benefit from Tantric practices if they were conducted under the instruction of a guru, and that one should be prepared for them by a process of initiation. There is a recognition that sexuality and the emotions are powerful forces and need to be carefully controlled, and that the means of doing this is by passing the tradition of Tantric ritual down from guru to pupil. Hence, in their written form they can appear quite bizarre and unintelligible and this (even though done for the best of reasons) has only fuelled the sense of esoteric attractiveness that hovers over all Tantric practices.

Note

Since Tantric practices developed within both Hindu and Buddhist traditions, with some uncertainty about which influenced which in the early stages, the basic elements of Tantra are not specific to either tradition. In this chapter we shall first of all look at the basis of ritual and meditation and then at the Hindu background in Shiva and Shakti, before examining Tantric sexuality. Following that, we shall look at the philosophical background to the Buddhist interpretation of Tantra – a tradition which has continued down to the present day within Tibetan Buddhism.

Rituals and meditation

Visualizations

Visualization is the basic method used in Tantra for engaging the emotions. Both Hindu deities and Buddhist images of Buddhas and Bodhisattvas have rich iconography in terms of colours, clothes, hand positions, number of limbs, attendant creatures and so on, and these features can be rationalized and related to particular qualities that the deity represents.

But the analysis of images, as might be set out in a textbook, does little to show their place within the religion or their impact on the overall view of life taken by their devotees. What happens in a visualization is that a person who is familiar with a particular image is able to reconstruct that image imaginatively at will. Images can appear in the mind's eye and then dissolve again, and particular features of the image can be mentally enhanced and appreciated. In doing this, the worshipper may start to 'see' the deity not as an external image, but as a living person with whom he or she can have a relationship.

This is, of course, common to many religious traditions, but what is distinctive about Tantra is that a person may then go on to visualize himself or herself as the deity. In other words, in the process of visualization and meditation a person imaginatively adopts those qualities that are admired in the deity.

In other words

Through visualization, you become what you aspire to be. You explore imaginatively what your emotions would be if you were that Buddha or Bodhisattva or deity. You take a short-cut to enlightenment by imagining what it would be like to be enlightened.

Is this cheating? Is it the deliberate acceptance of illusion as fact? Well, consider the nature of self-understanding generally. It may be partly based on reason and an objective assessment of one's situation, but one's aspirations, values and fears, one's inherited characteristics even, play a large part in the interpretation of reality. A person also changes as he or she engages emotionally in various situations in life. Why then, in principle, should it not be a valid exercise to engage imaginatively with an image that represents one's highest ideals?

Comment

Even if philosophers do not appreciate the importance of imaginative identification with images, those who control media advertising certainly do! If you were this sort of person, what sort of coffee would you be drinking or what sort of car would you be driving? An advertisement invites you to enter imaginatively into a fantasy realm in which certain values are suggested and (if the advert works as intended) this will influence your subsequent choices in terms of buying coffee or cars. In this respect, a visualization is like a successful television advert.

There are four levels of Tantra. The first three are Action Tantra, Performance Tantra and Yoga Tantra. They involve ritual actions and are referred to as the Lower Tantras. The fourth is the *Anuttara* (Highest) *Tantra*, and requires no external action – everything takes place in terms of visualization. At the first level the meditator engages in what amounts to gazing on a beautiful god or goddess. The final level, however, involves the visualization of oneself as the deity, engaged in sexual union with a consort.

And, of course, such meditations were considered only suitable for those who had received formal initiations into the appropriate level. Without that, Tantric visualizations could be considered at best ineffective and at worst, harmful.

Mandalas

A *mandala* is a pattern which integrates various elements to form a single unified whole. So, for example, you can have the Buddhist mandala of the five Buddhas, where each of the Buddha images is set in relation to the others, so that together they form a total view of spiritual reality. A mandala may simply be viewed and visualized, or the value may be in the constructing of it. Even very elaborate mandalas may be temporary, discarded after use as a symbol of the transience of all life.

In terms of emotional engagement, the mandala particularly features a sense of wholeness and integrity. It serves as a spiritual map.

Mudras

Images of buddhas, bodhisattvas or deities generally convey their meaning through the position of the hands (the *mudra*) – meditation, generosity, fearlessness and so on. It is natural, therefore, that in Tantric ritual the worshipper should adopt the same mudras. By making the gesture representing fearlessness and determination, the practitioner generates those emotions.

This is of central importance for the place of Tantra within philosophy as a whole. Whereas most philosophy is an intellectual process of examining questions that arise as a result of our encounter with life – questions about what we can know for certain, or the nature of the self, or what it means to say something is just, or true or beautiful – Tantra seeks to manipulate life itself.

In other words

Tantra is not a process of observation and reflection, but one of engagement. Tantric rituals create what other philosophies only think about. But Tantra sets the things it creates within an overall context of meaning – and that is what enables it to be considered a philosophy.

Shiva and Shakti

In the chapter on Hinduism, we saw that ultimate reality was represented by a triad of gods – Brahma, Vishnu and Shiva. Shiva was there described as the destroyer, but that is only a small part of what he represents.

Long before Tantra developed, there had been an established tradition of energy and balance within Shaivite iconography – seen particularly in the image of Shiva Nataraja. Shiva dances within a circle of flames, treading upon a demon. He expresses a balance of creation and destruction, holding chaos in check.

There are many aspects of Shiva. He is shown as an ascetic, but also as the 'Lord of Animals', ruling in the natural sphere. But alongside this, he is generally represented by the lingum – representing the sexual power of the erect penis, and it is this sexual iconography which relates the older Shaivite tradition to Tantra.

Sexuality and asceticism

Shiva is presented as having a consort, representing female creative energy. This energy is generally referred to as Shakti, which at one level can refer to a goddess and at another to the general sense of feminine power.

But there is a curious polarity within this Shiva/Shakti tradition. On the one hand, they represent the sexual pair, and on the other, Shiva is seen as the ascetic who disengages himself from sexual and other domestic concerns. How can asceticism be related to sexuality?

It is in the elements of balance and control that sexuality is able to be employed as a means of self-discipline. This is seen, for example, in the retention of semen following sexual arousal – a tradition which, from quite another philosophical starting point, was also practised in some Taoist circles (see page 76). Sexuality may therefore be seen as an area of life within which there are powerful forces, the understanding, sublimation and control of which may be of spiritual benefit.

In terms of Tantric philosophy, the essential element taken over from the older Shaivite tradition would seem to be the idea that Shiva is able to utilize the power represented in sexuality in his pursuit of the ascetic path. Sex is not denied, but is utilized, transformed and transcended.

Kundalini

Within the Hindu Tantric tradition, it was believed that the power of the feminine resided in a point at the base of the spine, and that, with appropriate ritual, this 'Kundalini' could become active. Unlocking this power therefore became the whole purpose of Tantric yoga.

Comment

The problem with any philosophy that appears to be based on a feature of human biology is that it may appear dated, with the advances in scientific knowledge. Awakening the feminine power is unlikely to be located at the base of the spine, but might today be phrased in Jungian terms as an integration of the anima. On the other hand, in meditation a practitioner may become aware of various chakras, or circles at different parts of the body. Language about raising the kundalini from the base of the spine is therefore more likely to make sense in terms of a meditator's centres of awareness rather than straight biology.

Philosophically, however, this is of little importance. The key feature, as far as an appreciation of Tantra is concerned, is the need for a balance between male and female energies – a balance that finds parallels with the ancient Chinese Yin/Yang tradition.

The union of matter and spirit

Notice one important metaphysical assumption in this approach – the union of matter and spirit. Spirtuality comes to be explored within the physical world, not by escaping from it. Compare this with Sankhya philosophy (see page 17), where we have a metaphysics which presents the world as a union of *prakriti* (matter – feminine) and *purusha* (souls – masculine). But, for Sankhya, the aim is for a release in which the soul extricates itself from matter. Thus, within that tradition, you have a dualism in which the spirit is effectively trapped within the material and seeking to escape from it.

The implications of Tantric ritual are quite different. On the one hand, physical actions are thought to bring about spiritual change; on the other, spiritual intentions are thought to have a literal and therefore physical effect on the material world.

In other words, Tantra integrates spirit and matter – they are part of an interconnected whole. Hence one could describe the basic metaphysics of Tantra as *monistic*, rather than dualistic.

Comment

Tantra could also be contrasted with the dualism of Jain philosophy (see page 82).

If Tantric rituals are to work, they require a single reality, encompassing both what we would normally think of as the separate realms of the material world and the personal, spiritual or human world of people's aspirations and desires. Tantric ritual therefore implies a complete, single, interconnected world, where physical, mental and emotional reality reflect and influence one another.

Tantric sex

The Tantric texts, as we have them today, are very difficult to interpret – and deliberately so, since what they contain is meant to be reserved for the initiated and interpreted by a guru. Some of them describe sexual acts of different kinds, and do so in ways that leave the reader in little doubt about what is happening. On the other hand, some writers suggest that the actions described should be interpreted symbolically, and would not generally have been acted out physically. Others point to the texts as giving a script for visualization – so that the Tantric practitioner enters into what amounts to a guided fantasy.

The texts may be interpreted in ways that are valid and appropriate for the spiritual traditions of both Hinduism and Buddhism. The act of copulation (*maituna*) is indeed symbolic – representing (depending on your tradition) either the integrative power of matter and spirit or of wisdom and compassion. It is clearly the case that these actions and images have been used as the basis of meditation and visualization. The issue remains, however, as to whether, and how widely, the sexual rites described took place literally.

What seems clear is that there were levels of Tantra in which sexual intercourse took place as part of the rituals, and probably involved lower caste women who were effectively working as prostitutes. There is also the tradition within Tantra of married gurus who are able to act out the Tantric rites with their wives.

Western

The physical and literal nature of much of what is described seems obvious – techniques for maintaining an erection whilst avoiding ejaculation are hardly necessary in an entirely symbolic context! But that need not detract from the philosophical significance of what is taking place. Participating in the sexual act, in a narrowly Western context, is neither part of religion nor philosophy. But within Tantra, such participation has profound significance. It is not that sex is irrelevant to or trivializes philosophy and religion (as might be imagined from a Western perspective), but that a narrow appreciation of the scope of philosophy and religion trivializes the awareness that comes through sexuality!

Comment

If it is thought beneficial to calm one's mind through giving attention to one's breathing, or gently observing the arising of emotions or thoughts, why should it not also be beneficial to enhance the awareness of the balance of male and female energies in life through an appreciation of physical sexuality?

Tantra is a form of yoga – but it is a form part of which can be practised with a partner rather than individually. Although, as we have seen, part of the idea of Tantra is to break down conventional thinking and taboos, there are also guidelines for how it should be practised, no doubt set down in an attempt to regulate the potential misunderstandings and excesses of the practice. The *Mahanirvana Tantra*, for example, specifies the sexual practices should only be performed with one's own spouse.

What you have here is an identification of the cosmic process with those forces that shape the individual. The expression of the awareness of oneself and one's partner in the sexual act parallels out the balance of creativity and asceticism and of wisdom and compassion – and this, in turn, is seen as reflecting a balance throughout nature – as, for example, in the image of Shiva Nataraja dancing creation and destruction, and holding chaos in check by doing so.

Western

In Western philosophy, Ethics considers the criteria by which individual actions are to be justified, and one of the ways in which this might be done is using a Natural Law argument, where an action is considered right if it is in keeping with the rationally ascertained end or purpose, established by God, within the context of the overall purpose of the world. In other words, individual actions are regarded as either expressing and being in line with an overall cosmic purpose, or as going against such a purpose. The task is to align individual action with an overall cosmic aim.

Now consider what is happening within sexual Tantra. The sexual act is seen as participating in and representing forces that are universal. Whether it is Shiva and Shakti, or the Buddhist concepts of compassion and wisdom, it is placing a profound human action at the centre of a cosmology – such that control and awareness within the act leads to universal awareness. Whereas in Western Natural Law arguments, the purpose and therefore only justification of the sexual act is the potential it has for the conception of children, in Tantra, the sexual act mirrors the universal, and is therefore valued quite apart from the possibility of conception.

Buddhist Tantra

In terms of its basic philosophy, Tantra took over the key features of the Mahayana Buddhism within which it developed. In the Madhyamaka tradition we saw that there was the initially surprising claim that the ever-changing world of samsara was also nirvana (in other words, there is only one world, and it can appear simultaneously as samsara and nirvana); there was also the important idea that there is a Buddha nature within every creature (the Tathagatagarbha doctrine). Together, these ideas enabled Buddhist practitioners to see present physical reality as a stage on which the aspiration to enlightenment could be acted out.

In other words

If you already have a Buddha nature, and if this world of samsara can also be experienced as nirvana, then it follows that you can use physical actions as a means of expressing and realizing the enlightened state.

The Tantric tradition in Buddhism is generally known as the Vajrayana. Vajra is a word that has two meanings, it can stand for a diamond, or for a thunderbolt. Both are appropriate, since the Vajrayana tradition seems to engage directly and immediately in experience, rather than use logical argument or discursive thought. It is therefore seen as powerful and threatening, hard and precious.

The term **vajra** is also used for an object used in Tantric ritual. Vajras are generally small enough to be held in the hand. They comprise a central sphere, out of which, at each of the opposite poles there come five shoots – like the petals of a lotus – curving outwards and then coming together again in a point. Each part of the vajra is symbolic. The sphere is a symbol of purity, and thus of the enlightened self. At the one pole, the lotus petals represent the five poisons (infatuation, aversion, conceit, passion and envy), and at the other, five perfections represented by five buddhas. Taken as a whole, therefore, the vajra is thus a symbol of transformation – the poisons that can impede one's progress being transformed into the very perfections one seeks. But its shape also reflects the unified view of Tantric Buddhism, namely that both the poisons and the perfections spring from the same central reality.

a vajra and a bell with a vajra handle

A basic assumption in Buddhist Tantra – and indeed throughout Buddhism in all its forms – is that there are not two separate worlds, one being an objective world 'out there' and another private secret world of the inner self. Ultimately, for Buddhism, there is no self; the idea of a 'self' is simply a conventional term and not one that can stand careful analysis.

In other words

The most fundamental philosophical assumption of Tantra is that the forces at work throughout the universe are also those found within the human heart – there is one world, not two.

Another important feature of Mahayana philosophy for an understanding of Tantra is the claim, made in Yogacara philosophy (see page 109) that all reality is mental – what we know of the world, we know only in the form of experiences gained and assimilated through our own mind. Our perception of the world is therefore a mental phenomenon. The implication of this is that as we change, so our perception, and therefore the reality of the world as we know it, also changes.

This led, within Tantra, to a two-way relationship between what (in the West) we would call the inner and outer realities of the mind and the physical world. On the one hand, Tantra saw what happened mentally as having a profound effect on the external world. On the other, external actions and rituals could be a means of transforming one's mental state.

Comment

It is this two-way relationship that links Tantra with magic. Magic is the attempt to change external reality through mental activity – for example, by means of a particular chant, prayer or invocation of a deity. Religion is sometimes dismissed as magic when it claims to effect change in this way.

On the other hand, if ritual, prayers, chants and invocations are simply means of spiritual self-development – effective because enabling the self to be better aligned to fundamental realities – then no magic is involved.

But this reflects a very Western view of the self and the world – mind and matter – as separate things. Buddhism, in particular, rejects this – everything is anatta, it lacks separate inherent existence, it interconnects.

The crucial philosophical question for Tantra is therefore this:

Is an experienced change the same thing as an actual change?

In other words: through various practices, one may experience the world differently. But does that actually make the world different? To put the question crudely from a Western perspective – On a sunny day, one may become accustomed to the more comfortable view through sunglasses, but has the sun thereby been dimmed?

Wisdom and compassion

The Buddhist interpretation of what is represented by the sexual pair is very different from the Hindu. For Hinduism they were two fundamental forces within nature. For Buddhism, the male represents compassion (and also 'skilful means') and the female represents wisdom, the union of the two producing the ultimate goal of enlightenment.

Within Buddhist iconography, this union is represented by what are generally known as the *Yab-Yum* (literally 'Father-Mother') images, in which male and female are locked in sexual embrace facing one another, the male in the traditional posture of meditation with the female sitting in his lap with her legs locked round his body. The image often represents one of the archetypal Buddhas, for example Buddha Akshobya with his consort Lochana, representing aspects of clear-sighted wisdom.

Note on Akshobya

Akshobya is one of the archetypal Buddhas represented in 'The Mandala of the Five Buddhas'. His particular wisdom is 'mirror-like', seeing reality just as it is. The philosophical implication is that conventional wisdom sees only distortions, brought about by a false idea of the self, but the removal of those distortions leads to the natural, primordial state of wisdom. In what is known as 'The Great Seal Tradition', the pure mind is thought of as an undistorted mirror, reflecting exactly what is before it – which is exactly the role played by Akshobya in Buddhist iconography.

Within the overall Buddhist philosophy the implication here is that insight and wisdom (represented by the female partner in the image) only leads to the spiritual goal when it is in union with appropriate action or skilful means (represented by the male). Within the Buddhist tradition, sexuality can be a cause of craving (*tanha*), which is the root of suffering. Therefore, the challenge for Buddhist Tantra is to engage in sexuality without allowing this to be motivated by craving. It is sex without craving that is considered to lead to insight – again, in a union of wisdom and action.

Comment

Pornography turns sex into an object to be possessed or consumed. Pornography therefore encourages separateness – sex is no longer 'within here' to be enjoyed, but 'out there' to be sought. Notice how this is the very opposite of Tantric sex, for Tantric sex is the breaking down of conventional separateness. Unless the false ego is broken down, one remains a spectator as far as life is concerned; and (viewed in this way) sex remains pornography – to be craved and consumed. Without the sense of the separate ego, sexuality is simply a natural part of one's engagement in life, an immediate experience of universal interrelatedness.

Buddhist Tantra also sought to channel destructive urges into the destruction of all the hindrances to enlightenment. Hence, images of violent, threatening buddhas and bodhisattvas express the forcefulness with which a person is to break through all that limits his or her progress. In this spiritualization of the sexual and violent urges, Tantric Buddhism saw the potential of sexual power to enable the mind to develop the *bodhicitta* (the mind/heart determined to seek enlightenment), rather than simply to enable the physical body to produce semen. The moment of sexual climax becomes the moment of the *mahasukha* – the great bliss.

As was noted at the beginning of this chapter, the development of Tantra within Buddhism is complex and went through a number of phases, from the appearance of written records of mantric chanting from about the second century CE through to the appearance of independent non-monastic Tantric gurus who travelled about giving Tantric initiations. But this final stage was not reached until probably the ninth century. It is not possible, therefore, to give a straightforward account of Tantric philosophy, because at each stage it simply built on existing philosophical ideas, integrating them into the understanding of its rituals.

The Tantric tradition and philosophy is found mainly in Tibetan Buddhism, and also in Japanese Shingon Buddhism, although it should be noted that the Japanese form never accepted the sexual rites of the later (yogottara) Tantra, and anyone seeking the more extreme Tantric practices within modern Tibetan Buddhism are likely to be disappointed.

Note on Tibetan Buddhism

Buddhism had spread into China by the first century CE and into Japan by the fifth. These countries therefore received and developed a broadly Mahayana form of Buddhist philosophy. But, although there had been earlier Buddhist influence from both India and China, Buddhism really only made headway in Tibet from the eighth and ninth centuries, and by that time Tantra was well developed within India. So, for example, Padmasambhava, who arrived in Tibet in 747 CE and is seen as establishing Tibetan Buddhism, was already well known as a Tantric adept in India. Then, following a period of the suppression of Buddhism in Tibet (from the time of the ending of the Tibetan monarchy in 838 CE) it was introduced again in the eleventh and twelfth centuries. Hence, Tibetan Buddhism developed from the whole range of Indian Buddhist traditions and preserved them after Buddhism had died out in India. Tibetan Buddhism should not simply be identified with Tantra, but it is the one major branch of Buddhism which displays Tantric as well as earlier philosophies.

An important feature of Tibetan Buddhist literature is the *lam rim* tradition, which sees a cumulative progression from the earlier traditions to the later Tantric ones. In other words, Tibetan Buddhism is early Buddhism, plus the Mahayana developments, plus the Tantric elements.

Some philosophical implications of Tantric sexual integration

Within Buddhism, the aim of most spiritual practice is to break down the false notion of a separate self, and therefore to be able to overcome the craving associated with seeing the world 'out there' as a separate entity to be grasped and used. This is reflected in an awareness of a fundamental unity between inner and outer, between what is experienced personally and that which is universal – all things lack inherent existence, all arise in dependence upon conditions.

The integration of the sexual imagery into that overall view of reality is therefore part of that process of breaking down the sense of self. Whereas the conventional 'self' is likely to be possessive and craving in terms of sexuality, the enlightened self finds in the sexual act a natural blending of wisdom (which, for the Mahayana, is practically identified with the sense of shunyata, 'emptiness') and compassion – a dispassionate affirmation of the other person.

In other words

In the sexual act, wisdom and compassion come together. Wisdom recognizes the falseness of seeing separate selves, compassion is the emotionally positive response to that wisdom, going out to others because all are recognized as part of a common arising. Good, non-manipulative sex therefore reflects the very heart of Buddhist awareness. The moment of orgasm being also a moment of letting go, of becoming at one with one's partner.

But, as we have already seen, integration is represented in other aspects of Tantric iconography as well. Thus the image of the vajra – with both poisons and perfections springing out from opposite sides of the central sphere – represents the power to transform even those things that would generally be considered poisonous.

Tantra touches on a fundamental issue for all philosophy. Intellectual debate depends upon concepts, and concepts depend on seeing objects as discrete entities to be related to one another. Buddhist philosophy describes this process as being merely conventional and argues that, at a deeper level, all things interpenetrate, and that none possesses separate or inherent existence.

The actual and immediate awareness of the Buddhist description of reality is enlightenment, and in the earlier Buddhist traditions this was seen as the final goal at the end of a long process of spiritual development. The Tantra short-circuits this process by entering imaginatively into the situation of being a Buddha.

The moment of sexual release, described in Tantric texts as the moment of 'great bliss', coming about (in the cryptic language used in the texts) through the union of the *vajra* (penis) and the *lotus* (vagina), strives – whether literally (if the act is to be performed) or mentally (if this is used in meditation) – to enter imaginatively into a situation of union, and use that as a basis for a universal awareness.

Western

In the West, it is rather assumed that one's behaviour should follow from one's beliefs and should be justified subsequently in terms of them. Emotion and action follow thought. The problem with this is that, in everyday experience, thought is often led by emotion and action, rather than the other way round!

In the East – and in particular in Tantra – emotions and actions enable reality to be engaged and understood at a level that is deeper than that of conceptual thought. Concepts follow along afterwards and (from a Buddhist point of view) are merely conventional. It is not that you are able to give a rational justification of sexuality; rather, sexuality provides an immediate experience of that to which your concepts are subsequently attempting to point.

At what point can one actually experience the interpenetration of things? Where is there an appropriate expression for a sense of loss of self at the very point at which the self acts? Where is there a sense of a distinctive other, but not one that is separate from oneself? The sexual act would seem to be exactly suitable as a vehicle for exploring this view of reality.

Sexual integration, in the sense of taking part in the sexual act with full awareness of the partner as somehow distinct from the self and yet as not separate, and the awareness of the deep biological urges that make sexuality so powerful, is surely a most instructive expression of shunyata (emptiness). In the West the moment of orgasm has been described as 'the little death', but it is also the potential starting point of life.

Comment

It seems amazing that one could even attempt to put together an overall view of reality which did not take into account this moment of most immediate engagement with life. Sexual energy is such a powerful feature of life and it seems unrealistic to assume that one can simply sublimate it in order to strive for an intellectual grasp of things that leaves it out of account. Surely, it is more important that an intellectual grasp of things needs to be informed by and interpreted by such fundamental human phenomena as the experience of sexual union.

Western

Perhaps the nearest Western philosophy gets to Tantra is in the area of Aesthetics, where it explores what it is that can be considered beautiful, since that process is dependent upon the natural attractiveness of certain things that leads them to be called 'beautiful' in the first place, or the power of an image that leads it to be considered as a work of art. Philosophy thus stands back from and comments upon a process that most obviously is not based on reason alone, but on reason as interpreting emotional and intuitive resonance.

One Mind

Tantric Buddhism sees sense experience as essentially an illusion and reality as One Mind – and in this it follows Yogacara philosophy. But in probing the idea of One Mind, we find that it reveals another way into fundamental Buddhist philosophy:

- One Mind is a predicateless unity. In other words, the experience of 'One Mind' is an awareness of reality that goes beyond all distinctions, beyond the separation of one thing from another, and therefore beyond the conventional perception of time and space.
- One Mind is therefore timeless, changeless, eternal. One Mind represents total reality, before it is subsequently divided up by our conventional experience of it. It also gets beyond the self/non-self division.
- Entering into the experience of One Mind is therefore self-liberation, since it takes a person beyond those things in the world of samsara that cause suffering.

In Tantric visualization, a person enters into a relationship with the visualized image of his or her personal deity (a *yidam*), and this might give rise to the impression that there is a separation between the deity and oneself. But the Tantric tradition insists that one should not become over-enthusiastic about the visions of the yidam, since they are only manifestations of one's own mind.

Thus, even in those aspects of Tantric Buddhism in which it resembles a conventional religion with worship of gods and goddesses, there is the reminder that this is simply a process of mental cultivation. But this should not be emphasized as being 'only' in the mind – since that would be to make the self/non-self division that Buddhism as a whole wants to get beyond. There is a single reality, and one's mind is part of it.

Comment
Notice that, however elaborate Tantric ritual and language may become, it can still be related back to the fundamental Buddhist perspective.

Milarepa (1052–1135)

Milarepa – the second part of whose name means 'cotton clad', a title given to Mila because he is said to have practised a form of heat yoga that enabled him to wear only light clothing even in conditions of extreme cold – was an ascetic, a philosopher and also a poet. He brought together both Madhyamaka and Yogacara philosophies into his practice and outlook, insisting on both shunyata (the emptiness) of individual things and also the absolute nature of mind. In what is called the Mahamudra Yoga, he sets out four stages:

1 Establishing inner focus and quietness.
2 Moving beyond conceptual thought to direct experience of reality.
3 A singleness of purpose as the infinite is experienced in and through everything.
4 The ending of practice, as meditator and meditation become one and the same, and one goes beyond even the idea of spiritual practice.

After enlightenment, all separate objects are seen as shadow plays, devoid of inherent existence, but at the same time they become 'helpful friends' in that they can assist one to make progress. It is described as a point in which there is no fear of death or of anything in life.

Western
Notice the parallels here with Plato and the simile of the cave in *The Republic*. Like Milarepa, the person who is freed from the restraints that previously kept him bound in the cave emerges into the daylight and realizes that all he had previously known was no more than a sequence of shadows cast upon the wall of the cave. Seeing the infinite in and through the finite is also a key theme in Schleiermacher's view of religion.

Conclusion

Inevitably, perhaps, this chapter has focused on the sexual elements within Tantra, partly because it is so different from any Western philosophy, and also because it highlights issues that are there for all human action and emotion *vis-à-vis* an overall view of reality.

Nevertheless, if there is one single thing to grasp in terms of the importance of Tantra for philosophy it is this: that without Tantra it is possible to have an idea of the self that is for ever a spectator – looking out at and trying to analyze an external world. That same spectator tries then to look inwards and objectify its own emotions, making them, too, part of an external world. And in the midst of all that, the self becomes lost, it vanishes. It appears to have no reality, because the elusive 'I' cannot become simultaneously an observer and part of the observed world.

Tantra will have nothing of all this. For Tantra, the self and the world, emotions and experience, are part of one and the same process, and between the two aspects of that process there is a constant interaction.

Shunyata, the fundamental Mahayana concept, is here experienced directly. There are no boundaries between one thing and another, or between the human heart and the external world – all interpenetrate, and all therefore influence one another. Sexual or destructive urges, which from the perspective of the limited, false self can lead to suffering, can, from the perspective of the shunyata doctrine, become a vehicle for the harmonious balance of the inner and outer parts of reality.

Perhaps the last word here should be from Lama Anagarika Govinda, a great twentieth-century practitioner and writer on Vajrayana Buddhism. Here he points to the effect of a changed vision that comes through meditation:

> By seeing the world from the perspective of our limited little ego and our ephemeral aims and desires, we not only distort it; we make it a prison that separates us from our fellow beings and from the very sources of life. But the moment we become truly selfless, by emptying ourselves of all ego-tendencies, of our power hunger and all possessiveness and craving, we break down the walls of our self-created prison and become conscious of the immensity and boundlessness of our true being.

Creative Meditation and Multi-Dimensional Consciousness,
1976, p. 104

This, of course, is religious vision rather than philosophy. But look at the implication of that vision. Govinda is arguing in effect that it is only once one's narrow self view is surrendered to something wider in the practice of meditation, that one can understand the true nature of the self. In other words, experience rather than rationality is the starting point of the journey of self-discovery.

Comment

This, then, is the justification of examining Tantra within a book on philosophy. Tantra raises the fundamental question about the adequacy of rationality alone for understanding either oneself or the world. It recognizes that human beings are psycho-physical entities, for whom sexuality and aggression are important features to be taken into account, as well as energies to be harnessed.

08

Zen

In this chapter you will learn:
- the origins and development of Zen
- some key features of Zen Buddhism
- twentieth-century attempts to relate Zen to Western thought.

Introduction

All Buddhist traditions use meditation as a tool for spiritual development, and in this Buddhism simply adopted what had previously been practised within the Hindu religious milieu. The Chinese term for meditation is *Ch'an*, and the Japanese form of this is *Zen*. Zen simply means 'meditation'.

As we shall see, however, Zen goes beyond other traditions in that it rejects the possibility of using concepts to describe what is perceived in a moment of insight. Zen is the quest to break down our tendency to conceptualize and to deal with reality directly.

It might be tempting therefore to ask what Zen is doing in a book on Eastern Philosophy, since philosophy is primarily about the use of concepts. There are three reasons why it should be included:

- It explores the parameters of logical thought. By showing what concepts cannot do, it points to their proper use
- It is a reminder that 'wisdom' – the true object of philosophy – is not simply conceptual, and in doing this it reinforces the breadth of understanding of wisdom in the East, in contrast to the more narrowly defined function of philosophy in a western academic context
- It has influenced a number of thinkers who have consciously attempted to develop Eastern Philosophy in ways that relate it to Western thought.

Origins and development

Kasyapa's smile

Although the practice of Zen might be geographically and historically far removed from the teachings of Siddhartha Gautama, it claims to trace its origins to an incident that occurred while the Buddha was teaching. Instead of attempting to explain the Dharma in words, the Buddha was said simply to have held up a flower, turning it in his hand. Kasyapa, one of the disciples present on that occasion, saw the flower and smiled. That smile, devoid of all concepts or explanation, is claimed as the origin of Zen – a direct perception of the nature of reality.

Zen therefore claims to be a tradition of teaching going back to the Buddha himself, but one that was handed on verbally, by way of a tradition of training passed on from teacher to disciple, and not committed to writing. Indeed, Zen does not require acceptance of any written tradition – only the following of a pattern of spiritual teaching.

Bodhidharma

By tradition, Ch'an (Zen) was brought to China in 520 CE by Bodhidharma, to whom is attributed what amounts to a definition of Zen as a 'direct transmission of awakened consciousness, outside tradition and outside scripture'. He was the first of a line of Ch'an teachers – referred to as the patriarchs. He is portrayed as a fierce character with staring eyes and a number of legendary stories have gathered around him, including one that he sat in meditation facing a wall until his legs dropped off, and another that he cut off his eyelids to stop himself from dozing! What is clear, however, is that he did not initiate a totally new form of Buddhism, but rather developed aspects of meditation from Indian Mahayana Buddhism.

On the other hand, it was characteristic of Bodhidharma and later Ch'an and Zen, to present the Dharma in a slightly shocking way, breaking down conventional assumptions. Thus, when asked to give a summary of Buddhism, Bodhidharma is said to have replied 'Vast emptiness, nothing holy'.

Hui-Neng (638–713 CE)

Hui-Neng was the Sixth Patriarch in succession to Bodhidharma. A key feature of his philosophy was a rejection of all rituals as a means to salvation, or enlightenment. He also emphasized the possibility of sudden enlightenment. This was a departure from the earlier tradition, following the Indian approach, where enlightenment was thought to come gradually as a result of long training.

He presented important features of what developed as the Zen tradition – that nothing exists permanently, separately or independently (we saw this as a fundamental feature of all Buddhist traditions), but he took this a step further by claiming, as an implication of this, that nothing could be conceptualized correctly.

Comment

This is the logical conclusion of a loss of separate existence, since concepts discriminate between one thing and another. Once you start using concepts you divide your world up into separate entities. This, according to Hui-Neng, went against the fundamental idea of shunyata.

He believed that people were habitually attached to the notion of separate objects, and this obscured their light, like clouds obscuring the sun or the moon. What he sought to do was to get beneath the superficiality of concepts to a self-nature that was also pure Buddha-nature.

But what could be known in such a state? What can be conveyed if concepts cannot be used? Hui-Neng's answer is that one knows that there is nothing to be known. There is a sudden lightness and clarity; everything is empty.

Key features of Zen

When compared with other Buddhist philosophies, Zen has three important features which, as was said above, were originally attributed to Bodhidharma:

- it depends on verbal transmission: it passes directly from mind to mind
- it does not rely on scriptures
- it offers a method of dealing directly with each person's experience.

And to this we have now added the central features of Hui-Neng's teaching – namely, that it goes beyond all concepts, and that it is discovery of the Buddha Mind. Before looking at the two main branches of Zen and the techniques used, we need to clarify these two points.

Intuitive prajna

To appreciate Zen, one needs to remember two features of Buddhism in general:

1 That suffering results from grasping – and that it is possible to grasp and cling to ideas and concepts as well as to particular things. To attempt to systematize, categorize and conceptualize the world is to grasp at it, and that is to miss the point of the fundamental Buddhist intuition.

2 That everything is impermanent and is 'empty' of inherent existence (the idea of shunyata).

Once you start to think of yourself as separate from other things, once you start to rationalize and set out your world in terms of individual things, differentiating between them, then your thinking is conventional and not absolute. For in absolute terms, everything is shunyata.

Enlightenment comes with getting beyond the clutter of conventional thinking and having a direct perception of reality. But how is that to be done? Certainly not by forming concepts and arguments about the nature of existence, for such arguments only drag you further into the quagmire of conceptual thought and conventional differentiation and analysis.

How then can you think the unthinkable? Zen cannot tell you how to do that, but it can offer a set of practices that can shock the mind out of its conventional patterns, in the hope that *satori* (a term used for a moment of insight) will occur.

Western

The nearest parallel in Western thought to this deliberate setting aside of all conceptual thought and simply being aware of the whole universe just as it is, can be found in religious mysticism rather than philosophy.

In exploring any parallels with Western mysticism, however, it should be remembered that, like all Buddhist philosophies, Zen does not use the concept of God. Thus the experience that a Western mystic would describe in terms of union with God, a Zen practitioner might want to describe as the discovery of his or her own Buddha nature.

What you have in Zen, therefore, is a form of intuitive wisdom. It can be communicated without words (a tradition that goes back to Kasyapa's smile), it leads to spontaneous behaviour and a sense of immediacy, and it shows little respect for tradition.

Comment

One can explore parallels between Zen Buddhism and Taoism – and that is hardly surprising, since Ch'an Buddhism and Taoism developed side by side in China for so long. On the other hand, it does not imply that Buddhism developed in this direction simply because of its contact with Taoism since, as we have seen, aspects of Zen can be traced back to earlier Buddhist traditions.

One Mind

In the Zen tradition (as in all Buddhism) the main obstacle to enlightenment is the way in which our superficial ego relates to life – both in grasping and in its thinking. This is, as we have seen, the result of the false notion of the self as a separate, self-existing entity. But Zen sees this small, surface mind as something that we acquire after birth. It is conventional, based on what we learn from others, influenced by our feelings and needs. In contrast to this, it sees the Buddha mind as innate. We do not acquire a Buddha mind, it is ours already. We do not have to create it, only become aware of it.

Once the superficiality of the ego is realized, then the Buddha mind can act naturally, seeing everything immediately and intuitively, just as it is.

In other words

Our Buddha mind is natural and intuitive. The problem is that most of the time we smother it with our narrowly egocentric conceptual thinking. We are not content just to experience something, but must immediately start to conceptualize it, to love or hate it, to ask how it relates to us, to give it a particular value in our scheme of things. In this way, reality is lost in our clutter of thoughts and feelings.

How then do we get beyond our small mind and start to use the Buddha mind? How, in other words, do we get to that state of awareness that Buddhism generally refers to as enlightenment?

In the Zen tradition, enlightenment varies in the way it is described, as do the techniques used for achieving it, between the two main branches of Zen – Rinzai and Soto. Rinzai emphasizes the use of koans, mental challenges to conventional thinking (see page 209), and looks for sudden moments of insight (called satori), whereas Soto Zen concentrates on the more gradual process of *zazen*, or sitting meditation, leading to a general enlightened state.

The language used relates the small mind (one's own) to the universal, or Buddha, mind. In some ways this comes close to the earlier Yogacara traditions of all reality being mental. The state of enlightenment is one of transcending the self to the point at which one's own small mind is seen as at one with (and, indeed, *is*) the universal mind.

In enlightenment, the self and Buddha are no longer seen as two separate things. The Buddha nature is within everything, therefore seeing your own nature is also to realize Buddhahood.

Dogen (see page 212) said that what Buddhas call the self is the entire universe. In other words, the true self is not the surface ego; the true self is the 'original face' that a person has before he or she is born.

Comment

The 'original face' concept is central to this whole approach. Once we get a 'face' we become an individual, distinguishable from others. We think of ourselves as separate from the world out there, and from that comes the whole problem of facing our own fragility and the suffering and grasping that comes from it – the starting point of the whole of Buddhist philosophy.

Our 'original face' before we were born relates the idea we have of ourselves to the whole undifferentiated world out of which – through the process of change – we have emerged. The original face therefore represents the loss of ego, the universal perspective and the Buddha nature. Our original face cannot be described in concepts; cannot be distinguished. If we strain after it, we fail to grasp it. We are thrown back on recognizing the superficial and temporary nature of what we conventionally see as ourselves.

Rinzai Zen

Before its arrival in Japan, Chinese Ch'an had already divided into different traditions, two of which were Lin chi (which became Japanese Rinzai Zen) and Ts'ong tung (which became Japanese Soto Zen). Lin chi is named after a teacher who died in the ninth century, best known for his provocative saying: 'If you see the Buddha on the road, kill him.'

This, as we shall see later, is absolutely typical of the approach of Rinzai Zen, which aims to shock a person out of conventional thinking to a sudden realization of a deeper truth.

In this case, of course, the idea is that one should not identify the Buddha with any particular thing, or teacher, or idea, or scripture that one might encounter on life's journey. Any such identification destroys the idea of directly seeing reality as it is, limiting one's view. Therefore, all such Buddhas must be killed, in order to get beyond them.

Eisai (1141–1215)

Eisai, who is regarded as the founder of this form of Zen, first studied Tendai Buddhism, a form that involves a wide variety of Buddhist practices, and he used meditation (Ch'an) as it had been developed in China as part of his overall Tendai approach. However, it was this particular practice that came to be dominant and so Rinzai Zen became a separate tradition. This form of Zen, established with the first setting up of a temple in Japan in 1184, quickly established itself with the ruling Samurai.

Hakuin (1685–1769)

Hakuin revived Rinzai Zen after a period during which it had gradually become more of a cultural and artistic phenomenon than a philosophical and religious one. He seems to have been a ferocious and determined man, and yet one who was sensitive and artistic, producing calligraphy and a large number of paintings.

The starting point of Hakuin's philosophy is basic Zen: the world of ordinary experience is delusion; reality itself is a divisionless unity; no concepts can apply to this ultimate truth; the self/non-self division is ultimately unreal and is the cause of suffering.

He also insisted that we could all experience reality itself, simply because we are part of that reality. Our Buddha nature is our real nature; it is our original face, hidden beneath the clutter of conceptual thought and conventional ways of seeing.

The goal of Zen is 'no-mind'. This does *not* mean extinction, but rather achieving a level of awareness that goes beyond the ego-centred mind. We are all potential Buddhas, for we are all potentially able to see reality as it is. Hakuin uses the image of water turning into ice to illustrate this:

All beings are primarily Buddhas.
Like water and ice
There is no ice apart from water;
There are no Buddhas apart from beings.
(from the opening of *Zazen Wasan*, 'The Song of Zazen')

Like all Buddhists, he practised meditation, and extended it into all of life, suggesting that the whole universe should become one's meditation cave. He saw enlightenment as a state of absolute peace, absolute fearlessness and absolute joy.

But Hakuin is probably best known for promoting the use of koans to challenge conventional thinking and enable moments of satori (insight), which are a distinctive feature of the Rinzai approach.

Koans

A *koan* is the recorded question or saying, attributed to one of the Zen masters, which is designed to shatter one's conventional thinking, and indeed to show the inability of achieving any answer by conceptual thought. Insight is produced once the mind lets go of the attempt to make sense of the koan.

As well as gathering together existing koans, Hakuin created his own. His most famous is generally abbreviated to the single question:

'What is the sound of one hand clapping?'

Hakuin argued that, as you investigate your koan, you find that your ego-based thoughts are overcome. There may come a point at which you face a 'vast abyss' in which you feel suddenly free, and in which you let go of both your body and your mind. This is described as a moment of seeing into one's own mind.

So the more you think about the idea of clapping, the more you find the concept of a single hand clapping to be meaningless. There is no solution to the dilemma of what the single hand clapping can be.

The effect of a koan can be quite startling. Hakuin describes hearing another famous koan attributed to Joshu (778–897 CE):

A monk asked Joshu, a Chinese Zen master:
'Has a dog a Buddha-nature or not?'
Joshu answered 'Wu'.

(The 'Wu' (or 'Mu') here does not simply mean 'No' – Joshu was not saying that a dog does not have a Buddha-nature, rather he was barking back a 'nothing' indicating that the question itself is flawed. And, of course 'Wu!' is very much what a dog would say, if asked!)

Hakuin says that the effect this had on him was like being frozen in a sheet of ice extending thousands of miles in each direction, so that he was quite unable to move. He was quite out of his mind, just hearing the single word 'Wu'. Then suddenly he was brought out of this state by the sound of a temple bell, and achieved satori.

In a sense, once the koan has done its job, it can be set aside. The result is a sudden new insight into all reality, the koan is a valueless vehicle for bringing it about.

Comment

Koans can easily be taken superficially and misunderstood. Someone might feel that they have found a logical answer, for example – in which case the koan has failed to produce the right result. For this reason, koans are generally studied only under the guidance of a trained and experienced Zen teacher.

Alongside koans, Zen Buddhists explore their traditions through the recounted stories of the Zen masters, which often take the form of question and answer sessions between master and student. Such stories are generally termed *mondo*. As with the koan, the mondo is not to be treated as a scripture, but simply as the recording of a particular example of the teaching of a master, which one can appropriate by reading and reflecting. But again, as throughout Zen, it is considered best to do everything under the guidance of a *roshi*, or Zen master.

Satori

We have already used the term satori several times; it is the word used in Rinzai Zen for a moment of enlightenment. This is not seen as a once-for-all event, but a glimpse of reality that may be fleeting and may be repeated. It is described only in the most oblique way – as a sense of unity, of peace and of being beyond time and space, of suddenly knowing the truth.

Comment

If you can describe satori, it is not satori that you have described.

The only distinctive thing to be aware of with satori is that it is described as a flash of insight that can happen unexpectedly as a result of Zen practice. This contrasts with the more general term 'enlightenment', which is used in other forms of Buddhism for the general and ongoing state of awareness of reality as it is.

D.T. Suzuki (1870–1966)

Suzuki was particularly known for his *Essays in Zen Buddhism*, of which the first edition appeared in 1927. He followed the teaching of Hakuin, in insisting that all conceptual frameworks of space, time and identity are false, and are imposed on undifferentiated reality by the mind. Reality itself, he insisted, is non-dual. Apprehension of that reality is satori – and satori cannot be communicated, only experienced. In that book he sets out eight properties of satori:

1 irrationality – it cannot be achieved by reasoning, nor can it be described rationally;
2 noetic quality – it is not simply a void, but has content, although that content cannot be communicated in words;
3 authoritativeness – it is absolute for the person who has the experience and, of course, it cannot be refuted logically;
4 affirmation – although it goes beyond conventional awareness, it is certainly not a negative experience, but gives a very positive view of things;
5 sense of the 'beyond' – it goes beyond the normal distinction between self and other, although to try and take this further and describe the 'beyond' as 'God' or 'the Absolute' would be to try to bring concepts into what cannot be conceptualized;
6 impersonal tone – it is definitely not like a personal encounter, what is experienced in satori is positive but impersonal;
7 feeling of exaltation – this is the result of all the conventional hindrances falling away, giving direct experience;
8 momentariness – it happens suddenly, and is 'out of time'.

The last of these is particularly important, as the experience of satori is described as 'one thought' – it is a single insight, with no sense of movement or the passing of time. It is a moment that disrupts the normal awareness of time continuity. In this sense it is 'eternal'.

Comment

Notice that Suzuki has not done the impossible. He has not described satori, only spoken about what it is like to have satori. The content itself can be experienced, but not described.

Western

There are interesting parallels here with the moments of insight claimed by Western mystics. Suzuki himself explored these in a later work entitled *Mysticism, Christian and Buddhist* (1957).

His insistence that reality is non-dual, and that space, time and identity are imposed upon it by our conventional minds is also parallel to the work of Kant and his distinction between reality as it is in itself (noumenal) and as we experience it (phenomenal).

Soto Zen

In contrast to Rinzai Zen, with its challenging koans and sudden satori, Soto Zen placed its emphasis on enlightenment through the practice of sitting meditation – *zazen*. The key figure in the development of this tradition was Dogen.

Dogen (1200–1253)

Tendai, a form of Buddhism practised in Japan at the time when both Eisai and Dogen were developing their particular forms of Zen, had taught that people were originally enlightened, but that their enlightened nature (Buddha nature) was obscured. This led to the basic question – 'Why, if one is fundamentally enlightened, should one need to practise religion or asceticism at all? Should the enlightened state not be the natural one?'

In other words

There is a basic dilemma here: one tries to practise religion in the hope of one day becoming what one already is.

Dogen, having travelled in China and there encountered the Ts'ong tung tradition, returned to Japan to develop it there as Soto Zen. He believed that sitting meditation (zazen) was the right way to practise Buddhism and that, as a person sat in meditation, he or she was able to realize the enlightened nature. Nothing else was needed for enlightenment, so one could dispense with other religious or ascetic practices.

In coming to this conclusion, he did not see Zen as something new or different from the earlier forms of Buddhism, just the result of placing emphasis on a particular means of practising it. He also argued that everyday activities should be the basis of meditation leading to the exploration of the Buddha nature. Thus one could find realization through practice itself, not just as a result of having done the practice. For Dogen, the realization of the Buddha nature, and the actual practice of zazen that aimed to bring it about, were actually one and the same.

To put it simply: sitting in meditation is being enlightened – you don't develop awareness in meditation in order to move on to become enlightened afterwards.

Comment

A key thing to remember here is that Dogen did not think of the Buddha nature as something that a person could possess, as though it were some spiritual object. Rather he saw the whole of being as the Buddha nature – something to be realized here and now, once superficial distractions are removed and one could see clearly.

Dogen saw *mujo* (impermanence) as the Buddha nature. If you realize the one, you realize the other. In this way he sought to get beyond both samsara (the world of change) and nirvana (the original goal of peace and serenity for one who had gone beyond change). A person should not stay in either state, but, experiencing nirvana, should then freely enter into the ever-changing world of samsara again. But such a person will be enlightened – in other words, he or she will see and recognize the world of samsara for what it is.

Dogen and time

In *Shobogenzo Uji*, his main work, Dogen claimed that time, just as it is, is being and that being is all time. In other words, all phenomena – mountains and seas included – are a feature of time. They would not exist without time. All beings are impermanent, and all have Buddha nature, therefore even the Buddha nature itself is not unchanging.

He uses this argument for equating being and time:

- Time cannot be something that flies past, something that happens.
- If it were, it could only be known if it had gaps in it. In other words, you would need to see one thing and then another,

and then point to time as being the means of moving from one to another. But actually reality is not sliced up in that way.

- There is no passage from one state to the next – no gap that is created by something external called 'time'.
- Rather, time is the 'passageless passage' as one state flows into the next.
- So time is the name we give to the flow of being.

He also considered that the Buddha nature – fundamental reality – is always manifested in the present. In other words: the real is always present.

Hence, rather than have two separate entities – being and time – he has the single moving, flowing entity 'being-time'. There is no 'eternal' realm other than this present realm in which things change. Everything is manifested here and now. Every moment manifests eternity, for every moment reveals the passageless passage of time.

Western

It would be interesting to speculate on what Dogen would have made of the Theory of Relativity – sadly, he lived 700 years too early. Perhaps he would have seen Relativity as the application to the cosmic scale of the unreality of a separate 'time' which he saw as a feature of everything.

There are also parallels here with Process Philosophy, where the traditional, Western 'eternalist' approach is up against the reality of time and change. There are connections here all the way from Heraclitus through to Bergson and Whitehead and, on the theological side, with Teilhard de Chardin.

Comment

Dogen really does provide us with a most radical cosmology. If everything in the cosmos is impermanent and changing, time is simply the name we give to that process. The unity and ultimate nature of the universe is not something over and above or outside that process – as theistic religions claim, with their idea of God – but the recognition of the universal nature of change itself. He sees the logical outcome of the original Buddhist view of impermanence as a single space–time continuum in which everything interpenetrates.

Philosophically, it is interesting to put together this Soto Zen approach with the Rinzai view of satori, as it has been outlined above by Suzuki. For Suzuki, the moment of satori is outside time, whereas for Dogen awareness is of everything flowing through time, or being part of a process we call time. These seem to be contradictory, but need not be so. The moment of insight is a single thought, and the singularity of that thought takes us beyond all distinctions and therefore beyond time and space. On the other hand, the *content* of experience on which this single thought subsequently comes to bear – the result of that thought, in other words – would seem to be the universal awareness of the changing, flowing nature of reality.

Zazen

Zazen is generally performed sitting facing a blank wall. Sessions of zazen are interspersed with some walking meditation (*kinhin*). The task is just to sit with an absolutely clear, bright mind. This is far from easy, since the untrained mind naturally becomes cluttered with thoughts. In zazen it is common to focus on the process of breathing, and on the passing of thoughts as a means of entering into the calm, thoughtless state within which a direct, clear experience of reality can arise.

An image used for zazen is the clearing of a pool of muddy water. One's reflection is only seen once the water is clear and still. Zazen does not determine the content of the reflection, it merely clears the water so that a reflection can be seen, but the clearing of the water and the seeing of the reflection happen simultaneously, so sitting in zazen is the process of becoming enlightened.

Enlightenment in meditation

Unlike Rinzai Zen, which spoke mainly of moments of insight (satori) in which there is the sudden breaking through to a new form of awareness, Soto Zen emphasizes that, as one sits in meditation, one is already a Buddha. In other words, in meditation one becomes aware of one's true nature – one's Buddha nature. Therefore enlightenment is not something to be gained at the end of a long process of spiritual development, but is a present experience. To the extent to which a person practises meditation, to that extent he or she is already Buddha.

Comment

Remember, with all these traditions, that the goal is not
something to be grasped. Indeed, the very attempt to do so only
reinforces the false idea of the self. You have to become
enlightened almost as if by accident. What is sought is clarity for
the mind.

The Buddha nature

What has been said above about both the Rinzai and Soto
approaches to Zen has brought out two features of the nature
of the self in relation to Buddhism – characterized by the term
'Buddha nature'.

Introspection

The first key feature is that the Buddha, and our Buddha nature,
is not separate from our own self. If we see the Buddha on the
road, we are to kill him! Buddha nature, whether revealed as a
moment of satori, provoked by a koan, or as a result of zazen,
is essentially our own true nature, once the illusion of a separate
self has been set aside. The self and its Buddha nature are
therefore known through introspection (although through an
unconscious form of introspection, rather than a conscious
analysis of self – which would be quite contrary to Zen), not
through any external doctrines. It is, as we saw above in
connection with meditation, the clearing of water that has
formerly been muddied – it is the revealing of what has always
been there, not the discovery of something new.

Spontaneity

The Buddha nature is revealed through spontaneity. That is the
key to recognizing the difference between self-consciousness and
Buddha consciousness. Spontaneity is action that takes place
prior to any consideration of the illusory separate self. Devoid
of self-consciousness, it accords with the general Buddhist view
of the world, in which everything is connected to everything else
and arises in dependence upon conditions. Recognition of that
gives a lightness of touch, almost a playfulness in all creative
activity. As we shall see, this has a profound influence on Zen
practice and in particular on the Zen view of the arts.

Zen practice

Anarchy and discipline

Zen morality follows from its basic view of the mind. All evil actions are seen as the result of acting on the basis of the selfish ego-mind. The Buddha mind, being universal, cannot be selfish.

This is sometimes referred to as living in the 'unborn' – in other words, being at one with the One Mind that is beyond the changing surface of things. A person who dwells in the unborn, who has developed 'no-mind', will be totally spontaneous.

In other words

Whatever you are doing, once you stop and think about it, you become self-conscious and the absolute and spontaneous nature of that action is lost. To shoot an arrow perfectly, one should not be conscious of an 'I' that shoots at all, at the appropriate moment the arrow shoots itself – the mind is beyond the self, beyond that arrow and beyond the target.

Clearly, Zen requires great discipline, whether in the efforts to break down conventional thinking in the Rinzai tradition or in the disciplined sitting in Soto Zen. But the result of insight is that a person is freed to behave quite spontaneously. (Indeed, it no longer feels like 'a person behaving' but more just 'action taking place'.) This makes Zen action unpredictable and unconventional. Indeed, convention is the very enemy of Zen – for the conventional, by definition, has lost its spontaneity. Zen morality is certainly not based on rules, but on insight and intuitive response. In a way, that is anarchy. But it is not selfish anarchy, rather a totally selfless unpredictability, born out of the disciplines that help a person get beyond the narrow view of self.

Western

In moral terms, this is rather like Augustine's view that one should 'love and do what you want'. For Augustine, of course, to love was to know the mind of God and therefore all action that flowed from love was morally good. Zen has the same approach, but substituting 'love' and 'God' for 'egoless no-mind' and 'the unborn' or 'Buddha mind'. Both recognize the limits of conventional morality.

As with all Zen, the conventional is challenged in a very direct way. Here are verses from *Honshin no uta*, 'The Song of the Original Mind' (1653), by Bankei Yotaku:

> You think that good
> Means hating what is bad
> What's bad is
> The hating mind itself.
>
> Good, you say,
> Means doing good.
> Bad indeed
> The mind that says so!

Such verses reflect the paradoxical and challenging nature of Zen, always breaking down conventional patterns of thought.

Yet this feature of Zen might lead to the quite false impression that Zen is concerned in a narrow way with the self and not with issues of the wider world. Bankei Yotaku's verses could give that impression. But what is clear is that, in the end, the aim of Zen is to return a person to the everyday world with a new sense of clarity and selfless action. Two things might illustrate this aspiration.

The twelfth-century Chinese Ch'an master Kakuan devised a set of ten pictures depicting bulls (sometimes referred to as the 'The Bulls' and sometimes as 'The Ox-herding pictures'). In these, the relationship between the man and the bull depicts the human being and the Buddha nature. The herder spies the bull, goes after it, catches it, brings it back. But then both bull and self are forgotten, and in the last image the person returns to the marketplace of life, seeing everything alive and new and providing blessings on everyone.

There is also the traditional prayer used after evening zazen:

> Sentient beings are numberless,
> I vow to save them;
> Desires are inexhaustible,
> I vow to put an end to them;
> The Dharmas are boundless,
> I vow to master them.
> The Buddha way is unsurpassable,
> I vow to attain it.

In both the mastery of the dharmas (in other words understanding reality and gaining skills in dealing with it) and in the desire to save the innumerable beings, there is a sense of the ultimate altruism that comes once the self is transcended.

In other words

The *practice of Zen* aims at breaking down conventional thinking and the sense of self. The *result* of Zen practice should be unselfconsciousness, spontaneity and altruism. A key feature of Zen (and all Buddhism, in its various ways) is that if you simply aspire to become unselfconscious, spontaneous and altruistic, without following the practice, you may fail to do so, simply because all three may be sought as qualities to enhance the self (a subtle form of selfishness – caricatured in the West by the notion of the 'do-gooder'). Zen provides techniques to break down the notion of self – following which unselfconsciousness, spontaneity and altruism may arise quite naturally.

Zen and the arts

In the idea of hua yen (interpenetration), every spec of dust in the universe contains the whole universe. Everything is within everything else; separateness is illusion. Therefore the whole of Buddhahood can be found in a simple action. Whatever is done naturally and spontaneously flows from our own Buddha-nature.

In other words

Most of the time, our false idea of a separate self, the 'I' that tries to shape the world around it, masks our true nature and our actions are formal. Once we can set aside self-consciousness and act with naturalness and spontaneity, then the 'self' has vanished and we act through our Buddha-nature.

The arts, giving an opportunity for natural expression, are therefore vehicles for spiritual development. A simple flower, a sand garden, the naturally flowing and unselfconscious actions of the tea ceremony – all these are attempts to get beyond the self, to act at one with the universal Buddha nature. Zen has therefore influenced calligraphy, music, poetry, painting and gardening.

Comment

Zen aesthetics are very straightforward. The two qualities sought in any artistic production are naturalness and spontaneity. These spring from unselfconsciousness, which in turn is the result of getting beyond the illusion of a separate self, and a recognition of the natural interpenetration of all things.

Again, notice the parallels here with Taoism. One could say of a Zen creation that it is the product of wu wei (non-action) – because it is not the result of any conscious imposition of the self upon the material.

East meets West

Modern Buddhist philosophers have been concerned to explore parallels and differences between their own views and Western philosophy. D.T. Suzuki, for example, was critical of the dualistic, analytical and conceptual framework within which all Western philosophy was couched. He pointed out how very different this was from Zen, which sought an insight that was non-dualistic and therefore beyond concepts. He pointed out that Western contrasts – between man and God, for example, or between faith and reason – simply do not apply to Zen.

In *Reason and Intuition in Buddhist Philosophy* (1951) he made an important distinction between two terms – *vijnana* and *prajna*.

- Vijnana is best translated 'reason' and it is essentially analytical. In the West, philosophy is primarily concerned with vijnana.
- Prajna is 'wisdom' and, far from being analytic, its chief function is to integrate. It is coming to awareness as a whole, going beyond conventional distinctions.

Comment
The meeting of East and West in philosophy is essentially a dialogue between vijnana and prajna. From the Western point of view, Eastern prajna is too much bound up with religion, morals, culture and so on. From an Eastern point of view, Western analytic vijnana never gets beyond the conventional distinctions within which rationality is forced to operate.

Nishida Kitaro (1870–1945)

From the mid-nineteenth century, Japan came out of a period of cultural isolation and its philosophers were able to read western philosophy and to assess its relationship to their own tradition. This process is particularly well illustrated by the work of Nishida, who was Professor of Philosophy at Kyoto University from 1913 to 1928.

Nishida's work went through various phases as he took first one and then another set of Western concepts through which to articulate his thought. Basically he was trying to see if Zen could be articulated using concepts and, if so, whether any Western philosophy could provide a conceptual framework for it.

Comment

Notice what a difficult task Nishida set himself. Zen, like Western mysticism, is inherently non-conceptual. It works by breaking down conventional thinking. How then can concepts be used to illustrate it without at the same time destroying it?

His first approach was based in part on an interpretation of Hegel. In Hegel's 'dialectic' you have a process where thesis and antithesis are resolved in a synthesis. But that synthesis in turn moves on to become another thesis, and so on. At the risk of gross over-simplification, we may say that what he took from Hegel was the sense of the universe as a constantly moving process which worked by the resolution of opposites.

Now Nishida's basic question was how it could be that we experience the world in terms of the changes and contradictions of ordinary experience, given that Zen points to an underlying unity. What he suggested, in *An Inquiry into the Good* (1911) was that reality is pure experience, prior to any subject/object division, prior to any division between mind and matter, prior even to any sense of time. But, of course, the way we normally experience reality is not like that at all – that sort of experience would be satori, or enlightenment. What we actually see is a universe in a process of change, in time. We see a self-fulfilling process of opposition, beneath which there is a unity.

Western

Nishida's idea of 'pure experience' as the basic way of getting beyond the subject/object division can be related to such Western thinkers as Henri Bergson and William James, who took experience – whether the experience of being alive and moving forward in a headlong rush of evolutionary life, or distinctively religious – as the starting point, out of which philosophical concepts can be developed.

He then takes a bold step and introduces the concept of God (*An Inquiry into the Good*, 1911, p. 79). He argues that God is not something that transcends reality, but is the basis of reality – something which dissolves the distinction between subjectivity and objectivity, spirit and nature. Our 'true self' is the ultimate reality of the universe, and to know one's true self is therefore to be united with the will of God. The 'Good' which he seeks is the realization of that true self.

Comment

What you have here is a very bold attempt to bring together the Eastern non-conceptual experience of Zen, with Western concepts. In this and later work, Nishida is attempting to find a global philosophy.

In this attempt, Nishida went on to use two other concepts. By 1917, he was moving away from the idea of 'pure experience', as the basis for his work for that of 'absolute free will', and then moved on to 'the place of nothingness'. From 1927 he was much occupied with trying to develop a form of logic that went beyond Aristotle. This is fundamental to any appreciation of the dilemma of wedding Western and Eastern thought. For Aristotle, there are two very basic logical principles:

- a thing is itself and not something else
- 'p' and 'non p' cannot both be true at one and the same time.

But we have seen that the approach of Zen is exactly to break down this sort of logical analysis. It relies on paradox and opposition in order to force the mind to go beyond conventional analysis. What Nishida insists on is that the real is both one and many at the same time.

Nishida attempted to replace Aristotelian logic by what he called 'place or field logic'. Subjects are determined by their place. But that which is ultimate can have no place – it is 'nothingness'. If ultimate reality is 'nothingness', what is its place? In *The Logic of the Place of Nothingness and the Religious World View* (1945) he argued that religion is fundamentally about the true self and its relation to reality. He thought that religious consciousness is universal, and that religion is also about the nature of the self. His conclusion therefore is that God and the 'true self' are identical. In this, he was reaffirming a basic Zen concept that the Buddha-nature is present in everyone.

The key concept here is 'absolute nothingness', which Nishida sees as true reality. This is not a relative nothingness, which simply negates a particular being (i.e. 'Is it here or not?'), but an absolute nothingness that denies absolute reality to individual beings. This reflects the most fundamental feature of Buddhism, that everything lacks inherent selfhood (anatta in early and Theravadin Buddhism), that everything depends for its existence on everything else, that everything is interconnected. This 'nothingness' (shunyata in the Mahayana tradition) is central to the Buddhist view of reality, and so, in relating his thought to Western concepts, Nishida emphasizes the 'place of nothingness'.

In other words

If you tried to make 'God' (or reality) 'absolute being', you would start to describe it – and, as soon as you did that, it would no longer be 'absolute being', for once you define it, you objectivize it and limit it. Such an idea needs therefore to be balanced by making reality 'absolute nothingness'. This is not a negative thing, but a very positive affirmation of reality. It is that which is beyond objectivity and concepts. You can only have absolute being in terms of absolute nothingness. You have what Nishida called an 'identity of absolute contradiction'. Very Zen!

Western

Nishida's concept of God, as both transcendent and immanent, is probably closest to the Western concept of panentheism. It sounds, at times, as though Nishida wants a pantheism, with reality within everything, but yet, through the idea of 'absolute nothingness' this is always negated. He is using Mahayana Buddhist concepts to articulate a basic tension that is also found in Western concepts of God – as something that is said to exist, and yet to be beyond the existence that we would predicate of individual things.

One might explore Heidegger's idea of the nature of 'being', and also the theology of Paul Tillich with his concept of God as 'being itself'. There is also the 'Death of God' theology of Van Buren and others. These were Western attempts to prevent the concept of God being objectivized and limited. Nishida tries to accomplish the same thing using the basic Buddhist concept of 'shunyata'.

Comment

This section on Nishida claims to do no more than throw out a few hints about the relevance of his work. There is a vast area of exploration possible here in terms of both Eastern and Western traditions. What is clear, is that the Buddhist concept of shunyata can be applied to a whole range of Western problems including, for example, the elusive nature of the self. (In the spontaneity of Zen, the self both vanishes and acts at the same time.)

Much of Nishida's work concerned the mystical and personal aspects of reality, taking little note of the political and social dimensions, which probably reflected the concerns of the Western thinkers with whom his philosophy entered into dialogue. This lack was corrected by a follower of Nishida within the Kyoto School of Philosophy, Tanabe Majima (1885–1962), who insisted that individuals did not connect with the absolute directly, but did so through the medium of social and political structures. His earlier work was particularly concerned with the place of the nation state, but later he was more concerned with surrendering the self as a response to the past, and moving towards receiving power from the 'other power', identified again with the ultimate reality, which he related to the idea of Amida Buddha.

In its ethics, the Kyoto school has emphasized the need to negate the self absolutely – and that can work on two levels, either through losing the self by becoming integrated into society, or more generally as an experience of the 'nothingness' of the self. There are interesting parallels here with the Taoist idea of wu wei ('non-action'), as a description of what is done most naturally and spontaneously. Interestingly, the ethical thinking from within the Kyoto school emphasized the role of society, criticizing Heidegger for being too individualistic. This perhaps reflects a very important East Asian contribution also to Buddhist thought, which at times has been portrayed as being overly individualistic.

But is it philosophy?

Zen pushes philosophy to its limits, because Zen involves going beyond concepts and rational thoughts and aims at direct awareness. Many of the activities associated with Zen, along with the practices designed to deepen a person's appreciation of it, aim to break down conventional thinking and reasoning.

Having said that, Zen is an absolutely essential part of any appreciation of Eastern Philosophy, first because it is rigorous in setting the limits of what can be articulated, and second because it is from within a broadly Zen tradition that there have been these interesting attempts to articulate Eastern spiritual insights using western concepts. The subject of Zen and Western thought deserves far greater coverage than is possible here – all we have attempted to do is look briefly at some of the great thinkers in this tradition, the key elements that form the distinctively Zen approach to Buddhist philosophy, and at Nishida, whose work established the Kyoto school of philosophy, which has most obviously worked towards not just the interpretation of Eastern thought for the West (which task had been undertaken particularly by Suzuki) but in actually forming a global philosophy, utilizing concepts from both hemispheres.

Comment

In most of the material we have looked at in this book, it has been clear that the concepts and background are culturally conditioned, and that parallels with Western thought can be rather tenuous, simply because Western philosophers approach similar questions from a very different point of view. Naturally this is also true to some extent with Zen – it has influenced and been influenced by Japanese culture. On the other hand, the attempt to get beyond concepts, and its rejection of doctrines and rituals, gives it an immediate claim to be genuinely global.

postscript

This postscript is both an apology and an invitation.

An apology, because it is folly to try to give an overview of the whole range of Eastern Philosophy in a book of this length. Inevitably, ideas of subtlety and depth have received no more than a cursory mention or a brief sketch. I hope those who are coming to Eastern Philosophy for the first time will not take this book as the last word on any of the traditions included, and that those who have already studied this material will excuse the inevitable lacunae and accept it in the light of its intended purpose.

Which brings me to the invitation.

The purpose of this book has been to whet the appetite for Eastern Philosophy. Every one of the traditions outlined here could repay a lifetime of study and reflection. It is enriching both to see something of the ideas that have shaped cultures which now contribute so extensively to our global humanity, and also to have our own thoughts and assumptions challenged by those who may come to familiar topics from perspectives very different from our own.

Since this manuscript was written, in 1998, there have been a steady flow of books on Eastern Philosophy, and others have surveyed 'World Philosophy', highlighting the parallels between different philosophical traditions.

In a world where communications and economic influences are global, where ideologies, political or religious, impact on one another, sometimes in the most brutal way, it is both dangerous and unrealistic to divide up philosophy too rigidly. Unrealistic, because there are basic questions about life and its meaning, about morality and society, that transcend conventional cultural and religious differences. Dangerous, because failure to recognise common concerns across a range of philosophies, religions or ideologies may too easily lead to an 'us/them' view and an inability to appreciate the motives and aspirations of others.

The recognition of interconnectedness will come as no surprise to those who consider Buddhist philosophy, for cultures as much as individuals are temporary and 'put together' from elements that are found everywhere. The division of philosophy between East and West is no more than a conventional convenience, whereas the activity of thinking and asking questions is clearly global.

MT
September 2002

taking it further

Further Reading

For those who want to follow up on any branch of Eastern Philosophy with an authoritative, academic but readable survey of scholarship:

The Companion Encyclopedia of Asian Philosophy, ed. Brian Carr and Indira Mahalingam (Routledge, 1997)

There are also concise entries on a wide range of eastern philosophers and philosophies in:

The Oxford Companion to Philosophy, ed. T. Honderich (OUP, 1995)
The Concise Routledge Encyclopedia of Philosophy, (Routledge, 2000)

And for books that give a global perspective, and therefore include Eastern Philosophy, try:

World Philosophies, Ninian Smart (Routledge, 1999)
World Philosophy, ed. D. Appelbaum and M. Thompson (Vega, 2002)
A Companion to World Philosophies, ed. Deutsch and Bontekoe (Blackwell, 1997)

For general, illustrated guides to Eastern Philosophy and religion:

The Sacred East, ed. C. Scott Littleton (Macmillan, 1996)
The Illustrated Encyclopedia of World Religions, ed. C. Richards (Element Books, 1997)
Tantra: the Search for Ecstasy, Indra Sinha (Hamlyn, 1993)

There are classic texts in a variety of translations. Try, for example:

The Analects, Confucius (OUP, World's Classics Series, 1993)

That Which Is (the Tattvartha Sutra), Umasvati (trans. Nathmal Tatia) (HarperCollins 1994). This book gives a very clear exposition of Jain philosophy, as well as a translation of the principal Jain scripture.

Buddhist and Hindu texts are available in a number of translations, including *Penguin Classics*.

There are a good number of books on each of the philosophies included in this volume. Most examine them from a mainly religious perspective, but they will nevertheless include expositions of the underlying philosophy, and – as has been pointed out many times – it is difficult to separate out the religious from the philosophical in Eastern thought. Of the many books on branches of Eastern Philosophy, try:

Classical Hindu Thought: an introduction, Arvind Sharma (OUP, 2000)

Philosophy in Classical India, J. Ganeri (Routledge, 2001)

An Introduction to Hinduism, G. Flood (CUP, 1996)

A Short Introduction to Hinduism, K. K. Klostermaier (Oneworld, 1998)

The Foundations of Buddhism, Rupert Gethin (OUP, 1998)

Buddhist Thought, Paul Williams (Routledge, 2000)

Early Buddhism: a new approach, Sue Hamilton (Curzon Press, 2000)

Heart of the Buddha's Teachings, A, Thich Nhat Hanh (Rider, 1998)

History of Buddhist Philosophy, A, D. J. Kalupahana (University of Hawaii Press, 1992)

Concise History of Buddhism, A, Andrew Skilton (Windhorse, 1994)

Understanding Eastern Philosophy, Ray Billington (Routledge, 1997)

Thirty Five Oriental Philosophers, Diane Collinson and Robert Wilkinson (Routledge, 1994)

Websites

A useful glossary of terms is available from The Internet Encyclopedia of Philosophy, at:
www.utm.edu/research/iep/e/eastglos.htm

The Philosophy in Cyberspace site has a section on Eastern Philosophy, at:
www-personal.monash.edu.au/~dey/phil/eastern.htm

For a draft manuscript of a book on Eastern Philosophy by J. Fieser, from the site that hosts The Internet Encyclopedia, go to:
www.utm.edu/~jfieser/vita1/research/eastphil.htm

For information on Buddhist Philosophy, the BuddhaNet (**www.buddhanet.net**) gives a useful range of study materials from basic introductions to illustrations of Buddhist art. It covers all the main branches of Buddhism, and presents Buddhist teachings in a particularly accessible and straightforward way.

Also for Buddhist thought, the American-based Buddhist magazine Tricycle can be found on-line:
www.tricycle.com

To contact the author of this book with questions or comments, or for additional information of particular interest to students and teachers, log on to:
www.mel-thompson.co.uk

glossary

Hindu

advaita Non-dualist philosophy. Brahman/Atman is ultimately real; all else is illusion.

ahankara The individual ego (in Sankhya philosophy).

ahimsa Non-violence.

ananda Bliss (one of the three qualities of Brahman).

aparigraha Avoiding avarice (last of the yamas).

asat 'Non-being' or unreal.

asrama Stages of life.

asteya Not stealing (third of the five yamas).

astika 'Orthodox', used of schools or philosophies (c.f. nastika – unorthodox).

Atman Self or soul.

avidya Ignorance.

bhakti Devotion (one of the paths to liberation).

Brahman The absolute reality.

Brahmacarya Student stage of life.

cit Mind or consciousness (also quality of Brahman).

darshana 'Viewing', used in Hindu religion for the act of viewing the image of a god (a murti) or a spiritual teacher. It is also used in the sense of 'philosophy', a particular tradition of teaching, offering an insight.

Dharma *See* Sanatana Dharma.

dvaita Dualist philosophy.

Grhasta Householder stage of life.

gunas Three aspects of the material universe (Sankhya philosophy).

guru Spiritual teacher.

Isvara One's personal deity.

jnanamarga Knowledge.

jiva The individual person.

karma Literally 'action', used of actions that produce spiritual results.

marga Way (of release) – of which there are three: *karmamarga* (depending on action), *jnanamarga* (depending on understanding) and *bhaktimarga* (depending on devotion).

Mimamsa Branch of Hindu philosophy.

moksha Spiritual liberation, the goal of the Hindu life.

nastika 'Unorthodox', used of schools of philosophy.

Nirguna Brahman Ultimate reality, pure consciousness, beyond description.

prajna Wisdom.

prakrti The material universe (in Sankhya philosophy).

purusha The spiritual element, which (with prakrti) makes up the universe within Sankhya philosophy. Used also of the original 'cosmic man' out of whose body the various varnas are formed.

rta Early term for the principle of order within the universe.

Saguna Brahman Ultimate reality as it is manifested in and through thoughts that can be directly known and experienced (as opposed to Nirguna Brahman).

samsara The ordinary world as it is experienced, constantly changing.

Sanatana Dharma 'The eternal law; the way things are ordered in the universe.

Sankhya Branch of Hindu philosophy.

Sannyasa A renunciate or ascetic, the final stage in life.

sat Truth (quality of Brahman, also used in many other contexts).

satcitananda 'Truth, Consciousness and Bliss' – spiritual goal.

shakti Feminine power, personified in goddesses.

shruti Innate or self-evident spiritual knowledge, gained independently of texts or concepts.

smriti Knowledge that comes from texts of traditions.

Upanishads Final part of the Vedic scriptures, giving teachings aimed at those who 'sit near' to the teacher.

varnasramadharma Duty set according to one's stage in life and by one's 'colour'.

varna 'Colour'; used of the basic caste groups.

Vanaprasta The retirement stage of life.

veda 'Knowledge', used of the Hindu scriptures.

Vedanta Hindu philosophy, concerned with interpreting the Vedas.

Visistadvaita Qualified non-dualism; affirmed the existence of the world, a personal God, the individual souls.

Yoga Disciplines aimed at achieving liberation

Jain

ahimsa Non-violence.

anekantavada The Jain refusal to accept that truth is absolute, all being subject to a particular perspective.

Digambara Monastic sect within Jainism.

jina Conqueror (used of Mahavira and the other ford-makers)

jiva Soul (within everything).

karma-vada The Jain interpretation of the general Hindu view of karma.

kavala The state of recognizing that one's spirit is in fact the same as absolute reality.

moksha Liberation.

nigantha nataputta The title used of Mahavira in Buddhist scriptures.

sallekhana Preparing for death by meditation and voluntary starvation.

samsara The ever-changing world that we experience.

shramana Independent spiritual teacher.

siddha 'Perfect one'; one who recognizes the self as the absolute reality and is said to have infinite knowledge, vision, strength and bliss.

Svetambara Monastic sect within Jainism – 'white clad', whose monks wear three pieces of white cloth

tirthankaras 'Ford-makers', Jain teachers, the last of whom was the historical Mahavira.

Buddhist

Abhidharma Philosophical analysis of the Dharma.

alaya-vignana 'Store consciousness'; mechanism by which we remember and are affected by events in the past.

anatta 'No inherently existing or independent self', one of the three marks of conditioned existence.

anicca The first mark of conditioned existence, that all things are subject to change.

Arhat 'Worthy one', used of those who gained enlightenment following the Buddha's teaching.

avidya Spiritual blindness.

Bardo Used of a transitional state, especially that between one life and the next.

bhikku (bhikkuni) Buddhist monk (nun).

Bodhicitta 'The mind of enlightenment', used of the spiritual state in which a person is determined to follow the path towards enlightenment.

bodhisattva 'Being of enlightenment', used of Gautama prior to his enlightenment, also of other spiritual beings that aid enlightenment, also of the goal of the Mahayana.

dhyana Meditation; also the spiritual state achieved in meditation.

dukkha Suffering, unsatisfactoriness (first of the Four Noble Truths, and the third mark of conditioned existence).

Hinayana 'Lesser vehicle', used as a derogatory term by Mahayana Buddhists of the early schools of which the extant one is the Theravada.

hua-yen The interpenetration of all things (Japanese term for the original Buddhist idea of conditioned co-production).

magga The 'Middle Way' – fourth of the Four Noble Truths.

Mahayana 'Great vehicle', the Buddhist tradition originating in India but developed particularly in the Far East and the Himalayas.

mandala A spiritual diagram or map.

mantra A chant, repeated as an aid to devotion and meditation.

maya Illusion, used of the world of the senses.

nirodha 'Cessation'. It describes the exhaustion of the karmic fuel of the fires of greed, hatred and ignorance, and is equated with Nirvana.

Nirvana (**Nibbana** in Pali), the state in which the triple fire of hatred, greed and ignorance is extinguished.

paramita Perfection (used of the six qualities of an enlightened being).

prajna Wisdom.

pratitya samutpada (**paticcasamuppada**) The arising and ceasing of things in dependence upon conditions (conditioned co-production; dependent origination), or 'interconnectedness'; the fundamental feature of the Buddha's teaching.

punabhava Re-becoming (the Buddhist equivalent of reincarnation).

rupa 'Body', one of the five skandhas.

samadhi Meditation.

samatha Form of meditation which seeks to develop calm, one-pointedness of mind.

samjna 'Mental concepts', one of the five skandhas.

samsara The world of change and re-becoming.

samskara 'Desires', one of the five skandhas.

satya Truth (*samvrti* – conventional; *paramartha* – ultimate).

shunyata 'Emptiness'; used to describe that which is dependent, conditioned and liable to change.

sila Morality.

skandhas The five elements (literally 'heaps') of which the self is made up (matter; feeling; mental concepts; desires; consciousness).

sutra Literally 'thread'; used of a teaching of the Buddha. The Buddhist scriptures are divided into 'sutras'.

svabhava Inherent existence (things lack this).

tanha Craving, the cause of suffering.

tathagata 'One who has gone beyond'; used of the Buddha.

tathata 'Suchness' – the reality of things just as they are.

Vajrayana 'Diamond vehicle' or 'thunderbolt vehicle', incorporating Tantric elements.

vedana 'Feelings', one of the five skandhas.

vijnana 'Consciousness', one of the five skandhas.

vipassana Form of meditation which seeks to develop insight into the nature of reality.

Confucian

ch'i Morality.

chiao 'Teachings'; the term used for systems of thought, including Confucianism and Taoism.

dao (Also **tao**) used of the moral life.

de Inner passions and energies.

fa The principle of justice (legalist school).

hsin Trustworthiness (one of the five cardinal virtues).

jianai Respect; a term used particularly by Mo Tzu.

junzi 'Gentleman'; one who strives to do what is right.

li The rites that determine good conduct; in neo-Confucianism, li refers to the principle that governs the universe.

ming Destiny or fate.

ren (jen) The essential quality of a mature human being; also used as 'person'.

ru (ju) The scholarly class to which Confucius belonged; used also of the school of thought based on Confucius' teachings.

sheng-ren A sage; one who both embodies and teaches wisdom.

Tai Ch'i 'The supreme ultimate', representing the li of heaven and earth.

te Spiritual power.

T'ien 'Heaven'; a sense of order in the world.

xiao-ren 'Small man'; one who acts without reference to moral values.

yi The principle of right conduct; duty.

Taoist

ch'ang The eternal principle that governs the process of change.

ch'i The life force (literally 'breath').

hua Transformation.

jing Vital essence.

li 'Principle'; used by Chuang Tzu to describe the operation of the Tao.

ming State of enlightenment.

Tao (Dao) 'Way', used of the cosmic order and first principle of the universe.

Te Power; the Tao operating through individual things.

wu wei 'Non-action'; avoiding taking action that manipulates or goes against the natural laws of the universe – used positively in the sense of living naturally and harmoniously.

Yin/Yang Female/male; passive/active – balance of forces within nature (found within Taoism and neo-Confucianism, where it is seen as the cause of everything and means by which Principle is transformed into the world).

Tantra

Anuttara Tantra Highest form of Tantra, which requires no physical action, but is based entirely on meditation.

bodhicitta The mind that seeks enlightenment.

guru Spiritual guide; teacher.

mahasukha The great bliss.

mandala Pattern representing spiritual or metaphysical entities.

mudra Position of the hands, to convey a particular quality.

vajra Tantric symbol; literally 'diamond' or 'thunderbolt'.

Yab-Yum Literally 'mother-father', images showing male and female locked in sexual embrace.

yidam A personal deity, used in Tantric visualization.

Zen

Ch'an (Zen) Meditation (derived from the Sanskrit *dhyana*).

kinhin Walking meditation.

koan A recorded saying or question, designed to frustrate the application of conventional thought.

mondo Record of a question and answer session between master and disciple.

mujo Japanese term for impermanence.

roshi Zen master.

satori Moment of insight (in Rinzai Zen).

zazen Sitting meditation.

index

Index of Western thinkers, schools and concepts referred to in the text:

teach yourself

philosophy of religion
mel thompson

- Does God exist? If so, what is he or she like?
- Do you have a soul? If so, can it survive your death?
- Do miracles happen?
- Should we take religious language literally?
- Is providence just a matter of luck?
- Why is there suffering and evil in the world?
- What is religious experience and what can it tell us?
- How does religion relate to the scientific world view?
- Does the world have to make sense to us?

These are just some of the questions which are examined in this book. They are fundamental to any intelligent understanding of life, whether or not a person is a member of one of the world religions. They are also questions which every believer needs to explore.

Dr Mel Thompson is a freelance writer and editor, specializing in Philosophy, Religion and Ethics.

- What can we know for certain about the world or ourselves?
- Can we prove the existence of God?
- How is the mind related to the body?
- What is justice?
- How should society be organized?

This book is an introduction to the way in which these and other questions have been explored by some of the greatest minds in the history of Western thought. From Plato to postmodernism, Anselm to Ayer, it examines the central themes in philosophy which have shaped the way in which we think about the world.

Teach Yourself Philosophy explains philosophical terms, such as epistemology, metaphysics or existentialism in a straightforward way, providing an accessible outline of Western thought for the student or general reader.

teach
yourself

ethics
mel thompson

Ethics is about moral choices – the values that lie behind them, the reasons people give for them and the language they use to describe them.

Teach Yourself Ethics introduces some of the main ethical theories, and looks at the contribution of many thinkers, including Aristotle, Aquinas, Hobbes, Kant, Nietzsche, Moore, Ayer and Rawls. But it does not simply offer an historical survey of the subject. Rather, it explores key themes: whether we are free to choose what to do: what we mean by moral choice; whether we should judge actions by their results or by intentions. It also looks at important areas of moral thought – personal relationships, law and order and global issues, and illustrates them through lively, real-life situations and dilemmas.

By exploring moral issues in a systematic way, *Teach Yourself Ethics* offers a grounding for those who want to do further study in ethics, philosophy, or other humanities and arts subjects, or who are concerned with professional ethics in the fields of law, medicine or business.